ATKINS

Eat Right, Not Less

Your personal guide to
living a healthy **low-carb**
& **low-sugar** lifestyle

COLETTE HEIMOWITZ

Vermilion
LONDON

10 9 8 7 6 5 4 3 2 1

Vermilion, an imprint of Ebury Publishing
20 Vauxhall Bridge Road
London SW1V 2SA

Vermilion is part of the Penguin Random House group of companies
whose addresses can be found at global.penguinrandomhouse.com

Penguin
Random House
UK

Photography by Ellen Silverman

Interior design by Laura Palese

First published by Vermilion in 2017

A CIP catalogue record for this book is available from the British Library

ISBN: 9781785041648

Printed and bound in Italy by L.E.G.O. S.p.A

MIX
Paper from
responsible sources
FSC® C018179

Penguin Random House is committed to a sustainable
future for our business, our readers and our planet.
This book is made from Forest Stewardship Council®
certified paper.

The information in this book has been compiled by way of general guidance
in relation to the specific subjects addressed, but is not a substitute and not
to be relied on for medical, healthcare, pharmaceutical or other professional
advice on specific circumstances and in specific locations. So far as the author
is aware the information given is correct and up to date as at December 2017.
Practice, laws and regulations all change, and the reader should obtain up to
date professional advice on any such issues. The author and publishers disclaim,
as far as the law allows, any liability arising directly or indirectly from the use,
or misuse, of the information contained in this book.

I WOULD LIKE TO DEDICATE THIS BOOK

**to the brilliant and creative team
at Atkins Nutritionals,**

who believes that Atkins is not just a diet but a way of eating that has the power to improve not just your health but all aspects of your life. The Atkins team has worked tirelessly and passionately to incorporate the latest scientific research into Atkins' proven way of eating, develop innovative products to support this lifestyle, and sustains our robust community of people dedicated to living a low-carb lifestyle.

IN ADDITION,

**I would like to dedicate this book to the
late Dr. Robert C. Atkins,**

who established the nutritional principle of eating right, not less, which remains the core of the Atkins way.

CONTENTS

INTRODUCTION

THIS JOURNEY STARTED MORE than forty years ago, when an American cardiologist named Dr. Robert Atkins disrupted conventional wisdom by developing an approach to better health and losing weight based on eating right, not less. He discovered that when you take simple steps to cut back on carbs and sugar, you transform your metabolism from one that *stores* fat into one that *burns* fat.

Meanwhile, 'conventional wisdom' had us cutting calories and fat to lose weight, which turned into a vicious cycle that left us feeling deprived and then overeating. For years, we've been told that fat is the main culprit in the obesity epidemic. We ate low-fat cookies and drank skim milk. And we kept getting fatter. But fat is not the enemy. There is another culprit, one that hides in plain sight, concealed in many of the 'healthful' foods we eat and drink. And guess what: it's sugar and excess carbohydrates.

◆

When you take **simple steps** to **cut back on carbs and sugar,** you transform your metabolism from one that **stores fat** to one that **burns fat.**

Sugars and foods that become sugars in the body are arguably responsible for one of the biggest health epidemics we face today. According to the World Health Organization, 1.9 billion adults are overweight; in the UK, a staggering 58 percent of women and 68 percent of men are overweight or obese.

In 2015, the UK government's health advisory group, Public Health England (PHE), published a report called *Sugar Reduction: The Evidence for Action*, which stated that consumption of sugary food and drink is fuelling an obesity crisis that costs the National Health Service £5.1 billion a year. (Although it's worth noting that many sources put the cost to the NHS nearer to £10 billion per year, if treating the indirect complications of type 2 diabetes are included in this figure, too.)

PHE also reports that in England 3.8 million people (around 9 percent of the adult population) have diabetes, 90 percent of which cases are type 2 diabetes and are related to diet and lifestyle choices.

In addition to this, healthcare charity Diabetes UK predicts that 5 million people are prediabetic – they have non-diabetic hyperglycaemia (higher than normal blood glucose levels) – which puts them at high risk of developing type 2 diabetes. If the trend continues, one in three people in England will be obese by 2034, and one in ten will have developed type 2 diabetes.

In the USA the situation is even worse; one-third of adults there are obese, 29 million people have diabetes, and 86 million are prediabetic. In fact, someone is diagnosed with diabetes *every 30 seconds*. The US Department of Agriculture (USDA) confirms that the typical American now eats a staggering 59 kilograms of added sugar (including table sugar, high-fructose corn syrup, and other caloric sweeteners added to food products) a year. And that's in addition to the naturally occurring sugar present in fruits, vegetables, grains, dairy products, and other foods. It is also a whole lot more than your grandparents and probably your parents consumed when they were your age.

But sugar is just the tip of the empty carbohydrate iceberg. If you cut out sugar but continue to eat lots of refined grains, such as white flour, white rice and most breakfast cereals, you aren't going to have the dramatic weight-loss and health gains that people experience on Atkins. That's because those kissing cousins of sugar quickly convert to glucose, aka sugar, in your bloodstream. They are known as hidden sugars, and from your body's perspective, they are processed just the same as sugar. With Atkins, you'll completely rebalance your intake of protein, fat, and carbohydrates. You'll be eating dramatically fewer carbs but more protein and fat.

Because you'll be eating fewer carbs and primarily carbs that are full of fibre, your blood sugar level will remain relatively constant. That, in turn, will minimize hunger and cravings, making it easy to eat this way. Since you can eat foods cooked in olive oil, vegetables topped with a knob of butter, and salads garnished with avocado and olives, you'll find the fare filling and satisfying.

It's Time To Rethink 'Diet'

Today, thanks to the movement started by Dr. Atkins, nearly three out of four adults are actively managing their carb intake. But although many adults would like to lose weight, many people don't want to feel forced to adhere to a programme. *Diet* has become a four-letter word that is neither healthy nor sustainable. Yet almost 150 million people have adopted this low-carb approach to eating in some form – they want balance, moderation, and variety, and they want to make the right food choices that will have a positive impact on their health and life. The world is ready to embrace what those of us at Atkins have known to be true all along: eating right – not less – helps you lose weight *and* improve

The **world is ready to embrace** what those of us at Atkins have known to be true all along: eating **right – not less –** helps you to **lose weight** and **improve your overall wellness.**

your overall health and wellness. I've seen the transition from diet to lifestyle firsthand.

When I was studying to become a nutritionist, if I had been asked whether the following statements were true or false, I would definitely have said they were true:

- The only way to lose weight is to cut calories.
- To lose weight, you must eat small portions and forgo snacks.
- Hunger is the price you pay for paring pounds.
- Eating high-fat foods makes you fat.
- Atkins doesn't provide enough vegetables.
- It's virtually impossible to maintain weight loss permanently.

In the years since then, I've learned that in every case, these statements are *false*. Atkins has opened my eyes to a different but highly effective way of eating.

Eat Right, Not Less

Consider this book your guide to living a low-carb, low-sugar lifestyle. I'll give you an overview of how Atkins works and all the positive health benefits that you have the potential to achieve. Then I'll help you create realistic goals, which will help you decide exactly how you want to do Atkins. Whether you want to start small or prefer a more structured plan, Atkins is *not* hard. Start by making small choices, such as eating more fresh, colourful vegetables, flavourful protein sources, and healthy fats, reducing your sugar intake, and swapping out refined carbohydrates (which contain

*This book is about **changing your mind-set** about eating and food, and I'm going to share **simple solutions** that will allow you to embrace and sustain a **low-carb, low-sugar** lifestyle.*

those insidious hidden sugars – and I'll show you how to find them) for high-fibre carbohydrate sources.

For many of us, diets have been a temporary solution. This is *not* a diet book. This book is about changing your mind-set about eating and food, and I'm going to share simple solutions that will allow you to embrace and sustain a low-carb, low-sugar lifestyle. With Atkins, you eat right, not less. This book is packed with useful information showing you how to do just that, plus 100 delicious low-carb and low-sugar recipes perfect for every occasion, including breakfasts you can grab and go, whole meals in minutes, holiday favourites, and makeovers of popular recipes for when you're craving comfort food, salty snacks, chocolatey desserts, pasta, pizza and more. Preparing and eating food should be a joyful ritual of mouthwatering flavours, and you'll be proud to share these recipes with family and friends.

About Me

I spent ten years in private practice working in physicians' offices directing patients' nutrition programmes. For the last twenty years, I have been working in one capacity or another for Atkins. I

> There is a **sense of accomplishment** that you experience by **taking control of your health** – and therefore your **future** – that **spills over** into **every aspect of your life**

spent four of them at the Atkins Center for Complementary Medicine, where I worked for Dr. Atkins as a nutritionist with thousands of patients to help them slim down and deal with health problems. In my next sixteen years at Atkins Nutritionals, I've observed and advised thousands of members of the Atkins community in their weight control efforts. When it comes to eating habits and weight reduction, I've seen and heard it all. Now I'm excited to have the opportunity to guide you in your evolution toward making the right food choices, as you transform yourself and pave a way to better health. You can also communicate with me through the community at Atkins.com.

What I have learned is that not all of us need a 'programme' to succeed, but everyone needs a clearer perspective on his or her carbohydrate consumption. Though some of us need tight guardrails, others just want a guidebook for success: success in meeting and maintaining your goals concerning your health and the health of your loved ones, success in taking charge of your life, and, yes, success in attaining the body you've always wanted. There is a sense of accomplishment that you experience by taking control of your health – and therefore your future – that spills over into every aspect of your life.

Doing Atkins your way allows you enormous variety in the kinds of foods you can eat when you are aware of the impact that excess carbs have on your health. When you are able to control the quality and quantity of carbs you consume to suit your individual metabolism and needs, you can sustain this way of eating for life. Whether you want the instructions for a well-constructed Atkins or just the information you need to reduce your carb intake on your terms while savouring a variety of foods, I hope I can help you learn how to make doing Atkins second nature.

Are you ready? It's time to get started!

PART ONE

EAT
RIGHT,
NOT
LESS

1

THE

HIDDEN SUGAR

EFFECT

IT'S A HARD FACT TO SWALLOW:

nearly two-thirds of Brits are overweight or obese,[1]

and despite medical advancements in recent decades, millennials are actually unhealthier than their parents.[2] It comes down to what we've been putting into our mouths. The way we have been eating – where 50 to 60 percent of our calories come from carbohydrates[3] – has contributed to this health epidemic.

BACKED BY SCIENCE

Atkins is **backed by more than eighty** published, **peer-reviewed studies** conducted over the past few decades. You can see a full list of these studies in **Appendix F.**

FORTUNATELY, THERE IS A solution. Atkins' proven nutritional approach offers a better, smarter way to help you become healthier and fit. In this book, I'm going to show you how to live a low-carb, low-sugar lifestyle that involves making simple choices that will optimize your health, plus I've included 100 delicious low-carb, low-sugar recipes to help you along your way.

GET TO KNOW YOUR SUGARS

• **ADDED SUGARS:** These include sucrose, also known as table sugar, which is typically extracted from sugarcane or beet sugar and added to foods to make them sweeter (you'll find a list of some of the most common added sugars on page 9).

• **NATURALLY OCCURRING SUGARS:** These are naturally found in fruits, vegetables, grains, legumes, dairy products and other foods.

• **HIDDEN SUGARS:** Carbohydrates that convert to sugar in your bloodstream.

First of all, let's examine how the current carb-centric way of eating brought on this obesity-driven health crisis. Carbohydrates, protein and fat are called macronutrients. They provide energy, and your body needs them to function, but the customary way of eating, and even typical calorie-cutting 'diets' (the diet status quo for the last thirty years), are high in carbohydrates that convert to sugar, leading to blood sugar 'highs' and excess sugar that is stored as fat. After your body scrambles to remove the excess sugar, it can lead to blood sugar 'lows,' during which you feel tired and hungry and crave more carbs and sugar. Carbohydrates are the only macronutrients that have this profound effect on your blood sugar. Here's why: The human metabolism can circulate only 5 grams of glucose at one time, which is equal to about 1 to 2 teaspoons of sugar. If your blood is required to circulate much more than that, the resulting blood sugar high forces your body to 'dump' the excess sugar, leading to fat storage and weight gain. We call this the Hidden Sugar Effect.

Think of it this way: a typical breakfast of a bagel and a cappuccino can convert to ten times the amount of sugar in your bloodstream than your body can easily process. You don't see the sugar in carbs, but your body feels its effects and has to work hard to get rid of it. After years and years of consuming excess sugars and excess carbohydrates that convert to sugar, it becomes harder and harder for your body to handle the constant increase in blood sugar, which can eventually lead to prediabetes and type 2 diabetes. In fact, according to an article published in *The Journal of the American Medical Association*, if you combine the population diagnosed with prediabetes and diabetes, there are currently 52 percent of Americans with this deadly disease[4] and Brits aren't too far behind.

Remember that bagel and cappuccino you had for breakfast? Once you process the sugar in your blood

THE HIDDEN SUGAR EFFECT*

Bowl of Corn Flakes	Plain Bagel	Can of Soda	Beef & Veggies
7 tsp of sugar	7.5 tsp of sugar	7 tsp of sugar	1 tsp of sugar

*based on glycemic load rating

and your body dumps the excess, you may be stuck with low blood sugar and cravings for more carbs. By keeping an eye on the *quality* and *quantity* of the carbohydrates that you eat, you can prevent this blood sugar roller-coaster ride. I'll show you exactly how to do this, but first, let's discuss sugar.

Though you probably know that foods such as white rice and white bread convert to sugar in your bloodstream, the vast majority of people are unaware of all the other foods that convert to sugar. So-called healthy foods such as fruit juice; low-fat, fruit-sweetened yogurt; wholewheat bagels; and flavoured porridge cause spikes in blood sugar similar to those produced by eating a chocolate bar! And the carbohydrates found in quinoa, ancient grains and brown rice, when eaten in quantities larger than an 80-gram/2¾-ounce serving, may also cause blood sugar spikes.

I'll show you on page 25 how you can incorporate these healthier whole grains into your diet wisely so that you lessen the impact on your blood sugar, but what is important to understand right now is that sugar is sugar. Translation: an organic pressed juice or smoothie has the same impact on your blood sugar as a can of soda. Welcome to the world of hidden sugars.

BACKED BY SCIENCE

Of course, you know that **tempting treats** such as doughnuts, biscuits and sweets contain sugar, but more **sugar** than you know is hiding in plain sight everywhere, even in foods that are often deemed 'healthy'. In fact, the vast majority of adults have no idea that added sugars, carbohydrates and natural sugars all cause your **blood sugar** to rise and, in excess, lead to weight gain, prediabetes and **type 2 diabetes.**

THE HIDDEN SUGAR QUIZ

To get a better understanding of hidden sugars,
let's start by testing your knowledge of which foods have a
bigger effect on your blood sugar. You might be surprised!

WHICH HAS THE BIGGER EFFECT ON YOUR BLOOD SUGAR?	ANSWERS (NO PEEKING!)
A strawberry frosted cupcake OR a small baked potato	They **both** have the same blood sugar–raising effect as 6.3 teaspoons of sugar.
A chocolate bar OR a serving of macaroni and cheese	The **macaroni and cheese** has the same blood sugar–raising effect as 11 teaspoons of sugar, compared to 9 teaspoons for the chocolate bar.
A sports drink OR a small bowl of corn flakes	The **corn flakes** have the same blood sugar–raising effect as 6.6 teaspoons of sugar, compared to 4 teaspoons for the sports drink.
A chocolate bar OR 40g/1½oz raisins	The **raisins** have the same blood sugar–raising effect as 9.3 teaspoons of sugar, compared to 9 teaspoons for the chocolate bar.
A bagel OR a muffin	They **both** have the same blood sugar–raising effect as 7.5 teaspoons of sugar.

Before you throw your hands up in despair thinking about all the hidden sugars lurking out there, it's important to understand that not all foods are full of them. You can feast on Pear and Manchego Mesclun Salad with Caramelized Onions (page 195) or Lemon Pepper Prawns with Mangetout (page 233), and you'll be consuming only 2 to 2.5 teaspoons of hidden sugars, while feeling far more satisfied than you ever would after scarfing down a portion of macaroni and cheese. Meals and snacks that contain adequate amounts of protein, healthy fats and high-fibre carbohydrates have very few hidden sugars and help prevent blood sugar spikes and fat storage (i.e., weight gain) while keeping your energy levels steady.

Now that you have made it through the tricky part of learning what hidden sugars are, how they impact your blood sugar, and how to identify them, you should begin to have a better idea of how much of your diet they currently make up and their potential effect on your overall health.

How to Find Added Sugars

There are more than fifty names for sugar! Next time you're at the supermarket or perusing your pantry, you might be amazed at how many foods feature these names on their ingredients lists. Here are some of the most common:

Agave nectar	Honey
Barley malt	Icing sugar
Beet sugar	Malt syrup
Brown sugar	Maltodextrin
Cane juice	Maltose
Caramel	Molasses
Coconut sugar	Muscovado
Corn syrup	Rice syrup
Dextrose	Saccharose
Fructose	Sucrose
Glucose	Turbinado sugar
High fructose corn syrup	

A BETTER WAY
TO EAT

I WILL SHOW YOU how Atkins works and how carbohydrates, protein and fat function in your body. I will also show you how you can make simple changes to cut back on your carb and sugar intake, giving you the potential to reap major health benefits. You'll learn how this way of eating can help you reduce blood sugar spikes while putting less wear and tear on your metabolism, helping you avoid weight gain as you age. In addition, you'll reduce your chances of getting diabetes while experiencing steady energy levels.

This is not a diet book where you are forced to comply with a one-size-fits-all diet plan. You have seen how traditional diets continue to impact our rising obesity rate and associated health problems, and you have possibly experienced those effects firsthand. My goal is to show you how Atkins' low-carb, low-sugar nutritional approach is truly a better way to eat, with proven recommendations that are tailored to you and your needs.

My goal is to show you how Atkins' **low-carb, low-sugar** nutritional approach is truly a **better way to eat.**

2

HOW
ATKINS
WORKS

When you reduce your CARBOHYDRATE AND SUGAR INTAKE,

as you do with Atkins, while consuming an optimal combination
of protein, healthy fats and fibre-rich, low-sugar carbohydrates – eating right,
not less – you flip the switch on your metabolism so you burn both dietary
and body fat for fuel. In other words, you burn fat instead of storing it.

Reducing carb and sugar intake has been proven to improve health and to help lose weight or maintain weight while feeling constantly energized and experiencing less hunger and fewer cravings. There's a reason why this way of eating has become a lifestyle for almost 150 million people.

This is because your metabolism burns two different types of fuel for energy: carbohydrates or fat.

As you have learned, when you consume mostly carbohydrates (plus the hidden sugars in them) and cut calories, your body burns those carbs and sugar for fuel, leading to blood sugar spikes, fat storage, fatigue, hunger and more. Let's dig a little deeper into how Atkins works and why eating right, not less, makes so much sense.

FEEL THE BURN

Metabolism refers to the process of how your body turns food into **energy.**

ATKINS' MANY HEALTH BENEFITS

In addition to weight loss, a low-carb, low-sugar lifestyle has been shown to impact health in the following ways:

- Decreased risk of developing prediabetes and type 2 diabetes
- Decreased risk of developing cardiovascular disease
- Improvements in brain health
- Steady energy levels
- Improvements in epilepsy and related diseases
- Decrease in inflammation markers

HOW DOES ATKINS WORK?

LOW-CALORIE/HIGH-CARB DIET	VS	ATKINS

 UP AND DOWN SUGAR LEVELS

 STEADY SUGAR LEVELS

 INCREASED
- FAT STORAGE
- HUNGER/CRAVINGS

 LESS
- FAT STORAGE
- HUNGER/CRAVINGS

 BURN SUGAR & STORE FAT

 BURN FAT & LOSE WEIGHT

GET TO KNOW YOUR
MACRONUTRIENTS

THE ADAGE 'YOU ARE WHAT YOU EAT' is true, and with Atkins, it all comes down to macronutrients: carbohydrates, protein and fat. Macronutrients provide your body with energy (calories), and they are necessary for your body to function properly. The amount of carbs, protein and fat in any food is measured in grams. Here's more about macronutrients.

Carbohydrates

These are broken down by your body into glucose (sugar) and used as energy. Any excess carbs are stored as fat. Carbohydrates are found in all plant foods, including grains, cereals, nuts, potatoes, bread and pasta. All vegetables and fruit are considered carbohydrates, but their carb counts vary a lot. Berries, for example, are relatively low in carbs, while bananas are not. In general, leafy greens, along with many other vegetables, are low in carbs, while potatoes, sweet potatoes and grains are higher. Dairy products also contain some carbs, in the form of milk sugars. On Atkins you count grams of Net Carbs, rather than grams of total carbs, because fibre is a form of carbohydrate and has minimal impact on blood sugar levels.

Protein

Your body needs protein because it contains the amino acids that are the building blocks your body uses to repair and regenerate body tissues and cells. It helps maintain a healthy immune system and manufactures hormones. Plus, digesting and metabolizing protein burns twice the calories than digesting and metabolizing carbohydrates does. Protein is found in seafood, poultry, eggs, meat and dairy. Soy products, nuts and beans also contain protein as well as carbohydrates.

Fat

Your body uses fat to help improve brain development and cell function, protect your organs, and help you absorb the fat-soluble vitamins A, D, E and K, plus micronutrients in vegetables. Consuming fat stimulates the burning of body fat, and, like protein, fat keeps you feeling full longer. Since it carries flavour, it also makes food more palatable and satisfying.

HOW TO 'EYEBALL' YOUR PROTEIN PORTIONS

Calculating how much protein you eat is simple. There's no need to count calories or grams or weigh your food. You need only about 115 to 170 grams/4 to 6 ounces of cooked protein at each meal. Just use these visual comparisons, and soon you'll find that it's quite easy to 'eyeball' how much protein you need.

25 grams
meat, poultry, tofu, etc.

=

Small matchbox/ remote car key

85 grams
meat, poultry, tofu, etc.

=

Slim paperback book

225 grams
meat, poultry, tofu, etc.

=

Deck of cards/mobile phone

85 grams
fish

=

Chequebook

25 grams
hard cheese

=

An individually wrapped cheese slice or four dice.
(Note: Limit cheese to 115g/4oz daily)

What is a Net Carb?

Net Carbs are calculated by subtracting grams of dietary fibre from total carbohydrate grams on a food label. You can download the Atkins Carb Counter for free at www.atkins.com. This guide provides the Net Carb counts of practically every food.

Nutrition Facts

Serving Size 1 Bar (38g)
Servings per Container 5

Amount Per Serving	
Calories 150	Calories from Fat 90
	% Reference Intake
Total Fat 9g	14%
Saturated Fat 2.5g	13%
Cholesterol 0mg	0%
Sodium 170mg	7%
Total Carbohydrate 17g	6%
Dietary Fibre 10g	40%
Sugars 4g	

THE SKINNY ON FAT

All dietary fat is not created equal. Here's what you need to know.

- **Monounsaturated fats (MUFAs):** are found in olive oil, rapeseed oil and walnuts and most other nuts, as well as avocados. MUFAs are usually liquid at room temperature. *Cook with heart-healthy olive oil, add creamy avocados, and eat walnuts and most other nuts as garnishes or snacks.*

- **Polyunsaturated fats (PUFAs):** liquid both at room temperature and in the refrigerator. They're found mostly in oils from vegetables, seeds and some nuts. *Sunflower, safflower, flaxseed, soybean, corn, cottonseed, grapeseed, and sesame oils are high in PUFAs. So are the oils in fatty fish such as sardines, herring and salmon.*

- **Essential fatty acids (EFAs):** two families of dietary fats that your body can't produce on its own. Both omega-3 and omega-6 EFAs are PUFAs essential to your health and well being. Omega-3s are found in the fat of shellfish and cold-water fish. Omega-6s are found primarily in seeds and grains, as well as in chicken and pork. Unless you're eating a very-low-fat diet, you are most likely getting more than the recommended amount of omega-6s. *Eat foods (or supplements) rich in omega-3 fatty acids, such as shellfish, cold-water ocean fish and fish oil (salmon, tuna, sardines, herring and anchovies, as well as non-fish sources such as flaxseed, almonds, walnuts, and rapeseed oil). Limit your consumption of corn, soybean and peanut oils, which are all high in omega-6s.*

- **Saturated fatty acids (SFAs):** tend to remain solid at room temperature. Butter, lard, suet, and palm and coconut oils are relatively rich in saturated fat. *Fine to consume as part of Atkins' way of eating because we know that the body burns primarily fat on Atkins, and we know from published research that the level of saturated fat in the blood does not increase when you are following Atkins.*

- **Trans fats:** are the only dietary fats you should truly avoid. A high intake of trans fats is associated with an increased heart attack risk, and most recently they have been shown to increase the body's level of inflammation. Typically found in foods you should already be avoiding, including battered fried foods, baked goods, biscuits, crackers, sweets, snack foods, icings and vegetable shortenings. Check the list of ingredients, where trans fats are listed as 'shortening', 'hydrogenated vegetable oil' or 'partially hydrogenated vegetable oil'. *If you see any of these words in the ingredients list, consider an alternative.*

THE BASICS OF ATKINS

ONCE YOU GET THE BASICS OF ATKINS under your belt, you will realize that it is really quite a simple plan to follow. Before you get started, here are a few other things that will help you have a better understanding of Atkins.

Atkins is *not* a 'no-carb' plan. From the very beginning, you will be eating high-quality carbohydrates (many in the form of vegetables) that are rich in nutrients and phytochemicals and high in fibre, which means they are naturally satiating. In fact, with Atkins, you actually eat more servings of vegetables than most adults do.
You don't need to count calories on Atkins. The quality and quantity of the protein, fats and carbohydrates that you eat while on Atkins are most important. The only thing you count on Atkins is your daily grams of Net Carbs, which helps ensure that you are eating the high-quality, nutrient-rich foods that keep you full and satisfied, so your calories naturally fall into a healthy range.
Atkins is *not* a high-protein plan. Though you'll be eating adequate amounts of protein, Atkins' typical intake of about 65 to 175 grams/2¼ to 6¼ ounces of protein a day, depending on your height, is not considered high protein. I like to think

of Atkins as a nutritional approach that features 'optimal' amounts of protein. The ideal amount of protein should make you feel full after your meal, not uncomfortably stuffed and not hungry until your next scheduled meal.

Atkins has built-in portion control. You will be eating foods that are rich in protein and good fat and high in fibre, helping you achieve your goals while controlling your hunger. This is because these foods are naturally self-limiting. Almost everyone has probably scarfed down half a packet of biscuits or a family-sized bag of crisps in one sitting, but have you ever overdone it on hard-boiled eggs or steamed broccoli?

MORE MUSCLE IS BETTER

Muscle is more **metabolically acctive** than fat. This means that every pound of muscle you have uses more calories for **energy** than every pound of fat, even when you're **at rest.**

WHY VEGETABLES
MATTER

When you do Atkins, you'll be eating 12 to 15 grams of Net Carbs of what we call Foundation Vegetables (page 291) a day. Thus, you will probably eat more veggies than you ever have before, and for some very good reasons:

VEGETABLES HELP KEEP YOU FULL FOR LONGER. The fibre and water in vegetables fill you up far more efficiently than do processed carbs that are low in fibre. Combining vegetables with protein and healthy fats will keep you satisfied until it's time for your next meal.

VEGETABLES KEEP YOUR ENERGY LEVELS BALANCED. The fibre in vegetables also helps regulate your blood sugar. If you're eating all your allotted vegetables each day, you shouldn't experience the late-afternoon energy slump (and cravings for sugar) that you may encounter when eating processed carbohydrates.

VEGETABLES PACK A POWERFUL NUTRITIONAL PUNCH. Vegetables tend to be low in calories and high in fibre, which means you may tend to consume fewer calories, while still feeling as satisfied as – if not more satisfied than – when you rely on packaged foods and foods devoid of nutrients.

EATING VEGETABLES MAY ADD YEARS TO YOUR LIFE. Numerous studies[1] show that a diet rich in a variety of colourful vegetables may help decrease the hardening of arteries, help lower cholesterol levels, and help prevent inflammation, a component of many degenerative diseases, including obesity, diabetes, heart disease and Alzheimer's disease. Researchers believe that the antioxidants (vitamins C and E, plus selenium and the carotenoids) may be partly responsible for this effect.

LIVING A LOW-CARB LIFESTYLE
ON YOUR TERMS

———•———

THE AVERAGE PERSON CONSUMES 251 to 300 grams of carbohydrates a day, but very few of us actually realize that. Those carbohydrates, especially when consumed in the form of sugar and refined carbohydrates, have a negative impact on both your health and your waistline.

The majority of people do not realize that you should consume 100 grams of carbohydrates or less in a day. This is where Atkins comes in. Reducing carb intake is a healthy way to live, and I'll show you how you can customize your daily carbohydrate intake based on your needs and a choice of three options: Atkins 20, 40 or 100.

Atkins 20™

Atkins 20 is the classic Atkins plan that has been so successful for millions of people over the past four decades. If you have more than 18 kilograms/40 pounds to lose, have a waist circumference of over 89 centimetres/35 inches (women) or 1 metre/40 inches (men), or are prediabetic or diabetic, this is the plan for you. You'll see results quickly. Even after just a few days, your clothes may fit better. As you approach your weight loss goals, you'll add plenty of fruits, veggies, and eventually whole grains.

HERE'S HOW ATKINS 20™ WORKS:

- START WITH 20 grams of Net Carbs of carbohydrates a day, with 12 to 15 grams of Net Carbs of carbohydrates coming from Foundation Vegetables (see page 291).
- EAT three 115- to 170-gram/4- to 6-ounce servings of protein each day.
- EAT 2 to 4 servings of added fat each day.
- BUDGET the remaining 5 to 8 grams of Net Carbs from the entire acceptable carbohydrates food list (pages 290–294).

Atkins 40™

If you have less than 18 kilograms/40 pounds to lose, you want a wider variety of food choices or you are breast-feeding, Atkins 40 is for you. On this plan, you can enjoy a full range of carbohydrate food options combined with a variety of proteins and fats – while still losing weight at a steady pace and feeling satisfied, never hungry. Your carbohydrate choices includes vegetables, fruits, controlled portions of whole grains, and even potatoes, right from the beginning.

- START WITH 40 grams of Net Carbs of carbohydrates a day, with 12 to 15 grams of Net Carbs of carbohydrates coming from Foundation Vegetables (see page 291).
- EAT three 115- to 170-gram/4- to 6-ounce servings of protein each day.
- EAT 2 to 4 servings of added fat each day.
- BUDGET the remaining 25 grams of Net Carbs from the entire acceptable carbohydrate food list (see all appendices).

Atkins 100™

If you would like to start experiencing some of the positive benefits of reducing your carb intake by gradually making small, smart changes to your eating habits on a daily basis, start here. See how eating this way makes you feel. If you like the changes you are making and feel ready to make more, you can always take it to the next level and try Atkins 40 or even Atkins 20 if you have a significant amount of weight to lose.

HERE'S HOW ATKINS 100™ WORKS:

- START WITH 100 grams of Net Carbs of carbohydrates a day, with a minimum of 12 to 15 grams of Net Carbs of carbohydrates coming from Foundation Vegetables (see page 291).
- EAT three 115- to 170-gram/4- to 6-ounce servings of protein each day.
- EAT 2 to 4 servings of added fat each day.
- BUDGET the remaining 85 grams of Net Carbs from the entire acceptable carbohydrates food list.

IT'S TIME TO EAT RIGHT, NOT LESS

No matter what Atkins plan you choose to follow, stick with these tips for eating right, not less:

- **FAT IS YOUR FRIEND, BUT DON'T GO OVERBOARD.** Stick with three 1-tablespoon servings of healthy fats a day.

- **PROTEIN KEEPS YOU SATISFIED.** Go for 115 to 170 grams/4 to 6 ounces of protein at each meal, maybe a little more if you are tall.

- **GET YOUR VEGGIES IN AT EVERY MEAL.** The fibre from the minimum of 12 to 15 grams of Net Carbs of vegetables that you're eating every day will help fill you up.

- **DON'T SKIP MEALS.** If you do, you'll feel ravenous by the end of the day and be more likely to overdo it at your next meal. Focus on eating three meals and two snacks a day.

- **DON'T CONSUME ALL YOUR CARBS FOR THE DAY IN ONE MEAL.** Spread the recommended amount of carbs out over your meals and snacks.

See Chapter 4 for detailed information on each of these plans.

HOW MANY CARBS

ARE YOU *REALLY* EATING, ANYWAY?

———•———

DO YOU HAVE ANY IDEA how many carbohydrates you eat on a daily basis? Not many of us do, but you might be amazed when you discover that it is way more than you think. You can start by figuring out how many grams of Net Carbs you are eating now. You can do this by recording everything you eat in a food journal (or one of the many online tools or apps available) for a few days. Remember, Net Carbs are calculated by subtracting grams of fibre from grams of total carbohydrates on a food label. This is a valuable exercise to do anyway; once you start reading food labels, you may be surprised at exactly what and how much you are eating, especially foods containing hidden sugars, such as low-fat sweetened yogurt or instant porridge.

Now that you have a rough idea of how many Net Carbs you are consuming daily, start making some small, healthy changes. You can use this as an excellent excuse to clean out your cupboards of processed foods (biscuits, sweets, crisps, and all those other things you know you shouldn't be eating anyway); you can learn more about what foods to toss and what foods to keep beginning on page 32. Focus on lean

KEEP A FOOD JOURNAL

Not only will it help you keep track of your meals and snacks, how many and what kind of carbs you are eating, as well as your portion sizes, you can also use it to record when you are eating and even why. Sometimes we find ourselves eating out of boredom or due to stress, and recording such moments in your food journal can help you begin to understand and recognize your hunger cues. For more tips on how to get started, see page 110.

sources of protein such as poultry, meat, fish and eggs; make sure you add healthy fats (olive oil, almonds and other nuts and seeds, and avocados) and eat plenty of fresh fruits and vegetables. You can find sample meal plans in chapter 4 and Acceptable Foods lists in the appendices to help get you started. Begin with these smart carb swaps and you should start experiencing some of Atkins' positive benefits.

SMART CARB SWAPS

*Small changes lead to big results when you start with
these smart nutrient-rich carb swaps.*

SWAP	FOR
White rice	**Brown rice** or **fibre-rich grains** such as quinoa, which have more nutrients and are higher in protein
White bread or potatoes	**Nutrient-rich wholegrain bread,** or double your serving of fibre-rich veggies
Tortillas or bread slices	**Leaves of lettuce** or romaine (they're naturally low in carbs and will turn your taco or sandwich into a wrap)
Hamburger bun	**Portobello mushroom** (rich in potassium and the perfect low-carb vehicle for a juicy burger)
Fruit juice	**Fresh fruit,** which is higher in fibre and more filling
Low-fat fruit-flavour yogurt	**Full-fat Greek yogurt,** which is higher in protein and lower in sugar. Top with a few blueberries to get your fruit fix.
Crackers	**Almonds** or **pistachios,** which are more satisfying than high-carb crackers and give you an extra boost of protein and heart-healthy fats
Low-fat or fat-free salad dressings (which tend to have sugar added)	**Oil- and vinegar-based** dressings
Breakfast cereal	**Wholegrain porridge** or, even better, a couple of **scrambled eggs**
Sweets	**Fresh fruit** or 25 grams/1 ounce of **dark chocolate,** both lower in carbs and the chocolate is rich in heart-healthy flavonoids

DID YOU KNOW?

Combining vegetables
with protein and healthy
fats will keep you
satisfied until it's time
for your next meal.

ATKINS
YOUR WAY

E VEN IF YOU ARE NOT ready to take the leap into a full-blown low-carb lifestyle, with Atkins you can start at your own pace. Now that you know how Atkins works, in the following chapters I will show you how you can get started and pick the Atkins way of eating that works for you (with additional details on each option). I'll also tell you about more smart carb swaps; nutrient-rich snacks to keep your energy levels on an even keel all day long; food lists; meal plans; low-carb tips for eating out at restaurants, on the road, and even on holiday; and mouthwatering low-carb, low-sugar recipes.

HOW TO ID
HIDDEN SUGARS

Net Carbs are a very good way of determining the effect a certain food will have on your blood sugar. Stick with foods that contain 15 grams of Net Carbs or fewer.

3

LET'S
GET
STARTED

IF YOU ARE READING THIS BOOK,

most likely it is because you are interested in a better
way of eating – one that has the power to improve your health, boost
your energy and help you feel and look better.

I'm going to show you how
you can **get started** on
making small steps toward
**embracing a low-carb
lifestyle** and all the amazing
food you *can* eat.

IN THE PREVIOUS CHAPTERS, I have shown the negative impact certain foods may have on your health, as well as how Atkins works in a positive way to optimize your health. Now it's time to talk about the fun stuff – I'm going to show you how you can get started on making small steps toward embracing a low-carb, low-sugar lifestyle and all the amazing food you *can* eat.

Before you skip to the recipes in the second half of this book, first things first: having the right food available is your secret to success. It's time to clean out and organize your fridge, freezer and pantry and toss all foods containing hidden sugars, added sugars, and processed carbohydrates. Once you have a clean 'low-carb' slate, it's time to go grocery shopping. I will give you some important shopping tips so that you can stock your kitchen with fresh, delicious and naturally low-carb foods – carbohydrates rich in fibre, plus protein and healthy fats – that you will love to eat. And you will definitely want to keep reading to discover some essential tools and gadgets to help you along the way.

When you finish this chapter, you will have everything you need to get started on the Atkins plan of your choice based on your goals (you will learn more about Atkins 20, Atkins 40 and Atkins 100 in chapter 4) and all the tools and food you need at your fingertips so you can start cooking some of the mouthwatering recipes in this book.

HOW TO SET S.M.A.R.T. GOALS

If you are ready to embrace a better way of eating by reducing your carb and sugar intake and making small, healthy changes you can live with, it helps to set some goals so you can stay focused. You need to make sure your goals are S.M.A.R.T.: Specific, Measureable, Attainable, Realistic and Timely. This proven strategy will improve your chances of success. Here's how to get started:

SPECIFIC: You have a greater chance of achieving a specific goal than a general goal. A goal that is too general would be 'I'd like to eat fewer carbs.' A specific goal is 'I'd like to reduce my carbs to 100 grams of Net Carbs a day, five days a week."

MEASURABLE: Next you need to establish your criteria for success. If your goal is to reduce your carb intake to 100 grams of Net Carbs a day, this is something you can easily measure by tracking your daily grams of Net Carbs in a food journal or the Atkins app (see page 42) to gauge your starting point and your progress.

ATTAINABLE: You want to make sure you can actually achieve the goal you set, or you may become discouraged and quit. For example, cutting back to 100 grams of Net Carbs a day may be more attainable for you than deciding to cut back to 20 grams of Net Carbs a day right away.

REALISTIC: Get real! You want to challenge yourself, but you also don't want to set yourself up to fail. Perhaps cutting back to 100 grams of Net Carbs seven days a week is an unrealistic expectation, maybe due to your travel or work schedule. Start with 100 grams of Net Carbs a day five days a week and commit to achieving that!

TIMELY: Your goal should have a deadline so that you have a timeline by when you hope to accomplish it. At that point, you can evaluate your progress and set new goals.

Now that you understand the process of S.M.A.R.T. goal setting, your options are endless. Here's one more tip that will help you stay focused on successfully achieving your goals: review them daily! You can program reminders in your smartphone or even jot them down and post them on your computer or refrigerator. Display them wherever you think you will see a powerful and inspiring reminder.

CREATING YOUR OWN
LOW-CARB KITCHEN

———— • ————

WHEN YOU TOSS THOSE TEMPTING treats that have been contributing to blood sugar spikes, constant cravings, low energy, mood swings and more, you will begin to feel so much better. Start by giving your kitchen a low-carb, low-sugar overhaul. I will divide your kitchen into the categories of fridge, freezer, and pantry so you have step-by-step instructions for each. Giving your kitchen this kind of attention will set you up to begin eating right, not less.

Fridge

TOSS THESE NOW

- Your first (and easiest) step is to toss anything that is expired (hello, salad dressing that's three years old).

- Next, toss anything that doesn't look or smell good, including vegetables that are past their prime. Don't worry, I will show you some tricks for not letting food go to waste in the future.

- Now it's time to read some labels. You would be amazed at the sugar lurking in foods such as barbecue sauce, salad dressing, low-fat yogurt, spaghetti sauce (you should probably toss that two-week-old, half-full jar anyway), jams, and jellies. Now, I am not suggesting you throw out perfectly good food, but you could at least delegate a section of your fridge as a 'high-sugar/high-carb' zone if you have other household members who will eat it. Once those foods are gone, if you are on Atkins 20™ or Atkins 40™, I would suggest replacing them with low-carb options. Sauces (such as barbecue, pasta and steak sauces) should not contain more than 3 grams of Net Carbs per serving.

- Now that the shelves and drawers are cleared out, this is your chance to wipe down your fridge and clean up all those mysterious spills so you are truly starting with a shiny, clean slate.

WHAT TO KEEP

- Fortunately, many things in your fridge may be naturally low in carbs already, including most vegetables, some fruits, meats, eggs, dairy products and oils.

- You can also keep condiments such as salsa, hot sauce, mustard, low-sugar or sugar-free salad dressings, mayonnaise, horseradish, pesto, lemon or lime juice, and soy sauce or tamari.

Freezer

- Start by tossing anything that's expired, freezer-burned, or impossible to identify (including that mysterious thing wrapped in foil that has been lurking in the darkest depths of your freezer for years).
- It's time to read the labels again. Depending on their sugar and Net Carb content, you might need to say so long to processed frozen food, such as waffles, breakfast pastries, pizza, pasta, chicken nuggets, ice cream and more.

WHAT TO KEEP

- Keep frozen broccoli, cauliflower, peppers and spinach. Watch out for frozen vegetables that are high in carbs, such as potatoes and sweetcorn.

SMART LOW-CARB CHOICES FOR YOU *AND* YOUR FAMILY

If you are doing Atkins 100 or you have other members in your family who would like to make more healthful choices, look for foods that contain less than 5 grams of sugar and less than 15 grams of Net Carbs per serving. If there is any added sugar, make sure it is one of the last three ingredients on the ingredients list.

- Frozen berries are naturally low in carbs. Check the labels on other frozen fruit.
- Protein such as frozen meats, prawns, seafood and more are all perfect to keep.

Pantry

TOSS THESE NOW

- Canned soups are typically high in carbs, but you can keep tomato soup or chicken and vegetable soups, broccoli or vegetable cream soups, as well as squash soups, which are typically lower in carbs. Canned fruit is usually packed with added sugar and syrups, but you can keep canned fruit packed in its own juices; just drain off the juice before eating.
- It's time to toss breakfast cereal and instant porridge, unless you use a high-fibre bran or flax cereal with 15 grams of Net Carbs or less. Toss all those sneaky snacks: crackers, crisps, biscuits and more. Replace them with cheese crisps or flax crisps that contain less than 3 grams of Net Carbs or less per serving if you are on Atkins 20, 5 grams of Net Carbs or less if you are on Atkins 40, or snap pea chips that have 15 grams of Net Carbs or less if you are on Atkins 100. Next time you go to the store, seek out high-fibre seed crackers, which are typically low in Net Carbs.
- This is also a good excuse to go through your spice rack and toss anything that smells stale or that is years old.

- Since most of the food in your pantry is nonperishable, you can donate anything that is not opened to a local food bank. And if you have family members who will revolt in protest if you donate or toss those tempting treats, store them on a shelf that is easily accessible to them but not you.

WHAT TO KEEP

- You probably already have some great low-carb options in your pantry, including:

Canned seafood (tuna, salmon, crab)

Sardines

Anchovies

Canned tomatoes

Salsas

Pasta sauce or tomato sauce without added sugar or 5 grams of sugar or less per serving

Canned green chillies

Tomato purée

Canned pumpkin

Chicken stock or broth

Beef stock or broth

Vegetable stock or broth

Nuts

Roasted red peppers (rinse if there is sugar in the ingredients)

Sun-dried tomatoes in oil (a little adds lots of flavour)

Artichoke hearts

Jars of pesto or other vegetable-based sauces

Other canned low-carb vegetables and beans (read the labels)

Dill pickles

Italian pickled vegetables

Nut butters

Olives

Your 'Get Started' Atkins Grocery List

Once you have cleaned out your fridge, freezer and pantry, you should have a better idea of what low-carb foods you will need to buy to stock your kitchen. You can start with this general grocery list. In upcoming chapters, you will be able to add to and customize this list in much more detail based on how you decide to do Atkins (in Chapter 4, I'll give you more meal plans and Acceptable Foods lists to help you) and which recipes you want to start cooking – there are so many to choose from, I guarantee you will be inspired!

Let's Talk About Carbs (Again)

Let's remember that Atkins is not about eliminating carbs. What you have learned so far is that certain carbs have a negative effect on your blood sugar and your health, but there are also foods that are crucial to your well-being that truly make this a lifestyle. Think of these foods as the foundation of your new way of eating. Initially there may be some carbs you will need to steer clear of and others you will eat in moderation, ensuring that those you do eat are high-fibre carbohydrates balanced by sufficient protein and healthy fats. In reality, this is the way everyone should be eating. Now let's start working on that low-carb grocery list.

PRODUCE

You can eat a huge assortment of veggies on Atkins, and this list is just the tip of the iceberg; it includes colourful vegetables and plenty of other salad essentials. You should consume a minimum of 12 to 15 grams of Net Carbs of vegetables a day, and you can mix and match raw and cooked vegetables to suit your needs. The Net Carb counts of these vegetables range from 0 to a little over 5 grams of Net Carbs per serving, and I have organized this list in order from the smallest amount of Net Carbs to the largest.

HOW TO READ A FOOD LABEL[1]

SERVING SIZE

Watch out! The amount shown on the label, as well as calories per serving, refers to a single serving, and many packages contain more than one serving.

TOTAL FAT

You can consume higher levels of saturated, polyunsaturated and monounsaturated fat on Atkins because you are burning fat, instead of carbohydrates, for fuel. You should, however, avoid trans fats, because they have been shown to increase levels of 'bad' LDL cholesterol while decreasing levels of 'good' HDL cholesterol. If the ingredients list includes hydrogenated or partially hydrogenated oil, the product contains trans fats.

TOTAL CARBS

Remember to subtract grams of fibre from total grams of carbs to get Net Carbs. You will see grams of sugar, but keep in mind that food labels do not distinguish between added sugar and naturally occurring sugar. You will have to dig deeper into the ingredients list to discover that.

REFERENCE INTAKE

The Reference Intake (RI) is the recommended amount of each nutrient for average adults and is based on a 2,000-calorie diet. If the RI of a nutrient is 5 percent or less, the food is considered to be low in that nutrient; if it is 20 percent or higher, it is considered high.

INGREDIENTS

This includes everything in the food product in order of highest content. This is where you'll find added sugars and trans fats, as well as naturally occurring sugars and whole or refined grains.

Nutrition Facts

Serving Size 1 Bar (38g)
Servings per Container 5

Amount Per Serving

Calories 150	Calories from Fat 90

	% Reference Intake
Total Fat 9g	14%
Saturated Fat 2.5g	13%
Cholesterol 0mg	0%
Sodium 170mg	7%
Total Carbohydrate 17g	6%
Dietary Fibre 10g	40%
Sugars 4g	
Protein 8g	
Vitamin A	0%
Vitamin C	0%
Calcium	6%
Iron	6%

* Percent Reference Intake is based on a 2,000 calorie diet.

INGREDIENTS: ALMONDS, CHICORY ROOT FIBRE, SOLUBLE CORN FIBRE, SOY PROTEIN ISOLATE, SOYBEANS, PEANUTS, DRIED BLUEBERRIES, POLYDEXTROSE, SUNFLOWER OIL, PALM KERNEL OIL, WHEY PROTEIN CONCENTRATE, APPLE JUICE CONCENTRATE, CONTAINS LESS THAN 2% OF: NATURAL FLAVOUR, RAISINS, DRIED APPLES, WHEY POWDER, RICE STARCH, SALT, SOY LECITHIN, OAT FIBRE, CITRIC ACID, VANILLA POWDER, SUCRALOSE. 120202
CONTAINS ALMONDS, SOY, PEANUTS, MILK.
MADE IN A FACILITY THAT ALSO USES EGGS, OTHER TREE NUTS, WHEAT.

Sprouts

Chicory greens

Endive

Olives, green or black

Watercress

Rocket

Radishes

Spinach

Pak choi

Lettuce, all types

Turnip greens

Hearts of palm

Radicchio

Mushrooms

Artichokes

Celery

Pickle, dill

Broccoli raab

Broccoli

Sauerkraut

Avocado

Daikon radish

Red/white onion

Courgette

Cucumber

Cauliflower

Beetroot greens

Fennel

Okra

Rhubarb

Swiss chard

Asparagus

Broccolini

Peppers

Aubergine

Kale

Spring onions

Turnips

Tomato

Jicama

Yellow squash

Cabbage

Green beans

Leeks

Shallots

Brussels sprouts

Spaghetti squash

Kohlrabi

Pumpkin

Garlic

Mangetout

MEAT

You can have any kind of meat on Atkins. Here are some options:

Beef

Ham

Lamb

Pork

Veal

Venison

Poussin

Chicken

Duck

Goose

Pheasant

Quail

Turkey

Ostrich

Avoid chicken nuggets, breaded cutlets and anything that has been deep-fried, stuffed, breaded, battered or coated in flour.

SEAFOOD

You can also have any kind of fish or shellfish on Atkins.

FISH	SHELLFISH
Flounder	Clams
Herring	Crabmeat
Salmon	Prawns
Sardines	Shrimp
Sole	Squid
Tuna	Lobster
Trout	Mussels*
Cod	Oysters*
Halibut	

Avoid anything deep-fried, stuffed, breaded, battered or coated with flour.

Oysters and mussels are slightly higher in Net Carb counts.

DAIRY PRODUCTS

You can stock your fridge with these essentials. Eggs are a versatile and tasty part of Atkins, and you'll find some 'eggs-cellent' recipes in this book.

Large eggs

Double cream

Single cream

Half-and-half

Soured cream, full-fat

Mayonnaise

Unsweetened almond milk

Plain coconut milk

Unsweetened soy milk

You can use liquid cream or half-and-half in your coffee. Watch out for packaged creamers; many are full of sugar or high-fructose corn syrup.

CHEESE

Here are some cheeses to start with:

Parmesan

Romano

Goats'

Blue cheese

Cheddar

Gouda

Mozzarella, whole-milk

Swiss

Cream cheese, full-fat or plain

Feta

Havarti

Jarlsberg

String

FATS AND OILS

There are no carbs in these, just fat. A typical serving size is 1 tablespoon.

Butter

Mayonnaise (watch out for added sugar)

Coconut oil

Olive oil

VEGETABLE OILS
(look for cold pressed or expeller pressed):

Rapeseed

Walnut

Soybean

Grapeseed

Sesame

Sunflower

Safflower

Use olive oil for sautéing only. Walnut or sesame oil should not be used for cooking but can be drizzled on cooked veggies or salad.

BEVERAGES

Always check the Nutrition Facts for high sugar content. You can pump up the flavour of water with a few squeezes of lemon or lime.

Clear broth/bouillon (or you can make your own nutrient-rich bone broth from our recipe on page 161)

Club soda

Decaffeinated or regular coffee and tea, sugar-free iced tea

Diet fizzy drinks

No-calorie flavoured sparkling water

Herb tea without added sugar

Unflavoured soy/almond milk

WATER, INCLUDING:

Filtered

Mineral

Spring

Tap

HERBS AND SPICES

All fresh herbs work great with Atkins, and there are minimal amounts of carbs in dried herbs. If you need to restock your spice rack, this list is a great place to start, but your options are endless. Just watch out for spice mixes that contain added sugar.

Basil

Cayenne pepper

Coriander

Dill

Oregano

Tarragon

Parsley

Chives, fresh or dehydrated

Ginger, fresh

Rosemary, dried

Sage, ground

Black pepper

Salt

Garlic

SALAD DRESSINGS

Look for dressings with 3 grams of Net Carbs per serving or less. Even better? Make your own salad dressing – you can take your pick from the recipes in chapter 9.

Red wine vinegar

Caesar

Ranch

Lemon and lime juice

Blue cheese

Balsamic vinegar

Italian/Creamy Italian

French

NON-CALORIC SWEETENERS

You should count each packet as 1 gram of Net Carbs. Try not to consume more than three per day.

Sucralose (Splenda)

Stevia (Truvia)

Saccharin

Xylitol

SMART SHOPPING
STRATEGIES

THESE HELPFUL TIPS WILL HELP turn your grocery shopping excursion into a streamlined and effective experience.

Start with a plan. Review your schedule for the week; this will help you determine what meals and snacks you need to shop for. For example, if you know you have an evening full of pickups and drop-offs for kids' after-school activities, pick a recipe that uses a slow cooker so that you have an appetizing low-carb meal waiting when everyone gets home. If you have a busy day of meetings and you know you'll be eating lunch at your desk, make sure you cook an extra serving or two for dinner the night before, so you can take leftovers to work. If the weather looks nice, pick a meal that you can prepare on the barbecue.

Make a list. This helps you stay focused and avoid impulse buys. Shopping list apps make it a breeze to update your list whenever you need to. Some apps allow you to link your list with family members so everyone can update the list in 'real time'.

Pick a shopping day. I always like to do my grocery shopping for the week on Sunday. Pick a day when you won't be rushed trying to get everything you need and when you will have plenty of time to prep your food for the week.

Never shop when you're hungry. Make sure you're hydrated and have a low-carb snack before you go, so you're not tempted by impulse buys simply because you are starving. (You'll find a list of quick and easy low-carb snacks in chapter 5.)

Shop the perimeter of the store. This is where the foods that make up the 'foundation' of Atkins are located: fruits, vegetables, dairy, meat and fish. I start in the produce section and fill my trolley with a rainbow of colourful vegetables. From there I hit the deli counter for roasted meats and cheeses, then the meat and seafood counter, and finally the dairy section.

Steer clear of the centre aisles. The centre aisles usually feature the food you are trying to avoid – the processed stuff that is high in carbs and packed with hidden sugars. I usually need to hit the centre aisles only for canned tuna and salmon, canned vegetables, stock and bouillon, spices, oils and condiments.

PREPPING FOR THE WEEK

O NCE YOU GET HOME FROM the supermarket, you're not quite done! Spending a little time up front to prep your food for the week is another secret to success with Atkins. It makes it much easier to make healthy choices.

Slice and dice. Wash and cut up the veggies you bought, and store them in clear containers so you can grab a handful of veggies for a quick snack or throw together a salad in minutes. This is also the key to not letting those beautiful veggies go to waste.

Prep your leafy greens. Give them a spin in a salad spinner and store in a clear container or zip-lock plastic bag with a paper towel to soak up any extra moisture.

Cut up your cauliflower and broccoli. Remove the outer leaves from a head of cauliflower or broccoli and cut into florets. Store the florets in a loosely sealed plastic bag so it's easy to grab a handful any time you want to roast or stir-fry them. If you want to make cauliflower or even broccoli 'rice', pulverize the head of cauliflower or broccoli with a food processor and store in individual, sealed plastic bags or containers. You may also be able to find frozen or fresh cauliflower rice in your grocery store's frozen or produce section.

Shred or spiralize. If you bought summer squash or courgettes, you can spiralize or shred them in advance, drain the liquid, and store in an airtight container so you have fresh low-carb 'noodles' that you can use in place of pasta or as a side dish. You can even add them to soups or an omelette. If you don't feel like making your own, you might be able to find packaged spiralized vegetables in the produce section.

Check your eggs. This is a great opportunity to make one of the best (and portable) low-carb snacks ever, in my opinion: hard-boiled eggs. Hard boil and store a dozen in their original carton in the fridge, and you'll have everything you need for a quick egg salad, devilled eggs or a grab-and-go protein-packed snack.

Prep your poultry. If you have time, bake, sauté or barbecue a batch or two of chicken thighs or breasts in advance, which can be a lifesaver during the week. Once your chicken is cooked, let it cool slightly and divide into 115- to 170-gram/4- to 6-ounce portions and store in the fridge. Now it is ready for salads, wraps, soups or the low-carb recipe of your choice. After three to four days, freeze any leftover chicken until you're ready to eat it. You can use the same cook-in-advance method for minced beef or turkey.

LOW-CARB
KITCHEN GADGETS

These handy tools will make prepping, cooking and storing
your low-carb ingredients and meals a breeze.

SPIRALIZER: This gadget cuts vegetables into long noodles or strips, resembling spaghetti. 'Courgetti' (spaghetti made from courgettes) is your low-carb answer to pasta.

SLOW COOKER: If you want a delicious, hot, low-carb meal waiting for you after a busy day, you need a slow cooker. Prep the ingredients and throw them into your slow cooker in the morning, set the timer, and your meal is ready when you are. It's perfect for soups, stews, casseroles, curries and roasts.

IMMERSION BLENDER: This handheld tool lets you blend ingredients or purée food right in the container you are preparing it in. You can purée soups or use it to make whipped cream, mayonnaise, vinaigrettes or smoothies.

SALAD SPINNER: This is used to wash and remove excess water from your salad greens, because who needs a soggy salad?

MINI FOOD PROCESSOR: This gadget takes up hardly any room on a shelf or your worktop and can dice, chop and purée your ingredients in minutes.

STORAGE CONTAINERS: You will need these to store and transport leftovers. You can also use them to store cut-up veggies in the fridge, perfect for low-carb snacking.

COOKBOOK HOLDER: You might want a nice stand to display this book in your kitchen so you can easily refer to the tasty low-carb recipe of your choice while you are cooking.

ESSENTIALS
FOR A LOW-CARB, LOW-SUGAR LIFESTYLE

Discovering a better way of eating and moving more may inspire you to incorporate some other healthy habits into your life. These tools will help you do all of that.

ATKINS APP: Atkins provides this free tool, which has a host of helpful features, including:

- **Food search.** You can find nutritional info for grocery items, restaurant meals, and Atkins-friendly recipes and products.

- **Meal tracker.** You can track your daily grams of Net Carbs, and it also includes popular brands and restaurant dishes and a breakdown of fats, protein and Foundation Vegetables.

- **Progress tracker.** This helps you stay on track with your goals.

- **Atkins overview and Acceptable Foods lists.** If you ever need a refresher on what Atkins is all about or need to review a food list on the fly, you'll find the information right in the Atkins app. Plus, you have access to Atkins' database of more than 1,000 low-carb recipes.

ATKINS CARB COUNTER: This guide gives you the Net Carb counts of practically every food. You can download it for free at Atkins.com.

FOOD JOURNAL: There are many food journal apps you can choose from; some even let you upload photos of your meals and snacks so you have a visual diary of what you eat each day.

ACTIVITY TRACKER: A variety of activity trackers allow you to track your daily steps, workouts and even sleep. You can even sync your device with the Atkins app.

WATER BOTTLE: It's easy to mistake thirst for hunger, which is why it's important to stay hydrated. Plus, water helps flush toxins from your body and is important to your overall good health. You should drink at least eight 240ml/ 8fl oz glasses of water daily to prevent dehydration. This is much easier if you have a water bottle by your side and refill it often.

EXERCISE
HAS ITS BENEFITS

ATKINS WILL HELP YOU IMPROVE your health and boost your energy, even without having to exercise. But there are many benefits to getting out there and moving more – that is, if you're interested in maintaining your weight, sleeping better, managing stress, improving your mood, boosting your energy, building muscle (especially because a pound of muscle burns more calories at rest than a pound of fat), and decreasing your risk of heart disease, diabetes and metabolic syndrome. The American Heart Association recommends the following:[2]

FOR OVERALL CARDIOVASCULAR HEALTH:

* At least **30 minutes of moderate-intensity** aerobic activity at **least five days per week for a total of 150 minutes**

OR

* At least **25 minutes of vigorous** aerobic activity at least **three days per week for a total of 75 minutes**; or a combination of moderate- and vigorous-intensity aerobic activity

AND

* **Moderate- to high-intensity muscle-strengthening activity** at least **two days per week** for additional health benefits

FOR LOWERING BLOOD PRESSURE AND CHOLESTEROL:

* An average of **40 minutes of moderate-to vigorous-intensity** aerobic activity **three or four times per week**

Exercise is anything that gets your body moving and your heart pumping, including walking, jogging, biking, exercise classes, stair climbing and playing sports. Strength and stretching exercises are also good for building and strengthening muscles and increasing overall stamina.

The reason I call this a **'guidebook** for living a low-carb and low-sugar lifestyle' is that I'm here to **gently guide you** in the direction you want to go.

BECOME MINDFUL
ABOUT HOW YOU EAT

*Did you know that it takes about 20 minutes for your
brain to register that you are full?*

If you scarf down your meal too quickly or while you are distracted, whether it is because you are eating lunch in front of your computer again or you are busy updating your social media status, you may end up overeating. Some studies[3] are beginning to suggest that eating more slowly and thoughtfully may actually help you make healthier food choices. This is called mindful eating, when you bring your full attention to the ritual of eating and enjoying the flavours and the experience.

Listening to your body's physical cues will lead to recognizing your body's hunger signals, which should help you begin to understand when you are actually eating because you are hungry instead of for emotional reasons or out of boredom.

Fortunately, you have an advantage with Atkins, because the powerful combination of adequate amounts of protein, high-fibre carbohydrates and healthy fats naturally helps you feel more satisfied and able to recognize and control your hunger signals. Slowing down and being mindful of how and what you eat with Atkins has its benefits, such as:

- Controlling your appetite
- Preserving muscle tissue
- Regulating your blood sugar
- Improving your cholesterol
- Decreasing your risk of heart disease
- Preventing diabetes
- Keeping your energy levels steady all day long

MOVING FORWARD

IF YOU HAVEN'T ALREADY, TAKE a little time to review the tips on how to set S.M.A.R.T. goals. This will help give you focus and direction. Feel free to share your goals with friends and family; maybe you can inspire them to join you on your journey toward a better way of eating, because research[4] has shown that you are more likely to be successful at making healthy changes to your lifestyle when you have support and motivation of friends and family. Once you have set your goals and you've started overhauling your fridge, freezer and cupboards, following my grocery shopping tips, and figuring out everything you need to do to prep and organize your food for the week, you will be on your way toward living a low-carb lifestyle on your terms.

The reason I call this a 'guidebook for living a low-carb, low-sugar lifestyle' is that I'm here to gently guide you in the direction you want to go in, so you have all the facts you need to decide exactly how you would like to incorporate Atkins into your life. If you're ready for a little more structure, Atkins 20 or Atkins 40 may be the approach you choose. Or you can start with Atkins 100, which is a way to ease

slowly into reducing your carbs with small, healthy changes. As you can see, there are plenty of options to choose from, so let's learn more about them.

4

ATKINS
YOUR WAY:
ATKINS 20, ATKINS 40
OR ATKINS 100

In this chapter, you'll learn all about Atkins 20, Atkins 40 and Atkins 100.

It's important to learn about these options, because
Atkins is a way of eating that can be customized to your needs,
and you can easily move between Atkins 20, Atkins 40 and
Atkins 100, depending on your goals, which may change over time.

OVER THE YEARS, I'VE LIVED every aspect of the Atkins lifestyle, from classic Atkins 20 to Atkins 100 and everything in between. This way of living has benefited me in many ways. First, I do not have any signs of heart disease or diabetes (I lost both parents and two siblings to complications of those diseases), I am at a healthy weight, I never became overweight as everyone else in my family did as they aged, and I have great energy.

Once you decide how you want to do Atkins, you will be able to fine-tune your grocery list and meal plans based on the Acceptable Foods lists for each option. No matter which way you go, there are plenty of delicious food choices so that you will never feel deprived, plus ways you can customize Atkins to your needs.

DAILY TARGETS BY PLAN

STARTING POINT	ATKINS 20™	ATKINS 40™	ATKINS 100™
NET CARBS (grams) = total carbs minus fibre	20	40	100
PROTEIN	3 servings of 115–170g/4–6oz per serving	3 servings of 115–170g/4–6oz per serving	3 servings of 115–170g/4–6oz per serving
HEALTHY FATS	3 servings of added healthy fats per day: butter, salad dressings, olive oil, etc.	3 servings of added healthy fats per day: butter, salad dressings, olive oil, etc.	3 servings of added healthy fats per day: butter, salad dressings, olive oil, etc.
CARBOHYDRATES	LIMITED: 12–15g Net Carbs from low carb vegetables, AKA foundation vegetables (see page 291 for list). Remaining carbs from whole milk dairy (ie: hard cheeses, soured cream, cream) or low-carb products	ALL FOOD GROUPS: 12–15g Net Carbs from low carb vegetables, AKA foundation vegetables (see page 291 for list). Remaining carbs from fruit, nuts, legumes, dairy, and/or whole grains	ALL FOOD GROUPS: 12–15g Net Carbs from low-carb vegetables, AKA foundation vegetables (see page 291 for list). Remaining carbs from fruit, nuts, legumes, dairy, and/or whole grains

	ATKINS 20™	ATKINS 40™	ATKINS 100™
ADDING CARBS BACK INTO YOUR DIET	Add in 5g Net Carb increments starting with lower carb foods and gradually progressing to higher-carb foods • Nuts and seeds (not chestnuts) • Berries, cherries and melon (not watermelon) • Whole milk yogurt and fresh cheeses, such as cottage cheese and ricotta • Legumes, including chickpeas and lentils • Tomato and vegetable juice 'cocktail' (not fruit juices or dried fruits) • Higher-carb vegetables, such as winter squash, carrots and peas	Add 10g Net Carbs when you're within 10 pounds of your goal weight by increasing your serving size or adding more variety If you're still losing, you can continue to add 10g Net Carbs each week until you find the level of carb intake where your goal weight is maintained	Continue to consume 100g Net Carbs daily to maintain weight. If you gain weight, lower carbs.

	ATKINS 20™	ATKINS 40™	ATKINS 100™
VEGETABLES	12–15g Net Carbs from low carb vegetables, AKA foundation vegetables (see list on page 291)	12–15g Net Carbs from low carb vegetables, AKA foundation vegetables (see list on page 291) Remaining carbs from fruit, nuts, legumes, dairy and/or whole grains	12–15g net carbs from low carb vegetables, AKA foundation vegetables (see list on page 291) Remaining carbs from fruit, nuts, legumes, dairy and/or whole grains
PROTEIN	3 servings of 115–170g/4–6oz per serving	3 servings of 115–170g/4–6oz per serving	3 servings of 115–170g/4–6oz per serving
HEALTHY FATS	3 servings of added healthy fats per day: butter, salad dressings, olive oil, etc.	3 servings of added healthy fats per day: butter, salad dressings, olive oil, etc.	3 servings of added healthy fats per day: butter, salad dressings, olive oil, etc.
ADDING FOODS BACK INTO YOUR DIET	PROGRESSIVE: There are five important points to understand as you begin to reintroduce foods: • Count your carbs • Introduce new foods one at a time • Experiment with new foods so you don't get bored • Don't forget foundation vegetables • Write it down Continue to add carbs in 5g Net Carb increments until your weight stabilizes. Maintain carb intake to reach your goal.	ALL FOOD GROUPS: Continue to avoid/limit sugar, refined carbs, and any 'trigger' foods that cause you to consume too many carbs Continue to add carbs in 10g Net Carb increments until your weight stabilizes. Maintain carb intake to maintain your weight.	ALL FOOD GROUPS: Continue to avoid/limit sugar, refined carbs, and any 'trigger' foods that cause you to consume too many carbs.

HOW TO GET STARTED ON
ATKINS 20

———•———

ATKINS 20 IS BASED ON Atkins' classic nutritional approach, which has been popular and effective for forty years. Atkins 20 consists of four levels. You will start by consuming 20 grams of Net Carbs a day and gradually increase the amount as you reintroduce various foods. If you decide that Atkins 20 is the way to go, most likely you are ready to commit to giving the way you have been eating a total makeover. You are willing to embrace a clear-cut, step-by-step structured plan that leaves little room for guesswork and helps you kick carb and sugar cravings to the curb while eliminating blood sugar spikes and energy and mood swings and improving your overall health and wellness.

To start, you reduce your carb intake to 20 grams of Net Carbs a day, which, over the years, has been proven to be highly effective. In fact, for some people, going 'cold turkey' with carbs that quickly convert to sugar and added sugar may be the only thing that works. I've seen this firsthand with many of the folks I've worked with and talked to over the years (reducing carbs has certainly helped me control my cravings and my killer sweet tooth), but science also shows this to be true. Some studies suggest

DID YOU KNOW?

Atkins 20 is a clear-cut, step-by-step structured plan that leaves **little room for guesswork** and helps you kick carb and sugar **cravings** to the curb.

that reducing your consumption of these foods, and replacing them with protein, healthy fats, and fibre-rich carbohydrates low in sugar means you end up craving them less, if at all.[1] In fact, this way of eating has been shown to reduce your cravings in all food categories, including fatty, salty, high-carb and fast food, not just sugar and sweets.

Ready to get started? It's quite simple, actually. Just stick with the list of Acceptable Foods for each level, and you can expect some big changes as you learn how to eat right, not less!

ATKINS 20™

	PHASE 1 >>>>	PHASE 2 >>>>	PHASE 3 >>>>	PHASE 4 >>>>
	20-25g Daily Net Carbs	25-50g Daily Net Carbs	50-80g Daily Net Carbs	80-100g Daily Net Carbs

ACCEPTABLE FOODS:

	PHASE 1	PHASE 2	PHASE 3	PHASE 4
Foundation vegetables, proteins, healthy fats and most cheeses	●	●	●	●
Nuts and seeds	●	●	●	●
Berries, cherries or melon	●	●	●	●
Whole milk Greek yogurt, ricotta or cottage cheese	●	●	●	●
Legumes	●	●	●	●
Tomato juice	●	●	●	●
Additional fruits	●	●	●	●
Starchy vegetables	●	●	●	●
Whole grains	●	●	●	●

Your Personal Carb Balance

You will eventually discover the maximum daily grams of Net Carbs you can eat while continuing to improve your overall wellness, keep your appetite and cravings under control, and stay energized. This is called your Personal Carb Balance, and it is affected by your age, gender, activity level, hormonal status and other factors.

See Appendix A for the Acceptable Foods list for Atkins 20, Level 1, page 289.

Atkins 20, Level 1

In level 1, your goal is to shift your body from burning primarily carbs for fuel to burning primarily fat for fuel, and you will do so by reducing your daily grams of Net Carbs to 20.

You'll follow this level for a minimum of two weeks, but if you are motivated by fast results and appreciate the structure and carefully selected food choices, you can follow it for much longer.

TIPS FOR LEVEL 1

- **Eat three meals and two snacks a day.** There is no reason you ever need to feel hungry on Atkins, especially when you eat a delicious and filling meal or snack every three to four hours (check out the snack recipes in Chapter 7). Pair your carb snacks with either fat or protein. The key is to never let yourself get to the point when you're starving; that's when it's much harder to resist your craving for salty or sweet foods.

- **Eat 20 grams of Net Carbs a day.** This includes 12 to 15 grams of Net Carbs that come from Foundation Vegetables. From the very beginning, you'll be filling your plate with colourful nutrient- and fibre-rich vegetables, and you can pick other carb foods from the list of Level 1 Acceptable Foods (see Appendix A).

- **Make sure you get enough protein.** Protein is a natural metabolism booster. Aim for three 85- to 170-gram/3- to 6-ounce servings a day.

- **Don't fret about fat – too much.** Fat pumps up the flavour of your food. A serving size is 1 tablespoon, and you should eat two to four servings of added fat daily.

- **Drink at least eight 240ml/8fl oz glasses of water daily.** Water is great for your skin, digestion and overall health.

- **Watch out for hidden sugars.** Read food labels carefully, looking for grams of added sugar, particularly in foods such as pasta sauce, ketchup, marinades and salad dressings. In restaurants, request oil and vinegar or a creamy dressing for salad, and request sauces on the side.
- **Use sugar substitutes – in moderation.** That means no more than three packets a day.
- **Stick with the list.** Follow the Level 1 Acceptable Foods list, and you're good to go! If you decide to stay at this level for longer than two weeks, you can also add nuts and seeds.

After two weeks, if you're ready to explore more food choices while continuing to eat right, not less, and progressing steadily toward accomplishing your goals, you can move to the next level.

YOU BOOZE, YOU LOSE?

Although I don't recommend drinking alcohol in Level 1 of Atkins 20, as long as you count the Net Carbs as part of your daily total, an occasional glass of wine is just fine once you transition to Level 2, as well as if you're doing Atkins 40 or Atkins 100. Although alcohol is not stored as fat, your body burns it as fuel first, which postpones any fat burning. Once your body processes the booze, you're back to burning fat for fuel. You can drink Scotch, rye, vodka and gin, but watch what you mix them with. Seltzer, diet tonic water and diet soda mixers don't contain sugar, but juice, tonic water and non-diet soda do. And a drink or two may lower your resistance to that pile of nachos or a slice of pizza. To counteract the cravings, pair your drink of choice with one of our low-carb savoury bites or appetizers in Chapter 10.

Atkins 20, Level 2

In Level 2, you're continuing on the journey toward discovering your Personal Carb Balance. You'll start at 25 daily grams of Net Carbs and increase your overall carb intake in 5-gram increments. You might level off anywhere between 30 and 100 grams of Net Carbs a day.

TIPS FOR LEVEL 2

- **Keep eating those veggies.** Fill your plate with a minimum of 12 to 15 grams of Net Carbs a day of Foundation Vegetables. Sure, vegetables contain carbs, but they are the kind of carbs you should be eating.
- **Start adding carbs back one by one.** If a certain food triggers the cravings you're trying so hard to kick, hold off on that food and try another. For example, if you've decided to try almonds, or maybe chickpeas or strawberries, and suddenly your hunger is uncontrollable and you feel your blood sugar swings start to return, wait to reintroduce them. How the body reacts to certain carbs is different for everyone.
- **Watch your hunger.** Hopefully you're starting to learn how to recognize your hunger cues. When your stomach starts grumbling, have a low-carb snack or eat your next meal earlier than you otherwise might have.
- **Go slow with fruit.** Once you start eating fruit, such as berries, cherries and melon, you may find that it spikes your blood sugar and/or causes cravings. A quick fix is to pair the fruit with fat or protein. For example, you can have berries with double cream, cottage cheese or Greek yogurt or melon with prosciutto or provolone cheese.

When you're ready to start reintroducing even more foods, you can move to Level 3.

Do I Have to Reintroduce All the Acceptable Foods for Each Level?

Nope! If you can't stomach cottage cheese or lentils just aren't your thing, that's fine. There are plenty of other whole foods on Atkins that will add variety and flavour to your meals. And who knows? You might be tempted to try a recipe in this book that features a food you never thought you'd like. Next thing you know, you'll have changed your opinion from 'dislike' to 'like'.

Atkins 20, Level 3

At this point, you are getting closer to meeting your goals and determining your Personal Carb Balance. This level sets the stage so that eating right, not less, can become a way of life for you.

You'll gradually increase your daily Net Carb intake in 10-gram (or 5-gram, if you prefer) increments, continuing to introduce new foods and gauging how they affect your progress toward your goal.

TIPS FOR LEVEL 3

- **Add foods one by one.** Keep an eye on your progress as you reintroduce foods; your age, sex, activity level and metabolism may determine how they affect you.
- **Watch for your trigger foods.** As you continue to add foods back that you haven't eaten in a while, some foods (i.e., a banana, sweetcorn or brown rice) may trigger cravings and uncontrollable hunger. If this is the case, cut them out for a couple of days and then try again.
- **Be patient with plateaus.** The journey toward accomplishing your goals is not always a linear one, and it's totally normal to experience stalls in your progress. If you feel you are on a plateau, reduce your daily Net Carb intake by 10 grams.

If you have accomplished your goals, are in control of your cravings and hunger, and are ready to learn how to maintain the results you have achieved, it's time to move on to Level 4!

SCIENCE SUPPORTS ATKINS

See **Appendix F** for the peer-reviewed independent published **studies that support** Atkins 20, 40 and 100.

See Appendix B for the complete Acceptable Foods list for Atkins 20, Level 2 (page 295)

See Appendix C for the complete Acceptable Foods list for Atkins 20, Level 3 (page 298)

YOUR CARB CRIB SHEET

At this point, you are adding more and more foods that are
higher in carbs to your Atkins menu – more fruit,
plus starchy vegetables and whole grains.
Here are some tried-and-true tips I have found to be very helpful.

FRUIT

This sweet treat adds a burst of juicy flavour to your meals, but it may make your sweet tooth go out of control if you're not careful.

- **START WITH** lower-carb fruits, such as berries, cherries and melon, and progress slowly by swapping one serving of berries or melon for a serving of higher-carb fruit. In other words, don't go bananas over bananas.
- **STICK WITH** two servings of fruit a day, including berries.
- **TREAT FRUITS** higher in carbs as a garnish; for example, add orange slices to your salad or sliced grapes to cottage cheese.
- **PORTION OUT** your fruit. Cut an apple or pear into slices and share them with a family member or save what you don't eat for later.

STARCHY VEGETABLES

Up until now, you've been enjoying a wide variety of Foundation Vegetables. Now you can start adding starchy vegetables, which are also rich in fibre and antioxidants but higher in carbs. Treat them as an accompaniment to your Foundation Vegetables.

- **CRUNCH ON** raw carrots (I love to snack on them with hummus), add grated carrots to tuna or chicken salad, or include them in a cabbage slaw.
- **PINING FOR POTATOES?** Steam and mash potatoes and cauliflower (a Foundation Vegetable) together.
- **GET CREATIVE** with side dishes by sautéing 30g/1oz of peas with sliced spring onions and thinly sliced spinach leaves or stir-frying asparagus, mushrooms and peas together.
- **ROAST ONE CUT-UP POTATO** or sweet potato with an assortment of cut-up Foundation Vegetables, such as mushrooms, courgettes and cauliflower.

WHOLE GRAINS

Last but not least come whole grains. Not everyone can tolerate grains and products made from them, and you've also learned about the hidden sugars that convert to sugar in your blood, so it's best to proceed slowly as you learn how your body reacts to them.

- **DON'T CONFUSE** whole grains with refined grains, such as white flour and white rice. You'll still want to limit baked goods, including bread, pita, tortillas, crackers and cereals made with refined grains, but you can find low-carb versions of these products in Appendix E.
- **START SMALL.** Eat small portions of whole grains, or use them as a garnish. Once again, on Atkins 20, whole grains shouldn't be the star player in your meals but part of the supporting cast.
- **SPRINKLE** some cooked wild rice or quinoa on top of a tossed salad as you would sliced almonds.
- **TOSS** some cooked brown rice or wholewheat couscous with sliced mushrooms, red peppers, courgettes and cooked chicken, beef or pork. This is a nice alternative to traditional stir fry.

Atkins 20, Level 4

When you reach this level, you have succeeded in making significant changes to your eating habits. You should be feeling good, both physically and emotionally. Embracing this better way of eating – a nutritional approach that truly works – will allow you to achieve results that are sustainable for life. You've learned how your body reacts to certain carbs – which foods you can continue to enjoy, which you should eat in moderation, and which you might choose to eat only occasionally. You've also discovered (or rediscovered) how to listen to your body and recognize cravings before they hit, as well as how to satisfy your hunger before it gets out of control. You're in this for the long haul, and now you know exactly how to do it.

TIPS FOR LEVEL 4

Don't forget the basics:

- **Continue to consume** 12 to 15 grams of Net Carbs a day of Foundation Vegetables.
- **Remember to drink** plenty of water (eight 240ml/8fl oz glasses a day).
- **Stick with** two servings of fruit a day.
- **Consume** two to four servings of added fat a day.
- **Eat 115 to 170 grams/4 to 6 ounces** of protein at each meal.
- **Start or keep moving.** Regular physical activity provides a host of health benefits. Why wouldn't you want to take advantage of the boost in energy you may be experiencing?
- **Adjust your carb intake as needed.** You might need to tweak your daily carb intake if you increase or decrease your activity level.
- **Watch your portions.** You can ensure you don't overdo it on nuts or cheese by preportioning servings of these foods in advance.

You Can Always Go Back – to Level 1

Once you have successfully progressed though all four levels of Atkins 20, you can enjoy the results you have achieved and the healthy habits that have become a part of your life. But sometimes life gets in the way. Maybe you've had a stressful week at work, or, even better, you're on holiday. During times like these, it's easy to believe that you'll be just fine having a biscuit or doughnut or a fruity tropical drink. Then you get overly confident and think, 'Well, if I can handle one biscuit, another one or two will be just fine.' Sometimes that may be the case and you're able to bounce right back into your low-carb lifestyle without any undue effects. On the other hand, those foods have the potential to bring back all the cravings you've been trying to conquer. Watch out for carb creep! If you see your hard-earned results start to go south, there is a simple solution: return to Level 1 for a week or two to jump-start your progress and stabilize your blood sugar levels.

ATKINS 20 is easy to do, especially if you start out by following this meal plan (and the Acceptable Foods list), which features two weeks' worth of low-carb meals and snacks you can prepare in minutes, as well as tasty recipes from this book. Feel free to substitute the recipes in this meal plan for others in this book.

ATKINS 20 MEAL PLAN WEEK 1	MONDAY	TUESDAY	WEDNESDAY
BREAKFAST	Egg-filled Avocado with Prosciutto	Creamy Avocado Smoothie	Cauliflower Rice Scrambles
SNACK	Tuna-stuffed Devilled Eggs	Asparagus with Burrata Cheese and Kale Pesto	2 stalks celery, 2 tbsp Ranch Dressing
LUNCH	Ropa Vieja Soup	Baby Kale and Blue Cheese Salad with Warm Hazelnut Dressing	Old Bay Shrimp Salad
SNACK	Low-Carb Flax Meal Bread, 25g/1oz Cheddar cheese	Tuna-stuffed Devilled Eggs	Avocado Toast
DINNER	Chimichurri Steak Bites, Watercress Bacon Salad with Ranch Dressing	170g/6oz salmon, Steamed Artichoke with Homemade Lemon Mayonnaise	Fried Sage Chicken and Courgette
TOTAL NET CARBS	21g	20g	20.5g
TOTAL FV	15g	14.9g	11.9g

THURSDAY	FRIDAY	SATURDAY	SUNDAY
Power Mug Muffin with Cinnamon Butter	Salmon Eggs Benedict	Avocado Toast	Birdies in a Basket
Basic Bone Broth, 2 stalks celery	Asparagus with Burrata Cheese and Kale Pesto	Prosciutto-wrapped Prawns with Kale Mayo	½ Hass avocado, 2 tbsp mayonnaise, Coriander Parmesan Crackers
Mixed Power Greens with Prosciutto-wrapped Chicken Tenders	Smoky Habanero Chilli, ½ Hass avocado	Mixed Asian Greens with Shredded Sesame Chicken	Crispy Duck Spinach Salad with Warm and Tangy Dressing
Bourbon Pecan Pâté, Coriander Parmesan Crackers	Hot Crab Dip, 2 stalks celery	Tuna-stuffed Devilled Eggs	2 Salted Caramel Cheesecake Bites
Italian Stuffed Cabbage, For dessert: Double Chocolate Brownie	Lemon Pepper Prawns with Mangetout	170g/6oz bone-in pork chop, Cheesy Spring Onion Cauliflower Mash	Roasted Fennel & Cod with Moroccan Dried Olives
20.9g	19.3g	20g	20.4g
12.1g	12.9g	12.5g	12.5g

	MONDAY	TUESDAY	WEDNESDAY
BREAKFAST	Cauliflower Rice Scrambles	Avocado Toast	Egg-filled Avocado with Prosciutto
SNACK	Manchego Mini Muffins	Asparagus with Burrata Cheese and Kale Pesto	Tuna-stuffed Devilled Eggs
LUNCH	Roasted Fennel and Cod with Morrocan Dried Olives	Bone Broth Minestrone	170g/6oz chicken breast, Cauliflower Bisque
SNACK	½ Hass avocado, 2 tbsp mayonnaise, Coriander Parmesan Crackers	25g/1oz Monterey Jack cheese, 5 black olives	Chipotle Lime Courgette Crisps
DINNER	Mixed Asian Greens with Shredded Sesame Chicken	Italian Stuffed Cabbage	Smoky Habanero Chilli, ½ Hass avocado
TOTAL NET CARBS	20.7g	20.8g	21.7g
TOTAL FV	13.3g	15.8g	14.8g

ATKINS 20 MEAL PLAN WEEK 2

THURSDAY	FRIDAY	SATURDAY	SUNDAY
Creamy Avocado Smoothie	Power Mug Muffin with Cinnamon Butter	Birdies in a Basket	Salmon Eggs Benedict
25g/1oz Monterey Jack cheese, 5 black olives	Prosciutto-wrapped Prawns with Kale Mayo	Tuna-stuffed Devilled Eggs	2 stalks celery, 2 tbsp Ranch Dressing
170g/6oz white fish, Watercress Bacon Salad with Ranch Dressing	Wilted Brussels Sprout Salad with Warm Pancetta Dressing	Chilled Avocado Crab Gazpacho, Avocado Toast	Lemon Pepper Prawns with Mangetout
Asparagus with Burrata Cheese and Kale Pesto	Tuna-stuffed Devilled Eggs	25g/1oz Monterey Jack cheese, 5 black olives	Artichoke Dip–stuffed Mushrooms
Salsa Verde Chicken Soup, For dessert: Chocolate Chip Cookie	Chimichurri Steak Bites, Sautéed Spinach with Caramelized Shallots	Mixed Power Greens with Prosciutto-wrapped Chicken Tenders	Fried Sage Chicken and Courgette, For dessert: Salted Caramel Cheesecake Bites
20.7g	20.2g	21.6g	20.8g
14g	13.5g	15.1g	13.5g

HOW TO GET STARTED ON
ATKINS 40

ATKINS 40 IS A RELATIVE newcomer to the Atkins family. It has less structure than Atkins 20 but a few more guidelines than Atkins 100, and it is quite popular and effective. If you would like to reduce your carb intake while eating a greater variety of food, this is the way to go, especially if you're motivated and ready to see how making these changes to your eating habits can have a positive impact on your overall wellness and energy levels.

As you may have guessed, on Atkins 40, you eat 40 grams of Net Carbs a day. Here's what else you need to know about this simple and effective way of eating:

- As with Atkins 20, 12 to 15 grams of Net Carbs a day come from that extensive list of tasty Foundation Vegetables.
- You can take your pick from the Other Carbs list in Appendix D to bring your total grams of Net Carbs up to 40.
- Eat three 115- to 170-gram/4- to 6-ounce servings of protein a day.
- Consume two to four servings of added fat a day.

TIPS FOR ATKINS 40

- **Enjoy a variety of foods while continuing to limit some.** I need to emphasize that although you do get to eat a wide variety of foods on Atkins 40, there are still some that I suggest you limit or avoid, and I'm sure you can guess which they are:
  - Avoid or limit foods containing added sugars.
  - Avoid or limit refined carbs, such as white rice and anything containing white flour.
  - Avoid foods that might trigger cravings.
  - Avoid foods containing hidden sugars; I'll teach you how to watch your portions of these.

CRUNCHING THE CARB NUMBERS

To **make the math easy,** the foods on the Other Carbs list (Appendix D) are rounded up in **5- to 10-gram increments.**

ATKINS 40™

Each day, you'll enjoy a wide variety of delicious and filling foods. Allocate 40g Net Carbs throughout the day as follows:

3 Meals Per Day

  10g 10g 10g

2 Snacks Per Day

 5g 5g

Occasionally you can bump up a meal to 15g of Net Carbs.

FOUNDATION VEGETABLES
6–8 servings

15g
Net Carbs

PROTEIN
3 servings (115–170g/4–6oz per serving)

0g
Net Carbs

ADDED FATS
3 servings (1 tbsp each)

0g
Net Carbs

OTHER CARBOHYDRATES
3–5 servings (5 net carbs per serving)

25g
Net Carbs

When you're 10 lbs from your goal weight add 10g of Net Carbs/week from this list

When goal weight is achieved you can expand your list of acceptable carbs. Refer to our carb counter (download for free at www.atkins.com) to make sure you stay on track!

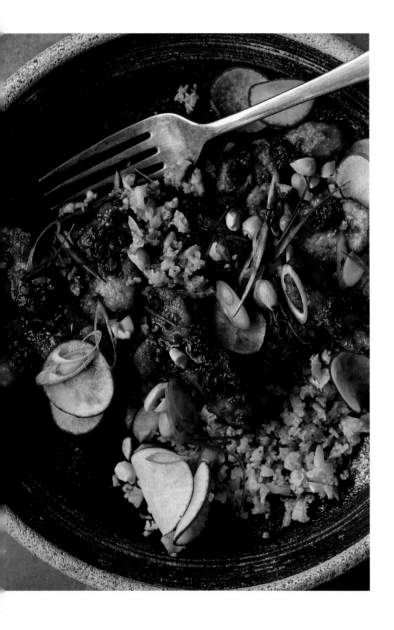

- **Speaking of portions . . .**
You'll notice that some of the recommended portions of foods are smaller than others. That is because these foods are higher in carbohydrates and lower in fibre, increasing the potential Hidden Sugar Effect in your body. By eating smaller portions of these foods, you can make the most of the nutritional impact of the 40 grams of Net Carbs you consume each day.

- **Don't sweat a slip-up.** Even with the added flexibility that Atkins 40 gives you, it's still possible you may slip up now and again, which is perfectly natural. Don't beat yourself up, but don't use it as an excuse to forgo this nutritional approach entirely. Make sure your next meal is a low-carb one, and put a little extra effort into planning some other meals and snacks, enjoying being able to choose from a delicious and satisfying variety of Acceptable Foods.

See Appendix D for the complete Acceptable Foods list for Atkins 40 (page 300)

FINE-TUNING
ATKINS 40

If you feel you are not making as much progress on Atkins 40 as you would like, remember that this is a more gradual way to reduce your carb intake while still eating a wide variety of food.

Ask yourself some questions: Are you feeling better? Do you have more energy? Have you noticed that you're no longer craving foods you used to? Are your clothes fitting better?

Keep up the good work! If you still think you need to make a few tweaks to speed up your progress, here are some tips that might help:

- Decrease the daily amount of Net Carbs you consume by 5 or 10 grams.
- Increase the amount of fat you eat, and decrease the amount of protein if you are consuming more than 115 to 170 grams/4 to 6 ounces of protein per serving.

If you would like to **reduce your carb intake** while eating a greater **variety** of food, **Atkins 40** is the way to go.

- Find and eliminate hidden sugars in the form of processed foods that may contain sugar.
- Increase your activity level.
- Drink at least eight 250ml/8fl oz glasses of water daily.
- Look at which higher-carb foods you've consumed recently, and try eliminating or limiting them for a week.

ATKINS 40 is practically foolproof if you start out by following this meal plan, which features two weeks' worth of low-carb meals and snacks. As always, you can swap out the recipes in this meal plan for others in this book.

	MONDAY	TUESDAY	WEDNESDAY
BREAKFAST	Antioxidant Berry Smoothie	Birdies in a Basket	Coconut Muesli Clusters, Greek yogurt
SNACK	1 stalk celery, 2 tbsp cream cheese	1 wedge honeydew, 60g/2oz prosciutto	1 stalk celery, 1 tbsp Ranch Dressing
LUNCH	Thai Tom Yum Soup, Crispy Brussels Sprouts with Sriracha Mayo Dipping Sauce	Green Goddess Salad with Lemon Tahini Dressing	Thai Peanut Buddha Bowl
SNACK	Flatbread with Two Toppings	Fried Green Tomatoes with Ranch Dipping Sauce	Chipotle Lime Courgette Crisps
DINNER	Bolognese Frying-pan Lasagne	Spicy Korean Soup with Spring Onions, For dessert: Lime Coconut Rum Cupcake	Grilled Miso Salmon, Turnip Fries
TOTAL NET CARBS	39.6g	40.5g	40.9g
TOTAL FV	15.8g	18.8g	20.1g

THURSDAY	FRIDAY	SATURDAY	SUNDAY
Grilled Huevos Rancheros, 1 wedge honeydew	Avocado Kale Berry Smoothie Bowl	Sunny-side Up Eggs with Cauliflower Hash Browns	Lemony Protein Pancakes, 5 large strawberries
50g/1¾oz sliced cucumber, 25g/1oz Monterey Jack	Basic Bone Broth, Coriander Parmesan Crackers, 25g/1oz Monterey Jack	Antioxidant Berry Smoothie	Chocolate Egg Cream, 12 walnut halves
170g/6oz turkey cutlets, Pear and Manchego Mesclun Salad with Caramelized Onions	Jalapeño Cheddar Broccoli Soup, Low-carb Flax Meal Bread	Kale Caesar Salad with Creamy Meyer Lemon Dressing	Cauliflower Mac & Cheese
Power Mug Muffin with Cinnamon Butter	1 carrot, 4 tbsp hummus	Avocado Toast	Artichoke Dip–stuffed Mushrooms
Mongolian Beef Wraps, Shishito Peppers with Hot Paprika Mayonnaise	Kung Pao Chicken with Cauliflower Rice	Super Fast Stroganoff, For dessert: 2 Chocolate Chip Cookies	Shellfish Cioppino
40.1g	39.5g	39.9g	40.4g
15.9g	17.3g	18.5g	16.6g

	MONDAY	TUESDAY	WEDNESDAY
BREAKFAST	Power Mug Muffin with Cinnamon Butter	Cauliflower Rice Scrambles, 1 wedge honeydew	Carrot Spice Smoothie Bowl
SNACK	Antioxidant Berry Smoothie	Low-carb Flax Meal Bread, 1 tbsp almond butter, 70g/2½oz sliced strawberries	50g/1¾oz sliced cucumber, 25g/1oz Monterey Jack
LUNCH	Salsa Verde Chicken Soup	Mixed Asian Greens with Shredded Sesame Chicken	Mongolian Beef Wraps
SNACK	1 carrot, 4 tbsp hummus	Artichoke Dip–stuffed Mushrooms	Avocado Toast
DINNER	Beef Bourguignon, 40g/1½oz baby spinach, 5 large radishes, 2 tbsp Blue Cheese Dressing	Roasted Fennel and Cod with Morrocan Dried Olives	Chicken and Dumplings, Cheesy Spring Onion Cauliflower Mash, For dessert: Double Chocolate Brownie
TOTAL NET CARBS	38.4g	38.8g	40g
TOTAL FV	16.5g	15.7g	14g

THURSDAY	FRIDAY	SATURDAY	SUNDAY
Sunny-side Up Eggs with Cauliflower Hash Browns	Coconut Muesli Clusters, 115g/4oz Greek yogurt	Chai Cinnamon Waffles	Sweet or Savoury Crepes (with raspberries)
115g/4oz Greek yogurt, 5 large strawberries	1 carrot, 4 tbsp hummus	1 wedge honeydew, 60g/2oz prosciutto	25g/1oz soft goats' cheese, Coriander Parmesan Crackers
Turmeric Carrot Ginger Soup, Low-carb Flax Meal Bread	Mushroom Spinach Egg Skillet	Lemon Pepper Prawns with Mangetout	Green Bean Chicken One-pot, 100g/3½oz mixed greens,35g/1¼oz grated carrot, 2 tbsp Ranch Dressing
Baked Sriracha Hot Wings and Kale Chips	Chipotle Lime Courgette Crisps	2 stalks celery, 1 tbsp Ranch Dressing	Portobello Pizza
Garlic Rosemary Pork Loin with Creamed Spinach, For dessert: Salted Caramel Cheesecake Bites	Smoky Habanero Chilli, Brushetta Duet (tomato/mozzarella)	Fried Sage Chicken and Courgette, Fried Green Tomatoes with Ranch Dipping Sauce	Parmesan Scallops, 50g/1¾oz mixed greens, 2 tbsp Mustard Vinaigrette
39.4g	38.7g	39.7g	40.7g
19g	16.5g	12.1g	21.9g

HOW TO GET STARTED ON
ATKINS 100

———————•———————

EVEN IF YOU HAVE THROWN in the towel on traditional 'diets', with Atkins 100, it's all about small changes leading to big results. You have the opportunity to pay attention to what kinds of foods you are eating and how they affect you both physically and emotionally, because this is not a diet, it is simply a better, smarter way of eating and living.

With Atkins 100, you'll consume 100 grams of Net Carbs a day. It's that simple! Here's what else you'll do:

- You'll eat a minimum of 12 to 15 grams of Net Carbs a day of Foundation Vegetables.
- You'll eat three 115- to 170-gram/4- to 6-ounce servings of protein a day.
- You'll eat two to four servings of added fat a day.
- You'll budget the remaining 85 grams of Net Carbs from the complete Acceptable Foods list in Appendix D, beginning on page 300

With **Atkins 100,** it's all about small changes leading to **big results.**

ATKINS 100 ACCEPTABLE FOODS LIST

Keep in mind that on Atkins 100, the Acceptable Foods list is simply a guideline to start you on your journey toward making smart, healthy choices since no food is really off limits. As a guideline, you can use the Acceptable Foods lists beginning on page 300.

ATKINS 100™

Each day, you'll enjoy a wide variety of delicious and filling foods. Allocate 100g Net Carbs throughout the day as follows:

3 Meals Per Day

 25g   25g 25g

2 Snacks Per Day

 10 to 15g   10 to 15g

FOUNDATION VEGETABLES
6–8 servings

12-15g
Net Carbs

PROTEIN
3 servings (115–170g/4–6oz per serving)

0g
Net Carbs

ADDED FATS
2–4 servings (1 tbsp each)

0g
Net Carbs

OTHER CARBOHYDRATES
3–5 servings (5 net carbs per serving)

85g
Net Carbs

When you're 10 lbs from your goal weight add 10g of Net Carbs/week from this list

When goal weight is achieved you can expand your list of acceptable carbs. Refer to our carb counter (download for free at www.atkins.com) to make sure you stay on track!

Just as with Atkins 20 and Atkins 40, I'm giving you a two-week meal plan and Acceptable Foods list with low-carb meals and snacks, plus recipes from this book that you can mix and match.

ATKINS 100 MEAL PLAN
WEEK 1

	MONDAY	TUESDAY	WEDNESDAY
BREAKFAST	Coconut Muesli Clusters, 240ml/8fl oz whole milk, ½ small banana	Sunny-side Up Eggs with Cauliflower Hash Browns, 1 wedge honeydew	Carrot Spice Smoothie Bowl, 2 mini oat bran muffins
SNACK	Coriander Parmesan Crackers, 1 tbsp cream cheese	2 carrots, 4 tbsp black bean dip	1 large tomato, 120g/4¼oz cottage cheese
LUNCH	Turmeric Carrot Ginger Soup, 100g/3½oz mixed greens, 1 large tomato, 40g/1½oz chickpeas, 2 tbsp Mustard Vinaigrette	Kale Caesar Salad with Creamy Meyer Lemon Dressing, 1 large slice wholewheat baguette	Smoky Habanero Chili, ½ Hass avocado, 80g/2¾oz black beans, 20g/¾oz crushed tortilla chips, 100g/3½oz mixed greens, 2 tbsp Mustard Vinaigrette
SNACK	70g/2½oz pineapple, 120g/4¼oz cottage cheese	Chocolate Egg Cream, 25g/1oz cashews	1 small apple, 25g/1oz Cheddar cheese
DINNER	140g/5oz steak, Turnip Fries, ¼ acorn squash, 60g/2oz wild rice	Fried Sage Chicken and Courgette, Crispy Brussels Sprouts with Sriracha Mayo Dipping Sauce, ½ small baked potato	Roasted Fennel and Cod with Moroccan Dried Olives
TOTAL NET CARBS	98.6g	101.2g	96.5g
TOTAL FV	23.9g	28.8g	19.5g

THURSDAY	FRIDAY	SATURDAY	SUNDAY
Grilled Huevos Rancheros, one 15cm/6in wholewheat tortilla	80g/2¾oz porridge oats, 240ml/8fl oz whole milk, 1 wedge cantaloupe	Chai Cinnamon Waffles, 1 small banana, 10 pecan halves	Salmon Eggs Benedict, 1 wholewheat English muffin
50g/1¾oz sliced cucumber, 25g/1oz Monterey Jack	Sweet or Savoury Crepes (with raspberries)	50g/1¾oz sliced cucumber, 2 tbsp creamy Italian Dressing	60g/2oz cherries, 115g/4oz Greek yogurt
Bone Broth Minestrone, 25g/1oz wholewheat pasta	Chimichurri Steak Bites, 40g/1½oz baby spinach, 80g/2¾oz black beans, 50g/1¾oz sliced cucumber, 35g/1¼oz grated carrot, 2 tbsp Mustard Vinaigrette	Hot-and-Sour Soup, 85g/3oz cooked rice noodles	Green Goddess Salad and Lemon Tahini Dressing, 1 large slice wholewheat baguette
1 small banana, 25g/1oz almonds	60g/2oz string cheese, 4 wholewheat crackers	1 large tomato, 115g/4oz cottage cheese	Brie-stuffed Grilled Jalapeños
Chicken and Dumplings, 55g/2oz sweetcorn, 40g/1½oz baby spinach, 2 tbsp Mustard Vinaigrette	Garlic Rosemary Pork Loin with Creamed Spinach, 45g/1½oz Brussels sprouts, 60g/2oz brown rice	Shellfish Cioppino, ½ medium sweet potato, For dessert: Apple Crumble	Green Bean Chicken One-pot, 60g/2oz brown rice, 40g/1½oz sweetcorn
101.2g	99.9g	101.3g	100.1g
20.6g	12.7g	21.3g	13.1g

		MONDAY	TUESDAY	WEDNESDAY
BREAKFAST		Power Mug Muffin with Cinnamon Butter, 1 small banana	Birdies in a Basket, ½ red grapefruit	Coconut Muesli Clusters, 240ml/ 8fl oz whole milk, 85g/3oz sliced mango
SNACK		1 large tomato, 115g/4oz cottage cheese	1 whole wheat English muffin, 2 tbsp cashew butter	50g/1¾oz sliced cucumber, 2 tbsp Creamy Italian Dressing
LUNCH		170g/6oz chicken breast, Watercress Bacon Salad with Ranch Dressing, 1 large slice whole weat baguette	Bolognese Frying-pan Lasagne, 100g/3½oz mixed greens,120g/ 4¼oz cooked sliced beetroot, 30g/1oz quinoa, 2 tbsp Mustard Vinaigrette	115g/4oz Salmon Pear & Manchego Mesclun Salad with Caramelized Onions, 2 mini oat bran muffins
SNACK		2 carrots, 4 tbsp black bean dip	120ml/4fl oz vegetable juice cocktail, 25g/1oz edamame	80g/2¾oz red grapes, 12 whole almonds
DINNER		Spicy Korean Soup with Spring Onions, 85g/3oz cooked rice noodles	Clam Linguine, 1 large slice whole wheat baguette, 40g/1½oz rocket, 2 tbsp French Dressing	Chicken Parmesan Meatballs, 155g/5½oz spaghetti squash, 100g/3½oz mixed greens, 1 large tomato, 40g/1½oz chickpeas, 2 tbsp Mustard Vinaigrette
TOTAL NET CARBS		99.4g	100.3g	98.3g
TOTAL FV		20.9g	26.7g	22.1g

ATKINS 100 MEAL PLAN
WEEK 2

THURSDAY	FRIDAY	SATURDAY	SUNDAY
Egg-filled Avocado with Prosciutto, 1 wedge honeydew, 1 whole wheat English muffin	Avocado Kale Berry Smoothie Bowl, 2 mini oat bran muffins	Cauliflower Rice Scrambles, 1 whole wheat tortilla, 2 tbsp salsa	Lemony Protein Pancakes, 70g/2½oz blueberries
Portobello Pizza	2 carrots, 2 tbsp black bean dip	2 carrots, 2 tbsp hummus	5 whole wheat crackers, 60g/2oz goats' cheese
Thai Tom Yum Soup, 60g/2oz brown rice	Superfast Stroganoff, 25g/1oz whole wheat pasta, 45g/1½oz Brussels sprouts	Crispy Duck Spinach Salad with Warm and Tangy Turmeric Dressing, 50g/1¾oz acorn squash, 60g/2oz lentils	Cauliflower Mac and Cheese, 100g/3½oz mixed greens, 1 large tomato, 40g/1½oz chickpeas, 2 tbsp French Dressing
70g/2½oz pineapple chunks, 115g/4oz cottage cheese	1 small banana, 24 whole almonds	4 whole wheat crackers, 60g/2oz string cheese	115g/4oz Greek yogurt, 60g/2oz cherries
Roast Beef with Greek Yogurt Horseradish Sauce, ½ small baked potato, 100g/3½oz mixed greens, 2 tbsp Mustard Vinaigrette	Mixed Power Greens with Prosciutto-wrapped Chicken Tenders, For dessert: Apple Crumble	Turmeric Orange Scallops, Turnip Fries, 30g/1oz quinoa	Beef Bourguignon, 25g/1oz whole wheat pasta, 155g/5½oz broccoli
99.2g	100g	98.7g	99.8g
12g	20.1g	19.8g	18.1g

HOW DO YOU
WANT TO DO ATKINS?

I N MY MANY YEARS OF clinical practice as a nutritionist and certainly in my role at Atkins, I've found that most people naturally fall into one of two categories foodwise: those who've discovered which foods they prefer and eat them regularly and those who thrive on variety and are always looking for ways to shake things up. Identifying which of the two groups you fall into can go a long way to making your experience on Atkins a positive one – complete with lasting results. So let's see which one you are.

ARE YOU A CREATURE OF HABIT?

Do you have your tried-and-true meals and snacks that you rotate through on a weekly basis? Maybe you're perfectly happy with scrambled eggs every morning, and you have some easy meals that you can mix and match for lunch and dinner. You're most likely a big fan of leftovers as a way to save money and time; what was delicious at dinner will certainly be lovely at lunch. You have your routine down, and trying out new recipes or foods may seem like a stretch to you.

If this sounds like you to a 'T', you'll probably be more comfortable following a structured version of Atkins, such as Atkins 20, so that your choices are carefully laid out for you right from the beginning, with a specific direction for how you can progress. You'll be in control of what you're eating; you'll know what you can eat, how much of it, and how your body responds to it. All you have to do is stick with the Acceptable Foods list and meal plan, and you're good to go.

ARE YOU A VARIETY SEEKER?

Do you get bored eating the same foods day in and day out? Are you always trying to come up with new ideas for lunch and dinner? Do you like to try new recipes and sample new ingredients? Do you get caught up in reading about food, recipes, and cooking techniques, and do you turn to Instagram and Pinterest for a daily dose of food inspiration or envy? A day at a farmers' market seems like a vacation, and a new kitchen gadget may bring you just as much excitement as a new pair of shoes. Cooking is probably a creative hobby for you instead of just a duty. Meanwhile, your family has become accustomed to the new tastes and combinations you present to them.

If this sounds like you, variety is the spice of your life, and Atkins 100 may be the way to go.

ARE YOU SOMEWHERE IN THE MIDDLE?

When time is tight, you have your go-to breakfasts, lunches and dinners down to a science, but when given the chance, you love to mix them up with new recipes and different flavours. Or you stick with a tight routine during the week, but on weekends you love to roll your sleeves up and get going in the kitchen.

If this sounds like you, Atkins 40 may be a great starting point.

HOW ABOUT ME?

I'm right in the middle. My weeks are pretty busy with travel and work, so I typically have an Atkins shake or smoothie not long after getting up and a second mini-breakfast, usually yogurt, flaked almonds and berries, after I get to the office. Once I'm at work, I find I am so busy I just don't want to have to deal with making a decision about what to have for lunch. My go-to choices are a big green salad with leftovers, or tofu, tuna, chicken or another protein source. For dinner, my husband and I usually have a huge salad and top it with chicken, burgers, salmon, or sometimes a steak. We usually make enough for more than one meal, so we often have the same meal twice in a week. But on weekends, I do like to try something new; we might explore the menu options at a new restaurant or enjoy leg of lamb, one of our favourites. We always have at least one vegetable with the meal and a side salad. If I have time on a Sunday, I like to try out the occasional new recipe – I've really been enjoying testing the ones from this book! And I'll always make extra, so we have leftovers to eat on Monday. After more than two decades following the Atkins lifestyle, this way of eating has become as natural as breathing. I barely have to think about it – other than to get myself to the supermarket!

IT'S YOUR CHOICE!

With Atkins 20, 40 and 100, you have learned how satisfying a low-carb lifestyle can be. Just by learning a few simple 'hacks' to guide your eating choices, you can avoid the sugars and hidden sugars that so many of us are unaware we are eating and that lead to blood sugar spikes and an energy-level roller coaster. You can learn to recognize your hunger cues, eat when you're actually hungry, and stop when you're full, because the foods you eat on Atkins and the recipes in this book are naturally filling and guaranteed to please your palate. Now comes the fun part as you discover how living a low-carb lifestyle is possible in every situation, whether you're eating out in a restaurant, hitting the fast-food drive-through, celebrating at Christmas or going on holiday.

HOW I DO
ATKINS

MOVING BETWEEN ATKINS 20, ATKINS 40 AND ATKINS 100

The wonderful thing about eating right, not less,
is that depending on your goals and what's going on in your life,
you can move between the various levels of Atkins with ease.
Here are some scenarios to consider:

- If you're going on holiday and you're doing Atkins 20, you can move up to Atkins 40 so you can enjoy a wider variety of food while travelling. And if you're doing Atkins 40, you might consider moving up to Atkins 100.

- If the food choices on Atkins 40 are causing 'carb creep', you might need the structure of Atkins 20 to help keep you honest and focused on your goals.

- Stressed out? Move up a level so you're still motivated to make healthy changes but have a few more options to choose from when time is tight and life is hectic.

- Are you still experiencing intense cravings and energy slumps, and do you feel that you really need to take control of the way you are eating? Buckle down and give Atkins 20 a try.

- Did you overdo it on holiday, and you're having a hard time getting back on track? Move down a level for the time being.

5

LIVING A
LOW-CARB AND LOW-SUGAR
LIFESTYLE

SMALL CHANGES = BIG RESULTS

Now that you know how your
LOW-CARB LIFESTYLE WORKS,

you can see how easy it is to incorporate small,
healthy changes into your life.

Instead of focusing on all the food you
think you can't eat, it's time to start
thinking about all the food you *can* eat
with Atkins, and how eating right, not
less, can change your life.

N OW YOU HAVE EVERYTHING YOU
need to start doing Atkins: a
sparkling clean kitchen stocked
with naturally low-carb foods, including
colourful vegetables, dairy products, fish,
poultry, beef and some pantry essentials.
Coming up, I'm going to show you my
smart carb swaps, easy low-carb snacks, my
favourite Atkins 'hacks', and some valuable
advice for eating out in restaurants,
travelling for work or while on holiday, plus
strategies for enjoying (not just surviving)
Christmas so that you can make this way
of eating a lifestyle.

EAT YOUR VEGGIES!

INCORPORATING VEGETABLES INTO THE MAJORITY of your meals or snacks may seem like a challenge, but there are endless options for every part of the day. Soon you'll wonder why you haven't been eating this way all along! Here are some suggestions.

BREAKFAST

- Add spinach, spring onions and a little tomato to your eggs and top with avocado.
- Make a low-carb breakfast wrap using turkey sausage, scrambled eggs, spinach and avocado and wrap it all up in a romaine lettuce leaf or a low-carb tortilla.
- Whip up a breakfast hash by sautéing minced beef, turkey or pork with spring onions, red peppers and cheese. You can top it with a fried or scrambled egg.
- Sautee 25g/1oz chopped broccoli and 35g/1¼oz chopped onion in 1 tablespoon real butter. Add two beaten eggs to the pan and stir over medium-high heat until the eggs are set. If you like, sprinkle 2 tablespoons grated Cheddar cheese over the eggs in the last 30 seconds of cooking.
- Add 135g/4¾oz chopped tomato and 85g/3oz chopped spinach or 35g/1¼oz chopped onion and 30g/1oz chopped mushrooms to 2 scrambled eggs.
- For a breakfast on the run, grab a couple of hard-boiled eggs, a slice of cheese, and one of the following raw veggies to crunch in the car: 175g/6¼oz chopped cucumber, 170g/6oz string beans (green beans), 160g/5¾oz chopped cauliflower, or 120g/4¼oz chopped green pepper.

LUNCH

- Combine deli meat, cheese and mayo and roll up with a pickle or cucumber.
- Pile spinach, tomatoes and mushrooms on a plate, drizzle with balsamic vinegar and olive oil, and top with sliced grilled chicken breast. Or start with 115g/4oz shredded romaine lettuce and add any of the following: 200g/7oz chopped cucumber, 100g/3½oz chopped jicama, 180g/6½oz sliced mushrooms, 120g/4¼oz chopped green pepper, 90g/3¼oz chopped red peppers, 230g/8oz sliced radishes, 90g/3¼oz chopped broccoli, 160g/5¾oz chopped cauliflower, 135g/4¾oz chopped tomatoes, 185g/6½oz sliced yellow squash. (If you want more than one added veggie in your salad, use half the measurement of one veggie, combined with half the measurement of another, such as 60g/2oz green peppers and 100g/3½oz chopped cucumber.) Plus, you can add 120 to 180ml/4 to 6fl oz of sugar-free salad dressing.

- Try raw or cooked veggies, cooked in butter, topped with your favourite protein.
- Top a tomato with cooked minced beef seasoned with chilli and cumin and Mexican-blend shredded cheese. Grill until the cheese is bubbling.

DINNER

- Experiment with your spinach salad; add various vegetables or dressings and top with grilled salmon, prawns, or sliced steak.
- Stuff half a pepper with turkey or pork sausage, cook at 180°C/350°F/Gas 4 for 45 minutes and top with grated cheese, no-sugar salsa, avocado or even a fried or poached egg.
- Grill a steak and serve with a side salad and mashed or riced cauliflower.
- Whip up a stir-fry by sautéing your choice of meat or poultry, and adding sliced red pepper, broccoli florets and mushrooms.
- Add butter or mayonnaise to hot cooked veggies for an instant flavour boost.

THE CURE FOR YOUR CARB CRAVINGS

Eating certain carbs may trigger cravings, hunger and blood sugar swings, which all have the potential to derail your progress, but it's natural to yearn for those foods at times. Whether you have a sweet tooth or you're all about the salty crunch, the recipes in this book are the cure. Here are a few you can choose from when the cravings hit:

FOR SWEET-TOOTH CRAVINGS

- Lemony Protein Pancakes (page 135)
- Double Chocolate Brownies (page 282)
- Coconut Muesli Clusters (page 136)

FOR SWEET AND CREAMY CRAVINGS

- Almond Butter Smoothie Bowl (page 228)
- Salted Caramel Cheesecake Bites (page 281)
- Creamy Avocado Smoothie (page 130)

FOR SALTY CRUNCH CRAVINGS

- Crispy Brussels Sprouts with Sriracha Mayo Dipping Sauce (page 141)
- Baked Sriracha Hot Wings and Kale Chips (page 147)
- Turnip Fries (page 222)
- Chipotle Lime Courgette Crisps (page 205)

FOR COMFORT FOOD CRAVINGS

- Cheesy Spring Onion Cauliflower Mash (page 151)
- Cauliflower Mac and Cheese (page 267)
- Bolognese Frying-pan Lasagne (page 258)
- Cream of Heirloom Tomato Soup (page 175)

IT'S SNACK TIME

SNACKING IS AN IMPORTANT PART of Atkins. When you nosh on two tasty snacks a day between your three meals, you are able to keep your hunger in check and your blood sugar levels right where they should be. I've put together a variety of easy options that you can mix and match, depending on whether you're hungry for something salty or sweet or somewhere in between. You can check out some additional snack recipes in chapter 7.

SNACKS WITH NO MORE THAN 3 GRAMS OF NET CARBS

- 25g/1oz of string cheese
- Celery stuffed with cream cheese
- Cucumber 'boats' filled with tuna salad
- Five green or black olives, perhaps stuffed with cheese
- Half a Haas avocado
- Beef or turkey jerky (cured without sugar)
- A devilled egg or hard-boiled egg
- A lettuce leaf wrapped around grated Cheddar cheese
- Sliced ham rolled around a few raw or cooked green beans

- Two slices of tomato topped with chopped fresh basil and grated mozzarella and grilled for one minute
- A pot of ready-made sugar-free jelly topped with a dollop of whipped cream

SNACKS WITH NO MORE THAN 5 GRAMS OF NET CARBS

- 120g/4¼oz of unsweetened whole milk yogurt mixed with 2 tablespoons no-added-sugar grated coconut and 1 packet sweetener
- Celery sticks stuffed with peanut butter or another nut or seed butter
- Cucumber 'boats' filled with ricotta and sprinkled with seasoned salt
- Two chunks of melon wrapped in slices of ham or smoked salmon
- A 'kebab' of two strawberries, two squares of Swiss cheese, and two cubes of jicama
- Nutty Cheese Dip: Blend 2 tablespoons cream cheese, 1 tablespoon grated mature Cheddar, a few drops of hot pepper sauce, a pinch of paprika, and 1 tablespoon chopped pecans. Serve with red pepper strips.

Low-Carb Product Buyers' Guide

For a list of recommended products for your low-carb lifestyle, see Appendix E. Follow these tips to make sure you're making smart choices when you're buying low-carb products:

• Look for 5 grams or less of total sugar

• Look for less than 15 grams of Net Carbs per serving

• Watch out for added sugars

• **Blue Cheese Dip:** Blend 2 tablespoons blue cheese into 3 tablespoons unsweetened plain whole milk yogurt. Serve with courgette spears or another vegetable.
• A scoop of cottage cheese topped with 2 tablespoons no-sugar-added salsa.
• Mix 120ml/4fl oz tomato juice and 1 tablespoon soured cream in a bowl, and you've got a refreshing cold creamed soup. Top with chunks of avocado, if desired.
• Mash 35g/1¼oz blueberries with 2 tablespoons mascarpone cheese and top with flaxseed meal.
• You can also enjoy 35g/1¼oz of blueberries while munching on a piece of string cheese.

SNACKS WITH NO MORE THAN 10 GRAMS OF NET CARBS

• Fruit other than berries, cherries and melon, as long as they're eaten with some cheese, cream, plain whole milk or Greek yogurt, nuts or protein
• 80g/2¾oz red or purple grapes with a couple of slices of sliced turkey
• An apple with some almonds
• Hummus with vegetables or low-carb crispbreads
• Baba ghanoush (aubergine dip) with vegetables
• Homemade popcorn topped with butter, olive oil or grated cheese
• Carrot sticks with aioli or ranch dip
• Soy crisps
• Single-size container plain, unsweetened Greek yogurt mixed with half a scoop of low-sugar vanilla protein powder and topped with sliced strawberries

WHAT YOU NEED TO KNOW ABOUT
COOKING WITH FATS

Healthy fats add flavour to the foods
you eat and make your meals satisfying and delicious.
Here's what you need to know.

Rapeseed Oil

This heart-healthy oil, made from the black seeds of the rape plant, is rich in omega-3 fatty acids, which lower blood pressure and heart rate.[1]

Use it for sautéing, baking and marinating.

Olive Oil

Olive oil is a staple in many households and for cooking international cuisines. Opt for extra-virgin olive oil, which is made from the first pressing of olives and is high in heart-healthy antioxidants called polyphenols.

Use it for sautéing vegetables, or combine with balsamic vinegar for an easy salad dressing.

Groundnut Oil

Made from unshelled peanuts, groundnut oil contains heart-healthy phytosterols, plant fats associated with lower cholesterol levels and cancer prevention.

Good for deep-frying (due to its high smoke point), as well as for roasting and sautéing.

Grapeseed Oil

Grapeseed oil, extracted from the seeds of grapes, is high in polyunsaturated fats and vitamin E.

Thanks to its high smoke point, you can use it for sautéing, stir-frying or roasting.

Coconut Oil

Coconut oil is rich in a type of saturated fat that may help boost your level of 'good' (HDL) cholesterol,[2] plus it is an excellent natural moisturizer for your skin and hair!

Use unrefined coconut oil for its subtle coconut flavour and in place of butter for baking. Use refined coconut oil for its neutral flavour in cooking or baking.

Non-hydrogenated Palm Shortening

Palm shortening comes from the tropical palm tree.

Use it for cooking or as a non-dairy substitute for butter.

MY ATKINS 'HACKS'

A hack is a trick or shortcut that makes your life easier. Since I have been living a low-carb lifestyle for going on twenty years and I'm constantly talking to folks who are doing the same, I've learned a number of hacks that help make Atkins pretty simple.

I DON'T ALWAYS DRINK PLAIN WATER. I carry a water bottle everywhere, and I like to boost the flavour with slices of cucumber, limes or lemons. When I need a boost of carbonation, zero-calorie and zero-sugar sparkling spring water flavoured with extracts of lime, berries and other fruit flavours is a refreshing change.

I FOCUS ON FRESH FLAVOURS. I love to add fresh herbs to my recipes. I'll make pesto out of basil and add coriander or chives to egg dishes or any main dish. Dill goes great on fish (or as part of a lemon aioli you can dip steamed artichoke leaves in), and rosemary boosts the flavour of chicken, fish, lamb and soups. I also enjoy frequenting farmers' markets during the warmer months and picking up an assortment of vegetables that are in season to add to my meals and snacks for the week.

I AM ALL ABOUT CONVENIENCE. When I don't have the time to spend a leisurely morning at the farmers' market or a relaxing evening at home preparing one of the recipes in this book, I have no problem hitting the deli and salad bar at the supermarket to fill up on sliced roasted meats, salad greens, marinated olives and fresh mozzarella, plus fresh veggies to garnish my salad and complete my meal. I'll also grab pre-washed salad leaves and packages of riced cauliflower and spiralized courgette in the produce section, a rotisserie chicken from the deli, and pre-made steak or chicken kebabs so that I can throw together delicious low-carb meals in minutes.

I EAT BREAKFAST FOR DINNER. Or dinner for breakfast. After a hectic day, sometimes a plate of scrambled eggs or an omelette filled with whatever veggies I have on hand is an easy and protein-packed evening meal. And if my meal of chicken, salmon or steak is delicious tonight, the leftovers are sure to satisfy me tomorrow morning.

I'M NOT AFRAID TO GO 'OFF THE MENU'. If I'm eating out, I have no problem politely asking the server for my sauce or dressing on the side, swapping a higher-carb side for steamed vegetables with butter, or even doubling up on two vegetable side dishes.

I EAT CARBS . . . in smaller portions. Though I've shown you that even foods such as wholewheat bagels and brown rice contain hidden sugars – carbs that convert to sugar in your blood – sometimes I just want a bagel. Instead of chowing down on a full bagel (and watching my energy levels and cravings go awry), I'll toast one-fourth of a wholewheat bagel, slather it with some nut butter and be perfectly satisfied.

ATKINS, FAMILY-STYLE

JUST BECAUSE YOU HAVE DECIDED to explore a low-carb lifestyle does not mean you're relegated to eating bland, tasteless meals while the rest of your family feasts. Nothing could be further from the truth, plus the healthy choices you are making will have a positive impact on everyone around you. Here are some family-friendly options that will turn rushed family dinners into experiences you can all enjoy:

- **Burger bar:** Cook a variety of burgers (beef, venison, turkey, chicken breast, or others; the choice is yours!), and lay out all the burger fixings so everyone can build his or her own burger. Skip the bun, and wrap your own burger in romaine lettuce leaves. Get creative with the fixings. In addition to tomato, lettuce and onion, you can include sautéed onions and mushrooms, bacon, avocado slices, jalapeños for some spice, and even a fried egg.

- **Salad bar:** Start with shredded rotisserie chicken or sliced steak. Put out a variety of salad leaves (romaine, spinach and/or kale), and go crazy with the toppings. You can include tomatoes and avocado, black beans, sliced mushrooms, broccoli florets, marinated artichoke hearts and sundried tomatoes, olives and grated cheeses.

- **Taco bar:** Begin with shredded rotisserie chicken, minced beef, or both. Let everyone fill his or her tortilla with a choice of taco toppings: beans, lettuce, tomatoes, avocados, fajita veggies, onions, jalapeños, cheese, salsa and soured cream. You can make your own taco with a low-carb tortilla or make a taco bowl instead, with lettuce as the foundation.

- **Chilli bar:** This can be a cozy make-ahead meal when your family's evening schedule is a bit hectic. Start some chilli in your slow cooker in the morning so it's ready to serve for dinner. Lay out grated cheese, olives, jalapeños and soured cream so all can garnish their chilli as they like.

- **Make-your-own pizza:** Grab some ready-to-cook pizza crusts (look for a low-carb version, or try a cauliflower or portobello mushroom pizza 'crust'), and let everyone pile on their choice of low-sugar (or homemade) tomato sauce, pepperoni, cooked and crumbled Italian sausage, ham, olives, sliced mushrooms, artichoke hearts, onions, peppers, sundried tomatoes and grated cheeses. Bake and enjoy!

LOW-CARB SWAPS
FOR HIGH-CARB FAVOURITES

*You can have your (low-carb) cake and eat it, too,
not to mention pizza and pasta. Keep reading for delicious
low-carb swaps for some of your favourite foods.*

Pizza

Did you think cheesy pizza was a thing of your high-carb past? You can still enjoy delicious low-carb pizza on Atkins, with the Portobello Pizza recipe (page 206).

French Fries

Crispy French fries fresh out of the fryer are hard to resist, but you can swap them out for baked alternatives that are lower in carbs, such as Turnip Fries (page 222) or sweet potato fries (stick with ¼ or ½ of a medium sweet potato).

Crisps

Skip the greasy fried potato crisps. You can satisfy your salty and crunchy cravings with Chipotle Lime Courgette Crisps (page 205).

Pasta and Noodles

Whether you're craving spaghetti and meatballs, lasagne or a steaming bowl of ramen noodles, you can substitute 'courgetti' for pasta and noodles to get your fix. Try our Thai Peanut Buddha Bowl recipe (page 230) and Bolognese Frying-pan Lasagne (page 258).

Brownies and Cookies

Good news! Swap out your traditional sugar- and flour-laden brownies and cookies for Double Chocolate Brownies (page 282) and Chocolate Chip Cookies (page 285). They feature the same rich chocolate taste, without the sugar.

EATING OUT

WITH ATKINS

NO MATTER HOW YOU DECIDE to do Atkins, eating out can be a delicious and guilt-free experience, if you arm yourself with my tips. Our options have expanded over the years because of an added emphasis on where our food comes from and how it's prepared. Whether you're vegetarian, gluten-free, reducing carbs or all of these, you'll find that many restaurants now cater to your way of eating.

Don't skip meals or arrive at a restaurant/ supermarket/party starving. This is my mantra before you do almost any activity that involves food. Try having a boiled egg, a few slices of cheese or a serving of almonds before you head out so that when you are faced with a basket of bread or a list of tempting happy hour appetizers, your appetite will remain in check.

Stay hydrated. Drink at least two glasses of water with your meal to help fill up.

Break out of your food rut. Whereas some people thrive on structure, others love the variety of being able to make different choices every day. If you prefer a clear-cut plan of action, review the menu online before you hit the restaurant and pick out one or two main dishes that fall into line with how you are doing Atkins. If you like to spice things up and need variety to help you stay on track, use this opportunity to be adventurous and pick a dish you've never had.

Skip the sides. Ask to have your dishes without the extras – rice, beans, potatoes, pasta – or ask for two sides of vegetables. Most restaurants will accommodate your request for a portion of vegetables or a side salad in lieu of such high-carb starches, and many restaurants now offer more nutrient-packed whole grains.

Go easy on the sauce. Ask for sauces on the side so you can decide whether and how much to consume. Instead of dousing your dish in sauce, dip a bite or two to get a hit of flavour.

Soup's on. I love soup, and it is a wonderful way to keep your appetite in check before your main course. Miso soup, many cream soups, vegetable purées and clear broth with meat or vegetables are satisfying and delicious ways to jump-start your meal.

Splurge on steak. Do you want to treat yourself while still making healthy choices? You can't go wrong with a steak house – it is a decadent mecca of naturally low-carb choices. Prawn cocktail? Check! Tender, juicy steak sizzling in butter? Check! Surf and turf? Check! Skip the mashed potatoes and go for asparagus drizzled with Hollandaise sauce, sautéed mushrooms or creamed spinach.

Don't save room for dessert. Go ahead and fill up on everything else so that you are pleasantly satisfied, but not stuffed, by the end of the meal. If your dinner companions insist on dessert, just savour a small bite of theirs, or stick with fresh fruit or a cheese plate.

Don't beat yourself up. If you stray off course before your main course even arrives, remember that one bite or one meal is no reason to give up on your goal of eating right, not less.

YOUR FAST FOOD CHEAT SHEET

Although hitting the drive-through is not always optimal because it usually means you're in a rush (or you forgot your lunch), you can still make healthy choices if you stick with these tips.

• **AT THE BURGER JOINT:** Order your burger without the bun and a side salad instead of fries. Most fast-food burger places also offer chicken sandwiches. Once again, skip the bun and go for grilled chicken instead of chicken that is battered or deep-fried. You'll usually find a few main dish salad selections that you can top with grilled (not fried) chicken. Watch out for the salad dressings, which may contain added sugar or corn syrup. Your best bet is usually vinaigrette, ranch or blue cheese.

• **AT THE TACO PLACE:** You can usually find a taco salad or bowl on the menu. Try not to eat the deep-fried tortilla bowl that your salad sometimes comes in.

• **AT THE FRIED CHICKEN TAKEAWAY:** Typically, you can select grilled or roasted chicken instead of fried chicken. Pass up the mashed potatoes dripping in gravy and the cheesy mac and cheese, and select sides such as steamed vegetables, creamed spinach, green beans (go with an 85g/3oz serving) or sweetcorn (have a 40–80g/1½–2¾oz serving).

AROUND THE WORLD
WITH ATKINS

———— ● ————

GET READY TO ENJOY A world of international flavours, because no cuisine is off limits with Atkins. In this book I've even included suggestions for Atkins-friendly versions of traditional recipes from a few of these cuisines.

Italian

Italian food is not just about pizza and pasta; it varies by region, and you have your choice of seafood, shellfish, poultry, pork and veal; tomatoes, garlic, olive oil, dark leafy greens; and whole grains; plus rich and creamy sauces. Herbs such as basil, flatleaf parsley, rosemary and oregano add flavour, and other important components of Italian cooking include salt, freshly cracked pepper, vinegar, anchovies, capers, olives and sundried tomatoes. Here are some smart choices:

- Start with an antipasto platter (assorted meats, cheeses, olives and marinated vegetables), caponata (an aubergine and caper salad) or a salad with shaved Parmesan cheese.
- Limit any seafood that's battered and fried (calamari, stuffed clams); order a seafood salad instead.
- You can have your fill of mixed grilled vegetables and grilled portobello mushrooms.
- Don't forget the soup course. Escarole soup features escarole, a lettucelike green, and meatballs or chicken. Stracciatella is an Italian version of egg drop soup made with eggs and spinach. While traditional minestrone is higher in carbs (it often contains pasta and beans), you can turn to page 164 to cook up our Atkins-friendly version, Bone Broth Minestrone.

●

DO YOUR RESEARCH

You can find the **menus for most restaurants** (including fast food) online, with many listing a full **nutritional breakdown** so you can make **healthy choices** in advance.

- Focus on grilled dishes, and order veal or chicken piccata or scaloppini (made with lemon and capers) instead of veal, chicken or aubergine Parmesan. Skip the pasta side dish, and ask if they can do broccoli or asparagus instead.
- You can satisfy your cravings for chicken Parmesan by making our Chicken Parmesan Meatballs on page 247.

Greek

Think of what's typically in a Greek salad: feta cheese, kalamata olives, tomatoes, cucumber and romaine lettuce, dressed with olive oil, oregano, lemon juice and black pepper. Those foods are staples of Greek cuisine, in addition to many varieties of fresh fish, lamb and beef. Here are some smart choices:

- Skip the skordalia (a garlicky dip made from potatoes) and try tzatziki, a sauce made from yogurt, cucumber and garlic, or taramosalata, a creamy spread made from heart-healthy fish roe. Enjoy these dips with fresh vegetables and olives. You'll often find tzatziki drizzled on beef, pork, lamb or chicken.
- Load up on cucumber salad, which is tossed with feta cheese, tomatoes and vinaigrette. Skip the pita and ask for cucumber and carrot sticks to dip in your tzatziki.
- Of course, there's always room for soup. You can try avgolemono, a chicken soup made with egg and lemon.
- Order beef, chicken or lamb souvlaki. These skewers of grilled meat are

naturally low in carbs and the perfect accompaniment to tzatziki sauce.
- Lamb is a Greek speciality and there are many options to choose from: roast leg of lamb, grilled chops and gyros.
- Choose grilled prawns, octopus or swordfish seasoned with garlic and lemon juice instead of battered and fried calamari. You can also try seafood baked with yogurt and herbs, cooked in rich tomato sauce, added to soups, or served cold as a side dish.
- Though honey-drenched baklava sounds heavenly for dessert, if you're still hungry after your Greek feast, a cheese plate is your best bet.

Indian

Indian food is complex and full of flavours influenced by a range of cuisines from the Far East to Europe. Vegetarian options often include rice, wheat or legumes, including peanuts. There are also plenty of dishes with protein and fibre-rich vegetables. Here are some smart choices:

- Vegetable samosas are fried or baked pastries – they are tempting but a better choice is paneer, which is a homemade cheese similar to cottage cheese that is cooked in a variety of ways. Shahi paneer is paneer cooked in a creamy curried sauce, and palak paneer is paneer cooked in a spinach curry.
- Pakora is a battered and fried fritter; opt for roasted aubergine with onions and spices instead.
- Vindaloo is a spicy dish that often

contains potatoes (to help cut the heat), while tandoori dishes do not. Tandoori dishes are very popular; you can choose from chicken, fish, prawns or lamb baked in a clay oven (called a tandoor) after marinating in yogurt, garlic, ginger, herbs and spices.

- Lentil or mulligatawny soup may be high in carbs, but you can try a bowl of chicken shorba, which is made with chicken, garlic, ginger, cinnamon, cumin and other spices.
- Instead of dal (made from lentils) or biryani (a rice dish), you can try korma, which is meat in a cream sauce, or any curried meat dish or meat or prawn kebabs.
- Watch out for saag dishes, which are prepared with spinach and spices but might be heavily thickened with flour or another starch.

French

French cuisine encompasses all the regions of France, from the coastal areas to the mountains and everything in between. Though French cuisine may seem decadent, it is based on a combination of protein, healthy fats and carbohydrates, and many traditional French sauces are perfectly acceptable if you're doing Atkins because they are made with butter or oil and thickened with egg yolks instead of flour. Here are some smart choices:

- French onion soup is traditionally topped with a large crouton of toasted bread under a layer of melted Gruyère

cheese, but you can request it without the bread.
- You can also enjoy some classic chicken, lamb and beef dishes without guilt. Coq au vin is chicken slowly simmered in a wine sauce. Just pass on the potatoes that may be included. Leg of lamb is roasted and rich in the flavours of garlic and rosemary, and boeuf bourguignon consists of cubes of beef slowly simmered in red wine, beef stock, onions, garlic and herbs. You can try our version of this classic French dish on page 261.
- Rather than the bacon, onion and egg pie called an Alsatian tart, try a frisée salad with thin strips of bacon and a poached egg.
- Enjoy coquilles St. Jacques, scallops in a cream sauce topped with cheese, instead of lobster in puff pastry.
- For vichyssoise, the famous French cream of leek and potato soup, substitute mussels in a white wine sauce or the equally famous fish stew called bouillabaisse.
- Order entrecôte or tournedos bordelaise, steak in reduced shallot and red wine sauce, instead of croque monsieur, an egg-dipped, fried ham-and-cheese sandwich.
- Rather than veal Prince Orloff, which is roasted and stuffed with rice, onions and mushrooms, have the veal Marengo, a stew with tomatoes and mushrooms.
- Instead of any potato dish, order buttered French green beans.
- If it's possible you still have room for dessert, you can't go wrong with a plate of French cheeses.

DATE NIGHT WITH ATKINS

While there are plenty of low-carb options
to choose from when you're lingering over a romantic meal
in a restaurant, sometimes it's even more special when you
can enjoy date night in the comfort of your own home,
especially when you have your pick of the following
mouthwatering menus featuring recipes from this book.

Vegetarian Delight

- Crispy Brussels Sprouts with Sriracha Mayo Dipping Sauce (page 141)
- Baby Kale and Blue Cheese Salad with Warm Hazelnut Dressing (page 189)
- Pear and Manchego Mesclun Salad with Caramelized Onions (page 195)
- Lime Coconut Rum Cupcakes (page 278)

Seafood Lovers

- Shishito Peppers with Hot Paprika Mayonnaise (page 157)
- Old Bay Shrimp Salad (page 182)
- Shellfish Cioppino (page 262)
- Lime Coconut Rum Cupcakes (page 278)

Farm to Table

- Cauliflower Bisque (page 167)
- Fried Green Tomatoes with Ranch Dipping Sauce (page 153)
- Crispy Duck Spinach Salad with Warm and Tangy Turmeric Dressing (page 185)
- Apple Crumble (page 286)

Paris Is for Lovers

- Steamed Artichoke with Homemade Lemon Mayonnaise (page 219)
- Turnip Fries (page 222)
- Beef Bourguignon (page 261)
- Salted Caramel Cheesecake Bites (page 281)

Surf and Salmon

- Garlic Butter Lobster Salad (page 198)
- Parmesan Scallops (page 242)
- Grilled Miso Salmon (page 235)
- Apple Crumble (page 286)

Mexican

There's more to this cuisine than tacos and burritos. You're probably quite familiar with the 'Americanized' or 'Tex-Mex' version of Mexican food, which often features enchiladas and tamales, and gets its spice from jalapeños. But Mexican cuisine is actually much more complex, with variations based on regions in Mexico, with some European, especially Spanish, influence and the flavours of garlic, chillies, coriander and cumin. Here are some smart choices:

- Start with guacamole, which is mashed avocado often flavoured with onions, tomato, coriander, lime and jalapeños. Plus, Atkins-friendly avocado is rich in fibre, heart-healthy monounsaturated fat and other nutrients. Instead of tortilla chips, ask for jicama sticks (a naturally sweet, crunchy root vegetable).
- Ceviche is a traditional Latin American dish made from raw fish marinated in lime or lemon juice, onion and chilli. This fresh, light appetizer is low in carbs or other raw vegetables.
- Sopa de albondigas (meatball and vegetable soup), is a much better swap for quesadillas.
- Enchiladas verdes are tortillas filled with spiced chicken and smothered in a tangy green sauce of tomatillos and coriander. Just ask for yours minus the tortillas.
- Fajitas can still be a favourite when you pile your plate with sizzling carne asada (marinated skirt steak), chicken or prawns, sliced onions and peppers, and skip the tortillas and beans; but keep all the fixings of guacamole, soured cream and pico de gallo.
- You can't go wrong with grilled fish, pollo asada (grilled chicken), camarones al ajili (prawns in garlic sauce), or chicken or turkey mole. (Mole is a rich sauce made from ground cocoa beans.)

Japanese

Since Japan is an island nation, its cuisine naturally emphasizes seafood. It's known for perfectly balanced flavours and a beautiful presentation, with ingredients including sesame seeds and sesame oil, shoyu (Japanese soy sauce), mirin (sweet rice wine), dashi (stock made from dried fish flakes), ponzu (dipping sauce made from shoyu, rice wine vinegar, dashi and seaweed), and wasabi, which is similiar to horseradish. When you think of Japanese food, you probably think of sushi, which is loaded with heart-healthy fats. The challenge? Watch out for the rice that accompanies it. Fortunately, Japanese cuisine offers some other good protein sources as well. Here are some smart choices:

- Start your meal with miso soup, which is a rich, light but flavourful soup made with fermented soybean paste (miso) and dashi stock. You'll often find it served with a few cubes of tofu and perhaps some seaweed, along with a garnish of spring onions.
- You won't get a traditional salad at a Japanese restaurant. Vegetables are almost always served crisp, and with the exception of tempura, which you'll want

to avoid because of the batter, vegetables are usually grilled or briefly blanched. Try burdock (a relative of the artichoke), daikon (a delicious radish), lotus root, Japanese aubergine, and edamame, which are steamed soybeans. Also sample the pickled vegetables, including seaweed, which are most often served as a snack or appetizer and are lower in carbs than other appetizers such as gyoza (fried dumplings).

- If you substitute sashimi for sushi, you won't be disappointed. Sashimi is artfully sliced raw fish, minus the white rice. Chances are it will be the very best the chef has available, because there's nothing to disguise any flaws in appearance and flavour.

- Shabu-shabu is thin slices of beef and vegetables that you cook at the table in a hot broth. It's a smarter choice than sukiyaki, which is seasoned with sugar.

- See if the menu offers any low-carb sushi rolls, which come wrapped in cucumber and avocado, minus the rice. Or ask if they can make you one.

Thai

Thai cuisine encompasses a delicate medley of flavours, including sour, sweet, salty, bitter and spicy. Fresh herbs such as lemongrass and coriander add brightness, and tropical influences come from coconut oil, coconut milk, tamarind and lime. There is an emphasis on seafood, and noodle and rice dishes are popular, as well as smaller portions of meat. Here are some smart choices.

- You've probably heard of pad Thai, a noodle-based dish with prawns or chicken, spring onions, eggs, dried tofu, beansprouts and chopped peanuts. The distinctive flavours of this dish can also be found in many without noodles: Naua yang nam tok, similar to a main dish salad, is sliced steak marinated in lime juice and mixed with chillies, onion, tomato, cucumber, coriander leaves and lettuce. If you're feeling adventurous, you can try yum pla muk, sliced squid. Similar dishes are made with pork, beef or other forms of protein and dressed with a fish sauce along with salt, lemon or lime juice, garlic or shallots, and chillies.

- Thai cuisine features some delicious soups that are naturally lower in carbs. Try tom yum goong, a hot-and-sour prawn soup with straw mushrooms, seasoned with lime juice, lemongrass and chillies; or gai tom kha, made with chicken slices in coconut milk. Our version of tom yum soup is on page 174.

- Instead of curries (which often contain potatoes), go with sautéed scallops and prawns with mushrooms, courgettes and chilli paste.

- Skip the fried rice in favour of sautéed mixed vegetables.

Korean

Korean food has some Japanese and Chinese elements, and fish, crab, prawns, clams, oysters and squid make up a large part of the typical diet. Some seafood is dried, pickled or used to make a paste. Fresh fish is usually grilled or stewed in a sauce. Vegetables (both raw and pickled) are a big part of Korean cuisine. The defining flavours of Korean food are garlic, ginger, soy sauce, rice vinegar, sesame oil and pastes made from fermented soybeans or chillies, which can provide considerable fire. Traditional Korean meals include soup and an assortment of tiny dishes featuring dried and pickled vegetables and seafood. Here are some smart choices:

- You can't go wrong with kimchi, one of Korea's best-known specialities, which is made by fermenting cabbage in pepper, garlic, ginger and spring onions. This spicy side dish is naturally low in carbs while having a high nutritional value and fibre content. Plus, fermented foods such as kimchi and sauerkraut have been shown to help improve digestion and boost the immune system.[3]
- Skip the rice noodle dishes and try bulgogi, a savoury dish of grilled marinated beef that you dip in a little sauce and wrap in a lettuce leaf. Samgyeopsal is grilled slices of pork belly meat wrapped in lettuce along with grilled slices of garlic and onion and shredded spring onions and kimchi. Some sauces are higher in sugar, so keep an eye on those.

- Some soups are full of noodles, but twoenjangguk, a Korean version of miso soup, is made from fermented soybean paste and baby clams. If you want to whip up a Korean-inspired soup at home, check out our Spicy Korean Soup with Spring Onions on page 168, which is a low-carb version of yukgaejong, a spicy shredded beef soup with vegetables, although in this case, we have swapped the beef for chicken.
- You can enjoy many of Korea's tofu dishes, and don't forget to try the variety of tiny vegetable- and seafood-based dishes that are traditionally a part of many meals.

Chinese

Four regions of China influence Chinese cuisine. Cantonese cuisine is probably the Chinese food you are most familiar with: light delicate sauces, roasted meats, and steamed and stir-fried vegetables. Szechuan is best known for its extremely hot dishes, such as kung pao chicken and double-cooked spicy pork. Hunan dishes are known for thick, rich sauces as well as complex and sometimes biting flavours, such as pepper chicken. Shandong cuisine emphasizes fresh ingredients and delicate flavours, sometimes brightened by the addition of garlic and spring onions. The one thing all these regions have in common is that rice is a part of every meal. Here are some smart choices:

- Beware of the buffet. You'll want to avoid sweet-and-sour dishes and anything breaded or battered. You can have any meat with sauce on the side and pile on the vegetables. If you miss Mongolian beef, which is typically doused in a sauce containing sugar, you can find our Atkins-friendly version on page 236.

- For an appetizer, try egg drop soup instead of fried wontons or an egg roll. The soup should be clear and thin, rather than thickened with cornflour.
- Instead of prawn, pork, beef or chicken fried rice, have a sizzling prawn platter.
- Substitute steamed tofu with vegetables or beef with Chinese mushrooms for any of the noodle-based dishes. If it comes with a sauce, request that it be served on the side.
- Rather than any of the sweet-and-sour dishes, try stir-fried pork with garlic sauce (sauce on the side, of course).

NAVIGATING THE WORLD OF FAST CASUAL FOOD

In today's world of fast casual restaurants, you can literally watch your meal made in front of you, choosing fresh ingredients as you go. If you've been paying attention up to this point, you should have an idea of all the choices available to you so you can enjoy a dish naturally low in carbs.

- **AT THE FAST CASUAL BURRITO RESTAURANT:** Go for a burrito bowl or salad, add the meat of your choice, pile on the fajita vegetables and salad leaves, stick with a 'garnish' of beans or rice, and pump up the flavour with your choice of salsas, guacamole, soured cream and cheese.

- **AT THE FAST CASUAL NOODLE RESTAURANT:** Very often you can replace your serving of noodles with extra veggies, or you can choose freshly made soup and a side salad or a main dish salad.

- **AT THE FAST CASUAL SANDWICH RESTAURANT:** You can fill up on soup and salad or skip the bread and turn a traditional sandwich into a salad.

- **AT THE FAST CASUAL BURGER RESTAURANT:** Savour that juicy burger, skip the bun, and wrap it in lettuce. I've even seen fast casual burger restaurants that offer options such as portobello burgers and grilled fresh fish. Keep your eye on the fries, although some places may offer veggie chips – strips of veggies that are flash-fried. Yes, they are still fried, but they are a better choice than French fries, which spend much more time in the deep fryer.

CELEBRATING (NOT JUST SURVIVING)
HOLIDAYS AND FESTIVALS

THERE IS NO REASON TO dread any holiday when it comes to embracing Atkins' nutritional approach of eating right, not less. If you stick with your routine of planning your low-carb meals and snacks (three meals and two snacks a day), it's easy to make smart choices, especially during times when temptations seem to be everywhere. When your hunger is under control, you'll be less likely to cave in under the pressure of unexpected treats, and you will be able to maintain your blood sugar levels so you don't suffer energy dips, especially when you need the extra energy to finish all those holiday errands. Many festivals (with the exception of Halloween) feature foods that are naturally low in carbs. Let's take a look.

- **Christmas:** Fill your plate with turkey or ham, and then focus on vegetable side dishes. Take advantage of any leftover turkey or ham and feast on roll-ups or add the meat to eggs, salads or soups.
- **Easter:** You can eat ham and all the hard-boiled eggs you would like, while taking advantage of spring vegetables such as asparagus, which you can smother in a rich hollandaise sauce. Turn the leftover hard-boiled eggs into devilled eggs for a low-carb snack.
- **Bonfire Night:** Skipping the potatoes and baked beans doesn't mean missing out on all the warming comfort foods on offer around bonfire night. Instead, try the Year-round Barbecued Brisket (page 268) with a side of Cauliflower Mac and Cheese (page 267).
- **Hanukkah:** You can enjoy brisket and try out latkes made from shredded courgettes instead of potatoes. Once again, take advantage of any leftovers.
- **Diwali:** Try to stay away from the carb-heavy snacks – sweet and savoury – and make your own courgette crisps (see page 205). Enjoy vegetable or paneer curries, or those with meat, if eaten, and serve with cauliflower rice or flatbreads (see page 215) instead of rice.
- **Eid:** A biryani is a classic Eid festival feast, so try stirring spices into cauliflower rice along with slow-cooked chicken or lamb to make a low-carb version. Try switching some of the festival's many sweet treats for some of those in Chapter 13.
- **Thanksgiving:** As for Christmas, focus on the turkey or ham, and fill your plate with the vegetable side dishes.

It doesn't matter if you're the host or the guest at a celebration, because you can enjoy this special time without the guilt if you stick with these suggestions:

Eat before you eat. Before you hit a celebratory lunch or dinner, a party, or an office social, fortify yourself with a filling Atkins-friendly snack (I've included some snacks on pages 87–88 in this chapter) before you go. Or you could have a small low-carb meal, such as a salad topped with grilled chicken. The combination of a small amount of carbs with either fat or protein will stabilize your blood sugar so you don't arrive famished. That way, you'll have the physical backup to your mental fortitude so you can pass up treat foods that are not on your low-carb meal plan while still partaking in the festivities.

Give it away. If you receive personal or business gifts that are high in carbs – biscuits, chocolate, fruitcake, flavoured popcorn, and the like – regift them to your child's school or a homeless shelter. If such gifts arrive at your office, simply put them in a public area such as the coffee break room. I guarantee that they will disappear fast.

Keep snacks on hand. If your workplace is awash in festive goodies, it's all the more important that you stick with your low-carb snacks to keep your appetite under control. If possible, avoid the parts of the office where bowls of sweets and plates of biscuits are set out. You might even want to talk to the office manager or whoever is responsible for this

festive custom and suggest some healthy alternatives such as fresh fruit and nuts.

Master the buffet. Buffets are actually full of Atkins-friendly options. Stick to the roast turkey, ham, roast beef, salmon fillet or other protein dishes, as well as tossed salads and Foundation Vegetables. Depending on if you are doing Atkins 20, 40 or 100, you can have modest portions of sweet potatoes, carrots, or other starchy veggies – or even some wholegrain bread. At sit-down meals, there's no rule against simply not serving yourself a food you want to stay away from. If the cook insists, take a small portion, have a tiny taste, and leave it at that.

Stay on track. No matter how 'good' you are when it comes to holiday temptations, the reality is that you'll probably take in a few extra carbs. The best way to deal with that is to get up the next morning and get back on track. The worst thing you can do is wallow in guilt and decide that you've blown it and need to wait until after the holidays to get back to your eating routine.

This is a time to enjoy family and friends and, yes, some favourite foods. If there isn't an Atkins-friendly alternative, enjoy a little bit of the real thing, and make sure your next meal or snack is low carb. I typically follow the 90/10 eating rule during the holidays: I make sure that 90 percent of the food I eat is on my low-carb plan and give myself 10 percent wriggle room to indulge. Finally, my mantra is to eat until I'm satisfied, not stuffed. A true sign of success is keeping your goals in sight while celebrating (not just surviving) the holidays.

ON THE ROAD

WITH ATKINS

WHETHER YOU'RE TRAVELLING FOR BUSINESS, road-tripping with the family, or enjoying a well-deserved holiday, here is a road map for navigating every twist and turn.

Plan ahead. Dining out at every meal can do damage to both your wallet and your waistline. If you're away with the family, rent or stay in homes or hotels that have kitchens or kitchenettes. If you're on an extended business trip, book a hotel room with a kitchenette or at least a fridge and microwave. Make a quick supermarket run as soon as you arrive at your destination so you have options for breakfasts, lunches and snacks. Forget fast food and hit the salad bar at the supermarket if you need a quick, convenient meal.

Pack a snack. Whether you're flying or driving, make sure you have low-carb snacks on hand such as jerky, trail mix, nuts, olives, turkey or ham roll-ups, and cut-up veggies and hummus.

Don't clean your plate. Stop eating when you're full, or split a salad and entrée. If you are staying in a place with a refrigerator, take your leftovers and have them for a snack or lunch the next day.

Make your splurge worth it. Save up for the delicious treats you won't be able to find at home. Cut out a snack in favour of the treat, and make sure you have your next low-carb meals and snacks planned out so your one splurge doesn't turn into a free-for-all. Or eat all your planned low-carb snacks and meals, and just indulge in a bite or two of the treat.

Stay hydrated. Bring bottled water, club soda, unsweetened tea, coffee or herb tea if you're driving or taking the train, or request it on the plane.

Find non-food distractions. Flight delay or hour five of a twelve-hour road trip? Instead of feeding your boredom with an overpriced coffee drink or bag of crisps, take a walk around the airport terminal or stop the car and do some stretches or a quick nature walk around a point of interest. You could also catch up on your reading or get the family involved in the 'license plate game'.

THE NEWS ON BOOZE

A **cocktail** or two very often go hand in hand with holidays and business dinners. Although that fruity tropical drink with the umbrella looks mighty tempting, it's **packed with sugar.** If you are going to have a drink, choose wisely, and stick with **lower-calorie drinks** such wine or light beer or drinks made with **sugar-free mixers.**

Get active. Build your holidays around activities that get your blood pumping. Research hikes in your area, hit the beach for volleyball, rent bikes, and explore your surroundings. Do you travel for business a lot? Pack your workout clothes and hit the hotel gym or go for a walk or run when you need to clear your head and boost your energy.

Do damage control. If you return from holiday a few pounds heavier, that's okay. Cut roughly 10 grams of Net Carbs a day from your intake until you return to your goal weight.

Exercise Your Right to Exercise

Exercise is a great stress reliever for me and helps me burn off any extra goodies I may have consumed. During the holidays, I always make a plan to keep pace with my exercise goals by scheduling fitness time on my calendar, just as I would a doctor's appointment or work meeting. I also suggest squeezing in some extra movement every day, even if it's as simple as taking the stairs instead of the lift, parking farther away in the car park or a taking brisk walk around the block.

MAKING ATKINS
WORK AT WORK

———— • ————

THE WORKPLACE MAY SEEM LIKE a danger zone of carbs, with the lure of doughnuts at coffee breaks, fast-food lunches, and tempting treats in office vending machines. But with some advance planning, you can make Atkins work at work.

Conquering Your Coffee Break

Eat breakfast. If you start the day with a breakfast of sufficient protein and healthy fats, it not only sets you up for a positive and productive day but keeps you from experiencing an energy dip and being ravenous by mid-morning. That will be your secret to success if you are trying to limit your visits to the vending machine, which is often full of sugary soft drinks, biscuits, sweets and other sneaky sources of hidden sugars, or the coffee shop, which might feature a trifecta of doughnuts, muffins and pastries. Even non-breakfast foods are good alternatives. There's nothing wrong with kicking off your morning with leftover chicken and salad from the night before or scrambling up that leftover chicken with some eggs, spinach, and cheese. See chapter 6 for a variety of breakfast recipes, including smoothies you can whip up in minutes and sip on the go if time is tight.

Curb your caffeine intake. If you have already had your morning coffee, decaffeinated coffee, tea or herbal tea are better bets so you don't experience the mid-morning jitters. Keep a water bottle at your desk and drink from it frequently.

Sneak in a snack. Good, convenient choices include wrapped individual cheese portions, or bring in homemade snacks such as hard-boiled eggs, ham roll-ups or celery stalks filled with cream cheese, as well as nuts, seeds and some fruits. When it's your turn to bring in the doughnuts, it's your chance to introduce your co-workers to delicious and hearty Power Mug Muffins with Cinnamon Butter on page 133. They may never ask for doughnuts again!

Lunch and Learn

Master the cafeteria. Skip the fried foods, sandwiches and desserts. Instead, scrutinize the hot mains and the salad bar for smart choices. Ask to substitute extra veggies for sides such as chips.

Bring your own lunch. This is a surefire strategy for success. If a fridge is not available, pack your homemade lunch in an insulated bag or small cooler. Transport tuna fish, chicken or egg salad in a plastic container; green salads can travel in a zip-lock plastic bag with dressing on the side. Baked chicken legs, slices of roast beef or turkey and steamed prawns are also highly portable. And it's time to learn to love leftovers: prepare extra servings of your evening meal, so you can heat up a delicious lunch the next day.

OVERCOME OVERTIME

Overtime carbs at the office may be the hardest of all to avoid, especially if you weren't able to plan ahead by packing dinner or an **extra snack.** As your workday stretches out, your **stress** level rises – as does your desire for something sweet or crunchy. Keep an **emergency stash** of snacks so that healthy choices are at your fingertips before you get too ravenous. When your co-workers are sending out for dinnertime food, go ahead and join in, making the **best choices** you can from the available menu.

DEAR DIARY: SETTING THE STAGE FOR
SUCCESS WITH ATKINS

I'VE ALWAYS THOUGHT THAT A food journal is a valuable tool when it comes to helping you stay on track with Atkins (and also jump-starting your journey with Atkins, as I have mentioned earlier), and now there is research to confirm this approach. According to a study by the Fred Hutchinson Cancer Research Center and published in the *Journal of the Academy of Nutrition and Dietetics*,[4] women who kept a food journal lost more weight than those who didn't.[4]

Whether you are tracking your daily food (and Net Carbs) intake on a sticky note or in a hard-copy journal, the Atkins app, or another food journal app, this type of accountability will help you be more successful.

Maybe you've been doing Atkins for a while, and you've been making steady progress toward accomplishing your goals – until you're not. Tracking your daily food and Net Carbs intake will give you an honest picture of what you are eating. Your Net Carbs may have been gradually increasing due to 'carb creep', and you haven't noticed it until you started writing it down. Seeing the hard facts on paper (or on the computer) will help you get right back on track.

A journal can also help you identify the trigger foods that have the potential of setting you off on a carb free-for-all. Maybe you've noticed that you are ravenous every day at 3 p.m. First, ask yourself why this is happening. Are you not bringing enough food each day? Does this seem to be the peak time for stress for you at work, or are you simply eating out of boredom? Once you figure this out, you can have an Atkins-friendly snack ready to eat before your hunger gets uncontrollable, or go for a walk or practice some deep breathing to distract yourself or ease your stress. A journal can help you time your meals, and help you track with accuracy how often and when you are eating. The moral of the story? Spend a few minutes each day with your food journal to set the stage for success with Atkins.

Atkins is all about the experience of **eating and enjoying food** and becoming **empowered** by making healthy choices.

Living the Atkins Lifestyle

It's never been easier to eat healthfully,
especially when you're armed with this guidebook. Now
that you understand how Atkins works and why it makes
so much sense to eat this way, it's your choice
what level of Atkins you would like to start with. Or just
try out a few of the mouthwatering recipes coming
up, and see how this way of eating makes you feel. The
bottom line is that Atkins is all about the experience
of eating and enjoying food and becoming empowered
about making healthy choices. Turn the page, because
now it's time to start cooking!

PART TWO

LET'S
GET
COOKING

6

BREAKFAST

EGGS AND MORE,

plus brunch basics

FOR LEISURELY MORNINGS

•

Breakfast does a body good! When you start the day off on the right foot
with a meal that features a good source of protein, healthy fats, and carbohydrates
rich in fibre and nutrients, you set the stage for a full day of satisfying, smart choices.
These hearty, savoury and sweet breakfast recipes are deliciously easy to make,
whether you're grabbing a bite on the go or have time to relax with family and
friends while savouring a meal worth lingering over.

RECIPES

EGG-FILLED
AVOCADO
with Prosciutto

41g
NET CARBS

SERVES 4

422
CALORIES

This novel approach to 'sunny-side up eggs with bacon' features softly poached eggs in avocado halves, served with a side of crisp prosciutto. Avocado with an 'egg surprise inside' is a great way to introduce both adults and kids to eating the healthier fats found in vitamin E–rich avocados, which also happen to be packed with fibre. For picture-perfect eggs, use poaching cups to help the eggs keep a nice oval shape when simmering.

TIME	PER SERVING
Active: **10 minutes**	*Total Carbs:* **16g**
	Fibre: **11.9g**
Total: **15 minutes**	*Protein:* **18.5g**
	Fat: **34g**
	FV = 3.6

- 170g/6oz watercress or baby spinach
- 2 tablespoons balsamic vinegar
- 8 eggs
- 4 ripe Hass avocados, halved lengthwise and pitted
- Olive oil spray
- 8 slices (about 115g/4oz) prosciutto

1 Place the watercress or baby spinach in a large bowl. Drizzle with the balsamic vinegar and toss well. Divide among four small plates.

2 In a large saucepan, heat 5cm/2in of water over medium heat until bubbles cover the bottom and sides of the pan. Crack each egg into a separate small bowl (do not use eggs with broken yolks). When a few bubbles have broken the surface of the water, gently pour each egg into the pan, leaving room between them.

3 Cook the eggs, without stirring, until the whites are just set and the yolks are still runny, 2 to 3 minutes. Use a rubber spatula to gently release the eggs from the bottom of the pan, if necessary. Using a slotted spoon, remove the eggs from the water and drain on kitchen paper.

4 Place a poached egg into each avocado half. Coat a frying pan with olive oil spray. Heat the pan over medium heat and add the prosciutto. Cook until crispy, about 2 minutes per side. Transfer two avocado-filled egg halves to each plate, and serve immediately with two slices of prosciutto.

DID YOU KNOW ?

The abbreviation **FV** stands for **Foundation Vegetables** in the recipe.

SUNNY-SIDE UP
EGGS

with Cauliflower
Hash Browns

7.4g
NET CARBS

SERVES 4

271
CALORIES

This low-carb hash brown swap is made with an antioxidant-rich superfood, cauliflower, which is high in vitamin C (for immunity), folate (important for breast cancer protection), and vitamin K (for bone health). When shopping for cauliflower, avoid florets with black spots that resemble smudges, which is the result of oxidation (prolonged air exposure) that could mean spoilage or even mould.

TIME	PER SERVING
Active: **15 minutes**	*Total Carbs:* **11.4g** *Fibre:* **4.1g**
Total: **20 minutes**	*Protein:* **20g** *Fat:* **16.3g** *FV =* **6.3**

1 small head cauliflower, cut into florets (see Tip)

4 slices bacon, chopped

1 green pepper, deseeded and diced

½ onion, finely chopped

½ teaspoon seasoning salt (see Tip)

½ teaspoon freshly ground black pepper

4 teaspoons olive oil

8 eggs

1 To prepare the hash browns: place the cauliflower florets in a food processor and roughly chop; you will need to do this in two batches. Warm the bacon in a large frying pan over medium heat, and cook for 4 to 5 minutes, stirring occasionally, until the bacon is well browned. Transfer to a plate. Add the cauliflower, pepper, onion, salt and black pepper, cooking for 5 to 6 minutes, stirring often, until the cauliflower is soft.

2 Add 2 teaspoons of the olive oil to another large frying pan. Place over medium heat and add 4 eggs. Cook for 1 to 2 minutes, until the edges of the eggs start to firm. Cover and reduce the heat to low. Cook for 1 to 2 minutes, until the whites are cooked through but the yolks are still soft. Repeat with the remaining oil and eggs. Set out four plates, spoon equal portions of cauliflower hash browns on each plate, and top with 2 sunny-side up eggs and two slices of bacon. Serve immediately.

TIPS

To save time, find **'riced' cauliflower** *in the produce or frozen food section, which is ideal for this recipe and many others throughout the book.*

Seasoning salts *are a mixture of tasty spices blended with salt – a simple way to add more interest and flavour to recipes with just a shake. When shopping for seasoning salt, check the ingredients list to be sure it is free of added sugar, as brands vary.*

SALMON
EGGS
BENEDICT

3.4g
NET CARBS

SERVES
4

383
CALORIES

This luscious brunch treat – hold the bread – has the same rich sauce that Benedict buffs love. Swapping heart-healthy smoked salmon for bacon or ham gives you filling fats that are skin-healthy, too. An immersion blender, an inexpensive tool for faster and smarter prep, whips up the Hollandaise sauce in seconds.

TIME	PER SERVING
Active: 20 minutes	*Total Carbs:* **4.6g** *Fibre:* **1.2g**
Total: 30 minutes	*Protein:* **25.5g** *Fat:* **29.1g** *FV=2.1*

Hollandaise Sauce

75g/2¾oz unsalted butter

35g/1¼oz grated sweet onion or shallot

½ teaspoon salt

¼ teaspoon freshly ground black pepper

1 tablespoon white vinegar

1 egg yolk

1 tablespoon lemon juice

Eggs

Olive oil spray

8 eggs

225g/8oz baby rocket or spinach

225g/8oz smoked salmon, thinly sliced

10g/⅓oz chopped fresh chives or coriander

1 Prepare the Hollandaise sauce: Melt 1 tablespoon of the butter in a small saucepan over medium heat. Add the onion or shallot, and salt and pepper, and cook for 1 to 2 minutes, until the onion or shallot begins to soften. Stir in the vinegar; reduce the heat to medium low, and cook until the vinegar is evaporated, 1 to 2 minutes. Reduce heat to low and continue cooking, stirring frequently, until tender and translucent, about 4 minutes longer. Transfer the onion mixture to a tall blender beaker or measuring jug. Set aside.

2 In the same saucepan in which you cooked the onion, melt the remaining butter over medium-low heat. Leave to cool slightly for 4 to 5 minutes. Add the egg yolk and lemon juice to the blender beaker, then add a few tablespoons of the melted butter and use an immersion blender to blend until a thick yellow cloud forms. Add the remaining melted butter, and blend again until fully incorporated.

3 Prepare the eggs: coat a large frying pan with olive oil spray. Place over medium heat and add 4 eggs. Cook for 1 to 2 minutes, until the edges of the eggs start to firm. Cover and reduce the heat to low. Cook for 1 to 2 minutes longer, until the whites are cooked through but the yolks are still soft. Repeat with the remaining eggs. Divide the greens among four plates, top with the smoked salmon and place the eggs on top. Drizzle with the Hollandaise sauce, sprinkle with the chives or coriander, and serve.

CAULIFLOWER RICE
SCRAMBLES

5.1g NET CARBS

SERVES 4

381 CALORIES

Your hearty appetite will breathe a sigh of relief when you feast your eyes on this well-portioned breakfast scramble. You can't go wrong with anything that features bacon, and jalapeños add a fresh and spicy kick.

1 small head of cauliflower, cut into florets

8 rashers bacon

2 jalapeños, deseeded and diced

8 eggs

80g/2¾oz Cheddar cheese, grated

4 teaspoons hot sauce (optional)

1 Place the cauliflower florets in a food processor and chop roughly; you will need to do this in two batches.

2 Warm the bacon in a large frying pan over medium heat, and cook for 4 to 5 minutes, stirring occasionally, until the bacon is well browned. Transfer to a plate. Do not discard the bacon grease.

3 Add the cauliflower and jalapeños to the pan and cook for 5 to 6 minutes, stirring often, until the cauliflower is soft.

4 Place the eggs and Cheddar in a large bowl, and gently whisk. Add the eggs to the frying pan with the cauliflower and cook for 3 to 4 minutes, stirring occasionally, until firm. Serve immediately with the bacon and hot sauce, if desired.

TIME	PER SERVING
Active: 10 minutes	*Total Carbs:* **8.4g**
	Fibre: **3.3g**
Total: 25 minutes	*Protein:* **28.1g**
	Fat: **26.2g**
	FV=3.7

CHAI
CINNAMON
WAFFLES

10.3g
NET CARBS

SERVES
4

400
CALORIES

Chai spice mixes, used to make our coffee shop caffè lattes so fragrant, actually hail from India and a long tradition of using healing spices, including cinnamon, cardamom, black pepper, ground ginger and nutmeg, in drinks and food. These waffles borrow the name and spices to liven up plain waffles. If you wish, garnish each serving with a few berries, but be sure to count their carbs!

TIME	PER SERVING
Active: 20 minutes	*Total Carbs:* **13.6g**
	Fibre: **3.1g**
Total: 30 minutes	*Protein:* **30.3g**
	Fat: **25.8g**
	FV=0

- 120ml/4fl oz whipping cream, chilled
- 30g/1oz unsalted butter
- 1 teaspoon vanilla extract
- 1 tablespoon stevia (see Tip)
- 1 teaspoon ground cinnamon
- 1 teaspoon freshly grated nutmeg
- 1 teaspoon ground ginger
- ½ teaspoon ground cardamom
- 100g/3½oz Atkins Flour Mix (page 126)
- 1 teaspoon baking powder
- ¼ teaspoon salt
- 2 eggs
- 360ml/12fl oz whole milk
- Olive oil spray
- ½ teaspoon ground cinnamon
- 4 teaspoons sugar-free caramel or vanilla syrup (optional)

TIPS

Stevia, *a natural sugar substitute extracted from the stevia plant, can replace sugar in baking. It is calorie free, although it is 200 times as sweet as granulated table sugar, so a little goes a long way!*

1 Place the cream in a large bowl and beat with an electric mixer on high speed until light and fluffy. Refrigerate until ready to use.

2 Place the butter in a small saucepan and melt over low heat. Stir in the vanilla extract, stevia, cinnamon, nutmeg, ginger and cardamom. Set aside to cool.

3 Place the Atkins Flour Mix in a large bowl along with the baking powder and salt, and stir well. Mix the eggs, milk and butter mixture together, and add to the bowl with the flour mix. Stir until just combined.

4 Coat a waffle iron with olive oil spray. Heat the waffle iron according to the manufacturer's instructions. Add 240ml/8fl oz of the waffle mix, and close the lid. Cook for 3 to 4 minutes, until the waffle is cooked through. Repeat with the remaining batter. Serve immediately with the whipped cream, cinnamon and sugar-free caramel or vanilla syrup, if desired.

GRILLED
HUEVOS
RANCHEROS

9g
NET CARBS

SERVES 4

396
CALORIES

Huevos Rancheros, or 'Rancher's Eggs' is the perfect brunch meal when breakfast time has passed you by, but you still crave eggs. Use chorizo, a spicy cured pork sausage flavoured with chillies, or substitute cooked hot Italian pork sausage links instead.

Olive oil spray

170g/6oz cured chorizo sausage, thinly sliced

1 bunch asparagus, trimmed and chopped

140g/5oz broccoli florets

140g/5oz cauliflower florets

8 eggs

130g/4½oz tomato salsa from a jar

1 ripe Haas avocado, cut into wedges

4 tablespoons soured cream

1 Set the oven to grill and coat a large frying pan with olive oil spray. Place over medium heat and add the chorizo, browning for 3 to 4 minutes, stirring well, until it renders its fat. Add the asparagus, broccoli and cauliflower,and cook for 3 to 4 minutes, until the vegetables start to soften. Crack the eggs on top.

2 Place the pan under the grill on the middle oven rack, and cook for 3 to 4 minutes until the whites of the eggs are cooked but the yolks are still soft. Serve immediately with the salsa, avocado and soured cream.

DID YOU KNOW ?

Don't confuse smoked **Spanish-style cured chorizo** with the soft **fresh version**, which needs to be cooked.

TIME	PER SERVING
Active: 15 minutes	*Total Carbs:* **16.6g** *Fibre:* **7.6g** *Protein:* **23.6g**
Total: 20 minutes	*Fat:* **27.2g** *FV=7*

BIRDIES

IN A
BASKET

6g
NET CARBS

SERVES 4

362
CALORIES

The title of this recipe, also known as 'eggs in a basket,' has its roots in 1930s Hollywood, where actresses such as Betty Grable requested sunny-side up eggs cooked in toast. This version uses vitamin C–rich red pepper in place of the toast and adds even more veggie power with the addition of detoxifying asparagus, which is rich in fibre and folate.

1 tablespoon olive oil

½ bunch asparagus, trimmed and sliced

½ teaspoon salt

2 large red peppers

4 eggs

160g/5¾oz Cheddar cheese, grated

130g/4½oz tomato salsa from a jar

1 Heat a large frying pan with a heatproof handle over medium heat, and add the olive oil. Add the asparagus and salt and cook for 3 to 4 minutes, until the asparagus softens. Transfer to a plate.

2 Preheat the oven to 180°C/350°F/Gas 4. Cut the peppers in half lengthwise, and discard the seeds. Place the peppers in the frying pan, stem side down, and sear for 1 minute over medium heat. Flip and crack an egg into each pepper half. Top with the asparagus and sprinkle with the Cheddar. Bake for 25 to 30 minutes, until the cheese is golden and the whites of the eggs are cooked through. Serve immediately with the salsa.

TIME	PER SERVING
Active: 10 minutes	*Total Carbs:* **8.8g**
	Fibre: **2.8g**
Total: 40 minutes	*Protein:* **21.6g**
	Fat: **27.3g**
	FV=4.9

ATKINS
FLOUR
MIX

5g NET CARBS

MAKES 300 GRAMS

191 CALORIES

This versatile low-carb flour mix is an important component of many of the recipes in this book.

15g/½oz wheat bran

125g/4½oz wholegrain soy flour

65g/2¼oz vanilla whey protein

25g/1oz golden flaxseed meal

80g/2¾oz vital wheat gluten flour

Combine all ingredients, and mix thoroughly. Use immediately, or store in an airtight container in the refrigerator for up to 1 month.

TIME	PER SERVING
Active: 10 minutes	*Total Carbs:* **8.2g** *Fibre:* **3.2g**
Total: 10 minutes	*Protein:* **31.3g** *Fat:* **4.4g** *FV = 0*

SWEET OR SAVOURY
CREPES

SERVES 4

These delightfully thin pancakes are oh, so versatile and can be eaten with sweet or savoury toppings. This recipe makes 12 crepes – make a double batch to freeze, and serve as the centrepiece of a fun brunch with eggs and a side salad. Crepes also make a great replacement for a standard high-carb wrap – just roll with a few slices of lean deli meat and cheese for a fast, portable lunch. Resting the crepe batter makes it easier to handle and stick less while cooking.

Crepes

4 eggs

2 tablespoons double cream

100g/3½oz Atkins Flour Mix (page 126)

30g/1oz almond flour

¼ teaspoon salt

180ml/6fl oz water

For sweet crepes: add 1 teaspoon vanilla extract

For savoury crepes: add ½ teaspoon salt

Olive oil spray

1 Prepare the crepe batter: Place the eggs, cream, Atkins Flour Mix, almond flour, salt, water and vanilla extract or salt in a blender. Blend until smooth. Let rest in the fridge for 1 hour. Coat a small frying pan with olive oil spray. Place over medium-high heat. Add about 4 tablespoons of the batter and swirl it around the pan to spread out in a thin layer. Cook for 2 to 3 minutes, until the edges start to brown, then flip it over. Cook for 1 minute more, until the crepe is firm, and transfer to a plate.

2 Repeat with the remaining batter, adding olive oil spray as needed.

RECIPE CONTINUES

SWEET CREPES	
TIME	**PER SERVING**
Active: 50 minutes	*Net Carbs:* **7.4g**
	Total Carbs: **12.5g**
	Fibre: **5.1g**
Total: 1 hour, 50 minutes	*Protein:* **32.2g**
	Fat: **22g**
	Calories: **370**
	FV = 0

SAVOURY CREPES	
TIME	**PER SERVING**
Active: 50 minutes	*Net Carbs:* **5.6g**
	Total Carbs: **8.8g**
	Fibre: **3.2g**
Total: 1 hour 50 minutes	*Protein:* **38.1g**
	Fat: **19.5g**
	Calories: **359**
	FV=0.1

Sweet or Savoury Crepes CONTINUED

SWEET TOPPING

80ml/2½fl oz double cream, chilled

120g/4¼oz fresh raspberries

½ teaspoon ground cinnamon

Place the cream in a bowl and beat with an electric mixer on high speed until soft peaks form. For each serving, fold 3 crepes into quarters on a plate. Top each with raspberries, a dollop of whipped cream, and cinnamon.

SAVOURY TOPPING

Olive oil spray

4 eggs

40g/1½oz watercress

Spray a frying pan with olive oil spray and heat over medium heat until hot. Break the eggs and slip them into the pan one at a time. Reduce heat to low, and cook slowly until the whites are set and the yolks begin to thicken but aren't hard. For each serving, fold 3 crepes into quarters on a plate. Top each with a fried egg and an equal portion of watercress.

CREAMY
AVOCADO
SMOOTHIE

5.3g
NET CARBS

SERVES
2

308
CALORIES

Not a fan of overly 'green'-tasting smoothies? This light, silky smoothie is the perfect way to get more greens into your morning, as avocado, a fruit packed with heart-healthy fats, mellows the flavour of spinach or kale. See Tip for more options for seasonal stir-ins.

20g/¾oz baby spinach or kale

½ ripe Hass avocado

2 celery stalks

65g/2¼oz plain protein powder

1 tablespoon lemon juice

½ cucumber, peeled

14 walnut halves

120ml/4fl oz water

8 ice cubes

Place the baby spinach or kale, avocado, celery, protein powder, lemon juice, cucumber, walnuts, water and ice cubes in a blender. Blend until smooth, and serve immediately.

TIPS

For a hint of freshness, add a pinch of mild chilli powder in the winter or 2 tablespoons mint leaves (which add only .5 gram Net Carbs) in the summer.

TIME	PER SERVING
Active: 10 minutes	*Total Carbs:* **10.9g**
	Fibre: **5.6g**
Total: 10 minutes	*Protein:* **32.2g**
	Fat: **16.2g**
	FV=2.6

ANTIOXIDANT
BERRY
SMOOTHIE

7.1g
NET CARBS

SERVES 2

348
CALORIES

Berries are bursting with anthocyanins, colourful antioxidant pigments also responsible for their beautiful colours. This same antioxidant is being studied for a wide range of detox benefits for organs, from your heart to your liver and even your skin.[1]

TIME	PER SERVING
Active: 10 minutes	*Total Carbs:* **14.7g** *Fibre:* **7.7g** *Protein:* **32.4g** *Fat:* **15.5g** *FV=0*
Total: 10 minutes	

- 60g/2oz mixed frozen berries (such as raspberries or blueberries)
- 180ml/6fl oz full-fat tinned coconut milk
- 65g/2¼oz plain protein powder
- 2 tablespoons chia seeds
- ½ teaspoon ground cinnamon or cardamom
- ½ teaspoon ground turmeric
- 1 teaspoon vanilla extract
- 120ml/4fl oz cold water
- 4 ice cubes

Place the berries, coconut milk, protein powder, chia seeds, cinnamon or cardamom, turmeric, vanilla extract, water and ice cubes in a blender. Blend until smooth, and serve immediately.

TIPS

Protein powder *is a good source of amino acids, which are the building blocks of muscle and may even be instrumental in weight loss and boosting your immunity. Most protein powders are made from two types of milk protein, although you can also find a blend of both.*

- *Whey protein is one of the most popular protein powders. It is fast acting, which means it is digested more quickly.*
- *Casein protein is a slow-acting protein powder, and is digested more slowly.*

In addition, there are non-dairy, vegetarian sources of protein powder:

- *Soy protein is extracted from soybeans.*
- *Rice protein is isolated protein that comes from brown rice grains.*
- *Pea protein is concentrated protein extracted from split yellow peas.*

POWER
MUG MUFFIN

with Cinnamon Butter

3.9g
NET CARBS

SERVES
1

363
CALORIES

The power of this muffin comes from three superfoods: flax, almonds and eggs, which deliver a lot of brain-boosting nutrients such as omega-3s, choline and vitamin E. This faux 'soufflé' blossoms before your eyes, making it a fun recipe for kids to make.

TIME	PER SERVING
Active: 10 minutes	*Total Carbs:* **11.3g**
	Fibre: **7.4g**
Total: 10 minutes	*Protein:* **12.6g**
	Fat: **31.1g**
	FV=0

Cinnamon Butter

- 1 tablespoon unsalted butter, at room temperature
- ½ teaspoon ground cinnamon
- ⅛ teaspoon salt
- ¼ teaspoon ground nutmeg

Muffin

- 2 tablespoons golden flaxseed meal
- 2 tablespoons almond flour
- ½ teaspoon baking powder
- ½ teaspoon stevia
- 1 teaspoon ground cinnamon
- 1 egg
- 1 teaspoon unsalted butter, at room temperature, or olive oil

1 Prepare the cinnamon butter: Place the butter, cinnamon, salt and nutmeg in a small bowl, and mix well with a spoon. Set aside.

2 Prepare the muffin: Mix the flaxseed meal, almond flour, baking powder, stevia and cinnamon in a coffee mug or ramekin. Mix the egg and butter into the dry ingredients. Microwave for 1 minute on high, until firm. Serve immediately with the cinnamon butter.

LEMONY
PROTEIN PANCAKES

5.5g
NET CARBS

SERVES
4

302
CALORIES

If you're a fan of lemon ricotta pancakes, you'll love these higher-protein pancakes that will remind you a little of them, minus the blood sugar roller coaster. If you want to pump up the lemon flavour even more, look for Meyer lemons, a sweeter breed of lemon with a slightly spicy fragrance.

50g/1¾oz Atkins Flour Mix (page 126)

40g/1½oz almond meal

2 teaspoons baking powder

3 eggs

120g/4¼oz cottage cheese

1 tablespoon finely grated lemon zest (from 1 lemon), plus thin strips of lemon zest to garnish

2 tablespoons lemon juice

3 tablespoons coconut oil

1   Place the Atkins Flour Mix, almond meal and baking powder in a large bowl. Stir well. In a separate large bowl, whisk the eggs, then blend with the cottage cheese, lemon zest and lemon juice until well incorporated. Add to the dry ingredients.

2   Melt the coconut oil in a large frying pan over medium heat. Using a measuring cup or ladle, drop 60ml/2fl oz pools of the batter into the pan. The batter will make about eight 10cm/4in pancakes. Cook for 2 to 3 minutes, until the edges start to firm and bubbles begin to form in the middle of each pancake. Flip the pancakes, and cook for another 1 to 2 minutes, until firm. Serve immediately.

TIME	PER SERVING
Active: 10 minutes	*Total Carbs:* **7.9g**
	Fibre: **2.4g**
Total: 20 minutes	*Protein:* **21.5g**
	Fat: **21.8g**
	FV=0

COCONUT
MUESLI
CLUSTERS

3.9g
NET CARBS

SERVES 8

358
CALORIES

Cereal lovers don't have to go without with this clever mock muesli. The protein powder and egg coating help satisfy your hunger while giving this cereal a more cohesive texture and pleasing crunch – much better for you than the high-sugar honey typically used in muesli or granola. To vary the flavour, replace the pecans with almonds and add ½ teaspoon almond extract.

TIME	PER SERVING
Active: 10 minutes	*Total Carbs:* **12.8g**
	Fibre: **8.9g**
Total: 20 minutes	*Protein:* **19.3g**
	Fat: **27.3g**
	FV=0

Olive oil spray

100g/3½oz plain protein powder

70g/2½oz unsalted sunflower or pumpkin seeds

120g/4¼oz whole raw pecans

30g/1oz unsweetened dried coconut flakes

90g/3¼oz chia seeds or ground flaxseeds

1 tablespoon stevia

2 teaspoons ground cinnamon

½ teaspoon ground turmeric

1 tablespoon coconut oil

1 tablespoon peanut butter

1 teaspoon vanilla extract

2 eggs

60ml/2fl oz water

1 Preheat oven to 180°C/350°F/Gas 4. Line a large baking tray with baking parchment. Coat with olive oil spray and set aside. In a large bowl, mix together the protein powder, sunflower or pumpkin seeds, pecans, coconut, chia seeds or flaxseeds, stevia, cinnamon and turmeric.

2 In a large saucepan, combine the coconut oil, peanut butter and vanilla extract and melt completely, then stir in the nut mixture. Turn the heat off and add the eggs and water, tossing well. Transfer to the prepared baking tray, and spread the mixture in a layer about 1cm/½in thick over the tray.

3 Bake for 10 to 15 minutes, until the mixture starts to brown and clumps together to make clusters. Cool completely on the baking tray, then store in an airtight container, refrigerated, for up to 1 week.

SNACKS AND SIDES

SATISFYING SNACKS

AND WINNING SIDE DISHES

On Atkins, we recommend eating two snacks a day
to keep your hunger nicely in check, and what better way than with these
salty, savoury, spicy, crunchy, cheesy and creamy snacks that will
satisfy any craving. And the side dishes? They could very well become
the star of any meal! You'll be able to mix and match these recipes
with a variety of other recipes throughout this book.

RECIPES

CRISPY
BRUSSELS SPROUTS

with Sriracha Mayo Dipping Sauce

7.5g
NET CARBS

SERVES
4

207
CALORIES

If you're seeking more flavour in your veggie sides, searing is the ticket to taste! Searing Brussels sprouts in hot oil, as you would meat, helps to caramelize them quickly for a slightly sweet flavour that is well balanced by the hot chillies and spicy dipping sauce. For best results, dry the sprouts in kitchen paper or a tea towel before you cook them.

TIME	PER SERVING
Active: 10 minutes	*Total Carbs:* **12g** *Fibre:* **4.4g**
Total: 20 minutes	*Protein:* **3.9g** *Fat:* **17.1g** *FV=6*

Brussels sprouts

1 tablespoon grapeseed or coconut oil

450g/1lb Brussels sprouts, dried, trimmed and halved

2 serrano or jalapeño chillies, deseeded and sliced

½ teaspoon salt or smoked salt

¼ teaspoon freshly ground black pepper

Sriracha mayo

80g/2¾oz mayonnaise

2 tablespoons sriracha hot sauce

1 Warm the oil in a large frying pan over medium-high heat. Add the Brussels sprouts to the pan, cut sides down, and cook for about 3 minutes, until nicely browned. Add the chillies and sprinkle with the salt and pepper. Reduce the heat to medium low and cook until sprouts are tender, about 8 minutes more.

2 While the Brussels sprouts are cooking, prepare the mayonnaise: Put the mayonnaise and sriracha in a small bowl, and stir well to combine. Transfer the Brussels sprouts to a platter, and serve immediately with the mayonnaise.

AVOCADO
TOAST

5g NET CARBS   **SERVES 8**   **318** CALORIES

It's no wonder the snack staple of rich avocado mash on crisp toast has been shared around the world for more than two decades. Creamy avocados are filled with healthy fats and fibre. They help you feel fuller longer while satisfying your 'creamy' comfort food craving. The versatile 'toast' is easy to make and can serve as the base for many snacks, including our flatbread recipe on page (215).

TIME	PER SERVING
Active: 10 minutes	*Total Carbs:* **13.1g** *Fibre:* **8.2g** *Protein:* **18.9g**
Total: 40 minutes	*Fat:* **28g** *FV=***1.6**

1 egg

1 tablespoon olive oil

60ml/2fl oz water

180g/6½oz almond flour

15g/½oz Parmesan cheese, grated

½ teaspoon baking powder

½ teaspoon stevia

¾ teaspoon chopped fresh oregano

¼ teaspoon crushed chilli flakes

Olive oil spray

4 ripe Hass avocados

4 tablespoons lemon juice

1 teaspoon salt

1 Preheat the oven to 190°C/375°F/Gas 5. Whisk together the egg, olive oil and water in a small bowl. Set aside.

2 In a large bowl, combine the almond flour, Parmesan, baking powder, stevia, oregano and chilli flakes and stir to blend. Add the wet ingredients to the dry ingredients, stirring to form a sticky dough.

3 Coat a baking tray with olive oil spray. Smooth the dough onto the prepared tray with a spatula, into a 40- by 20-cm/16- by 8-in rectangle. Bake for 20 to 25 minutes, until golden and crisp around the edges. Allow the toast to cool for about 20 minutes.

4 While the dough is baking and cooling, prepare the avocados: Place the avocados in a large bowl with the lemon juice and seasoning salt and mash well. Cut the toast into eight squares, and top with the avocado. Serve immediately.

PROSCIUTTO-WRAPPED
PRAWNS

with Kale Mayonnaise

6.9g
NET CARBS

SERVES 4

474
CALORIES

Prosciutto is a lean Italian cured ham that crisps like bacon when sautéed. In this recipe, it makes a flavourful, high-protein wrap for prawns that also helps to keep in moisture. Kale mayonnaise adds filling fat, plus all the goodness of kale, a superfood rich in a long list of detoxifying nutrients, including vitamins A, C, K and more.

Kale mayonnaise

60g/2oz kale, chopped

120g/4¼oz mayonnaise

1 teaspoon paprika

½ teaspoon freshly ground black pepper

Prawns

10 slices prosciutto (about 15g/½oz)

20 extra large prawns, peeled and deveined, with tail segment attached

Olive oil spray

1 **Prepare the kale mayonnaise:** Place the kale in a food processor and process until minced. Add the mayonnaise, paprika and pepper; pulse to combine. Set aside.

2 **Prepare the prawns:** Cut each prosciutto slice in half lengthwise. Wrap each half slice around a prawn and transfer to a plate. Coat a frying pan with olive oil spray. Brown for 3 to 4 minutes, turning occasionally, until the prosciutto is crisp and the prawns are cooked through. Serve 5 prawns per person with 2 tablespoons of the kale mayonnaise.

TIME	PER SERVING
Active: 10 minutes	*Total Carbs:* **8.4g**
	Fibre: **1.6g**
Total: 20 minutes	*Protein:* **20.1g**
	Fat: **28.4g**
	*FV=***5.4**

HOT
CRAB DIP

1g
NET CARBS

SERVES 4

298
CALORIES

Creamy, satisfying hot crab dip is a seafood restaurant staple that seems upscale, but this dish is incredibly easy to make. You can serve it with raw veggies, such as 1 celery stalk cut into matchsticks or 30g/1oz cucumber slices per person (for an extra 1 gram Net Carbs per serving) or our Coriander Parmesan Crackers on page 155 (for an extra 3 grams Net Carbs per serving).

225g/8oz cooked crabmeat, picked over for shells and cartilage

120g/4¼oz mayonnaise

60g/2oz Cheddar cheese, grated

1 tablespoon lemon juice

2 garlic cloves

Preheat the oven to 200ºC/400°F/Gas 6. Place the crabmeat, mayonnaise, Cheddar, lemon juice and garlic in a food processor, and pulse until the mixture is creamy. Transfer to a baking dish and bake for 20 to 25 minutes, until the mixture is hot and bubbly. Serve immediately.

TIME	PER SERVING
Active: 10 minutes	*Total Carbs:* **1g**
	Fibre: **0.1g**
Total: 40 minutes	*Protein:* **15g**
	Fat: **25.7g**
	FV=0

BAKED SRIRACHA
HOT WINGS
AND KALE CHIPS

5.9g
NET CARBS

SERVES
4

281
CALORIES

In this recipe, we take the American bar classic to a healthier level. Skip the breading and crisp the skin by rendering the fat in a frying pan, then bake the wings at high heat. A quick toss in a sauce made of spicy sriracha butter adds richness plus heat. The kale chips crisp up quickly alongside the wings and are a great source of vitamins A, B, and C, iron and potassium.

TIME	PER SERVING
Active: **15 minutes**	*Total Carbs:* **6.7g**
	Fibre: **0.8g**
Total: **40 minutes**	*Protein:* **17.3g**
	Fat: **20.5g**
	FV=2.8

60ml/2fl oz sriracha hot sauce

45g/1½oz unsalted butter

½ teaspoon garlic salt

½ teaspoon freshly ground black pepper

Olive oil spray

450g/1lb chicken wings

140g/5oz kale

½ teaspoon salt

1   Preheat the oven to 200°C/400°F/Gas 6. Cover a large baking sheet with kitchen foil.

2   Prepare the wing sauce: Place the sriracha, butter, garlic salt and ¼ teaspoon of the black pepper in a large saucepan. Bring to a simmer over low heat, stirring continuously, until the butter melts. Turn the heat off and set aside.

3   Coat a large frying pan with olive oil spray. Add the wings and cook for 5 to 6 minutes, turning occasionally, until they brown. Transfer to the prepared baking sheet and bake for 12 to 15 minutes, until the chicken is cooked through and no longer pink at the bone.

4   While the chicken wings are cooking, prepare the kale chips: Remove the stems from the kale and discard. Tear the kale into 10-cm-/4-in-wide pieces and arrange on another baking sheet. Spray the tops with olive oil spray. Flip the kale, and coat the other side with olive oil spray. Transfer to the oven and bake for 5 to 8 minutes, until crisp.

5   When the chicken is cooked, remove it from the oven and toss in the sauce. Season the kale chips with the salt and remaining black pepper. Serve the chicken immediately with the kale chips.

ASPARAGUS WITH
BURRATA CHEESE
AND KALE PESTO

2g
NET CARBS

SERVES 6

174
CALORIES

Move over, mozzarella, burrata has a smooth, elastic exterior and a creamy, buttery interior. Served over asparagus, burrata cheese creates an instant creamy sauce, made even more indulgent when topped with pesto. It's a good thing that this recipe serves six, because it is sure to be a crowd pleaser.

TIME	PER SERVING
Active: 10 minutes	*Total Carbs:* **4.1g** *Fibre:* **2.1g** *Protein:* **8.8g**
Total: 25 minutes	*Fat:* **16.3g** *FV=***1.9**

450g/1lb asparagus, trimmed

Olive oil spray

½ teaspoon salt

¼ teaspoon freshly ground black pepper

15g/½oz kale leaves

12g/½oz basil leaves

3 tablespoons olive oil

2 garlic cloves, crushed

2 to 3 tablespoons cold water

225g/8oz burrata cheese

DID YOU KNOW

Burrata is a ball of mozzarella cheese with a **creamy,** runny (think poached egg) centre. You'll find it packed in water with the other fresh mozzarella products at the supermarket and at Italian delicatessens.

1 Place the asparagus on a plate and coat with olive oil spray. Sprinkle with half the seasoning salt and the black pepper. Heat a large frying pan over medium-high heat and add the asparagus. Cook for 5 to 6 minutes, turning often, until the asparagus is tender. Transfer to a platter.

2 Add the kale and basil to a food processor, pulsing seven to eight times, until finely chopped. Add the olive oil, garlic, remaining ¼ teaspoon salt and water; blend until smooth and creamy.

3 Cut the burrata into 6 wedges. Top a serving of asparagus with a wedge of burrata, including its creamy insides. Drizzle with the kale pesto and serve.

TUNA-STUFFED DEVILLED EGGS

1g
NET CARBS

SERVES
4

290
CALORIES

Devilled eggs received their name in the 1800s, when foods stuffed with a spicy flavouring such as Dijon mustard were termed *devilishly* hot. This version gets its 'devil' from jalapeños, which also add a pleasant crunch and are rich in vitamin C. Add these Atkins-friendly eggs to your next party or brunch spread.

TIME	PER SERVING
Active: 10 minutes	*Total Carbs:* **1.5g** *Fibre:* **0.5g**
Total: 30 minutes	*Protein:* **23.5g** *Fat:* **20.4g** *FV=0*

8 eggs

170-g/6-oz tin tuna, drained

60g/2oz mayonnaise

1 jalapeño, deseeded and finely chopped

2 tablespoons capers, drained, rinsed and chopped

1 teaspoon hot or sweet paprika or ground chilli

1 Place the eggs in a medium saucepan, and cover with cold water. Place over high heat and bring to a boil. Immediately turn the heat off and cover. Remove from the heat and let cool for 1 minute. Place the eggs in a colander under cold running water for 1 to 2 minutes, until they are easy to handle. Peel them under cold running water, and transfer to a clean tea towel to dry.

2 Cut the eggs in half lengthwise and scoop out the yolks. Transfer the yolks to a small bowl along with the tuna, mayonnaise, jalapeño and capers. Stir well until combined. Place the egg whites on a platter, centre side up, and fill with the tuna mixture. Garnish with the ground paprika or chilli, and serve immediately.

TIPS

Hard-boiled eggs *make a great grab-and-go low-carb snack. All you have to do is follow the instructions in this recipe for hard-boiling eggs.*

CHEESY
SPRING ONION
CAULIFLOWER MASH

2.7g
NET CARBS

SERVES 6

78
CALORIES

Creamy comfort food such as mashed potatoes may seem like a high-carb treat of the past, but this cheesy cauliflower mash is just as satisfying in both flavour and texture. Pressing the cauliflower before whipping in a food processor is the secret to a mash that is light and fluffy.

1 small head cauliflower, cut into florets

40g/1½oz Cheddar cheese, grated

1 tablespoon unsalted butter

1 teaspoon garlic salt

¼ teaspoon ground turmeric

2 spring onions, thinly sliced

1 Place a steamer basket in a large stockpot, add 2 cups of water and bring to the boil over high heat. Add the cauliflower and steam 10 to 12 minutes until it is fork tender. (If you don't have a steamer basket, you can just add the cauliflower to the boiling water in the pot.) Drain the cauliflower in a colander, pressing down with a small pan lid to drain the excess moisture.

2 Working in batches, transfer the cauliflower to a food processor and chop. Once all the cauliflower is chopped, put it all in the food processor along with the Cheddar, butter, garlic salt and turmeric. Process until smooth. Top with the spring onions and serve immediately.

TIME	PER SERVING
Active: 10 minutes	*Total Carbs:* **5g**
	Fibre: **2.2g**
Total: 15 minutes	*Protein:* **4.1g**
	Fat: **5.2g**
	*FV=***2.6**

FRIED GREEN
TOMATOES
with Ranch Dipping Sauce

6.8g
NET CARBS

SERVES
4

392
CALORIES

Fried green tomatoes are a comfort food from the American south that you will fall in love with at first bite. If you can't locate green tomatoes (under-ripe red tomatoes), search out less ripe brown tomatoes, such as Kumato. Capers make a tart garnish, if you happen to have them handy.

TIME	PER SERVING
Active: 20 minutes	*Total Carbs:* **9.7g**
	Fibre: **2.7g**
Total: 30 minutes	*Protein:* **15.1g**
	Fat: **33.5g**
	FV= **4.5**

Ranch Dipping Sauce

120g/4¼oz mayonnaise

2 tablespoons coconut milk or double cream

1 teaspoon apple cider vinegar

½ teaspoon onion powder

½ teaspoon garlic salt

1 tablespoon chopped fresh dill or flatleaf parsley

¼ teaspoon freshly ground black pepper

Fried Tomatoes

50g/1¾oz Atkins Flour Mix (page 126)

½ teaspoon garlic salt

½ teaspoon sweet paprika

½ teaspoon freshly ground black pepper

450g/1lb green tomatoes

1 egg

3 tablespoons olive oil

1 Prepare the ranch dipping sauce: Combine the mayonnaise, coconut milk or cream, vinegar, onion powder, garlic salt, dill or parsley and black pepper in a small bowl and whisk well. Refrigerate until ready to use, or make ahead and refrigerate overnight.

2 Prepare the fried tomatoes: Place the Atkins Flour Mix, garlic salt, paprika and pepper on a plate and toss with a spoon until well incorporated. Slice the tomatoes into four 1-cm-/½-in-thick rounds. Place the egg in a shallow bowl and whisk. Dip the tomato slices into the egg, then dredge in the flour mixture and transfer to a plate.

3 Warm the oil in a large frying pan and, working in batches, fry the tomatoes for 1 to 2 minutes per side, until crisp. Transfer to a kitchen paper–lined plate to drain. Transfer to a platter, and serve immediately with the ranch sauce.

SAUTÉED
SPINACH

with Caramelized Shallots

2.8g
NET CARBS

SERVES 6

62
CALORIES

Spinach and kale vie for the title of top superfood greens since they both contain high levels of many essential nutrients in just one small cup. Gentle sautéing doesn't destroy their nutrients, and it keeps the tender greens flavourful and fresh tasting, making this recipe an ideal companion for many of the heavier roasts and stews in this book. To prepare this recipe with either standard or Tuscan kale, substitute 450g/1lb of kale, stems removed, for the spinach.

TIME	PER SERVING
Active: 10 minutes	*2.8g* *Total Carbs:* **4.4g** *Protein:* **2.4g**
Total: 15 minutes	*Fat:* **4.5g** *FV=*2.7

1 tablespoon unsalted butter

1 tablespoon olive oil

3 shallots, thinly sliced

¼ teaspoon salt

¼ teaspoon freshly ground black pepper

¼ teaspoon stevia, optional

Olive oil spray

450g/1lb baby spinach or baby kale

1 Warm the butter and olive oil in a small frying pan over medium heat. Add the shallots, salt, black pepper and stevia. Cook for 10 to 12 minutes, stirring often, until the shallots are well browned, adding 1 to 2 tablespoons of water if the shallots stick. Transfer the shallots to a plate.

2 Coat the pan with the olive oil spray and, working in batches, add the spinach; cook for 1 to 2 minutes, until it is wilted and tender. Top with the shallots and serve immediately.

CORIANDER
PARMESAN
CRACKERS

1.4g
NET CARBS

MAKES 3 DOZEN

80
CALORIES

Watch these get snapped up at your next gathering, because these aren't your average crackers – they're fragrant taste bombs, thanks to fresh coriander mixed with Parmesan! See the tip for other savoury flavour combinations and serve with Bourbon Pecan Pâté (page 212) or Hot Crab Dip (page 145).

TIME	PER SERVING (4 crackers)
Active: 10 minutes	*Total Carbs:* **2.8g**
Total: 30 minutes	*Fibre:* **1.3g**
	Protein: **3.7g**
	Fat: **6.7g**
	FV: **0**

120g/4¼oz almond flour

1 egg white

3 tablespoons grated Parmesan cheese

1 tablespoon finely chopped fresh coriander

¼ teaspoon garlic salt

Olive oil spray

1 Place the almond flour, egg white, Parmesan, coriander and garlic salt in a medium bowl and mix well with a spatula until a soft, slightly crumbly dough forms.

2 Coat two sheets of baking parchment with olive oil spray. Roll out the dough into a large rectangle about 5mm/⅛in thick between the sheets of sprayed baking parchment. Freeze for 15 minutes to make the dough easier to handle.

3 Preheat the oven to 170°C/325°F/Gas 3. Remove the top sheet of parchment and discard. Score the dough into 36 rectangles, about 5-by-2.5cm/2-by-1in each. Leaving the dough on the parchment–lined baking sheet, bake for 15 to 20 minutes, until the crackers are golden and firm. Cool completely on the baking sheet. Break into crackers along the score marks. Serve or store in an airtight container at room temperature for up to 4 days.

TIP

Switch up your crackers with these other flavour combinations:

SWAP THIS	FOR THIS
Parmesan	*Pecorino, aged Gouda or grated Asiago*
Coriander	*Basil, parsley, chopped rosemary or ½ teaspoon crushed chilli flakes*

HOMEMADE
RED
SAUERKRAUT

with Fennel and
Caraway Seeds

6.9g
NET CARBS

MAKES
1.3
KG

44
CALORIES

Fermented foods such as sauerkraut are now all the rage in health circles, since we now know that eating cultured foods can help improve gut health. Other benefits include boosting your immunity and keeping your metabolism humming at optimal levels.[2] Another bonus: one batch of this fermented feast can last for up to 3 weeks.

TIME	PER SERVING (½ cup)
Active: 20 minutes	*Total Carbs:* **10g**
Total: 3 days, 15 minutes	*Fibre:* **3.1g**
	Protein: **2g**
	Fat: **0.4 g**
	FV=6.9

- 1 red cabbage (about 1.25kg/3lb), coarsely shredded
- 1 tablespoon fennel seeds
- 1 tablespoon caraway seeds
- 4 tablespoons apple cider vinegar
- 2 teaspoons salt
- ½ teaspoon ground turmeric

1 Toss the cabbage, fennel and caraway seeds, vinegar, salt and turmeric in a large glass bowl. Squeeze the mixture with clean hands for 4 to 5 minutes to soften the shreds and to release some juices to form part of the pickling liquid.

2 Transfer the cabbage and its juice to a large glass jar or pitcher, and press it down so the liquid covers the top. Add additional water if the natural juices of the cabbage don't completely cover the surface of the cabbage (this will protect it from moulding).

3 Cover with a clean tea towel and let rest on your worktop for 3 to 4 days maximum, until the mixture starts to bubble and reaches the desired tanginess. After 4 days maximum, transfer to airtight containers and store in the refrigerator for up to 3 weeks.

SHISHITO
PEPPERS
with Hot Paprika Mayonnaise

2.7g NET CARBS

SERVES **4**

245 CALORIES

Shishito peppers are long, finger-shaped peppers that hail from East Asia but are typically served at Spanish tapas bars. Shishitos are generally mild, but one out of every ten is a spicy zinger! Search for them in gourmet markets and farmers' market stands that specialize in chillies, or substitute with Padrón peppers or little mild peppers called 'ancient sweets' or 'mini sweets', which also work well in this recipe.

TIME	PER SERVING
Active: 10 minutes	*Total Carbs:* **7.1g**
	Fibre: **4.4g**
Total: 15 minutes	*Protein:* **2.2g**
	Fat: **23.7g**
	FV=2.3

450g/1lb (about 48) shishito peppers

120g/4¼oz mayonnaise

Zest of 1 lemon, finely grated

1 tablespoon tomato purée

1 tablespoon hot or sweet paprika

1 tablespoon grapeseed or coconut oil

1 Wash the shishito peppers and dry them well.

2 Prepare the paprika mayonnaise: Place the mayonnaise, lemon zest, tomato purée and paprika in a small bowl and stir well to combine.

3 Line a baking sheet with kitchen paper. Heat the oil in a large frying pan over high heat, and add the peppers. Cook for 2 to 3 minutes, stirring often, until the skins blister. Drain the peppers on the kitchen paper and serve immediately with the mayonnaise.

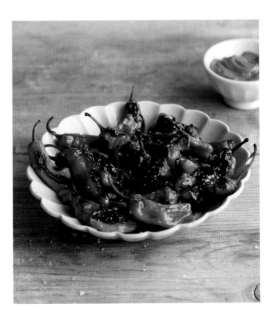

8

SOUPS AND STEWS

SOUPS, STEWS AND ANYTHING YOU CAN
SLURP UP IN A BOWL

The international medley of flavours of these soups and
stews will tantalize your taste buds. You can slurp on a smaller serving to
ease your appetite before your main meal, or indulge in a steaming
hot bowl as your main course, paired with a side salad.

RECIPES

BASIC
BONE BROTH

0g
NET CARBS

SERVES 8

164
CALORIES

Bone broth has become a health staple and rightfully so. It's a low-cal drink with 0 gram Net Carbs that boasts a boost of protein, plus a rich, comforting flavour that helps cleanse your system. The high gelatin content can help soothe your stomach and aid with digestion. This slowly cooked broth is used in recipes throughout this book to enrich your dining experience. If you wish, use a slow cooker to simmer while you sleep (or are at work).

TIME	PER SERVING
Active: 20 minutes	*Total Carbs:* **0g**
	Fibre: **0g**
Total: 8 hours, 20 minutes	*Protein:* **12g**
	Fat: **5g**
	FV=0

- 900g/2lb beef shank bones with marrow (see Tip on next page)
- ½ teaspoon salt
- ¼ teaspoon freshly ground black pepper
- 1 tablespoon unsalted butter
- 2 carrots, chopped
- 1 onion, quartered
- 2 garlic cloves, chopped
- 2 tablespoons white distilled vinegar
- 2 bay leaves
- 1 sprig fresh thyme

1 Sprinkle the bones with the salt and pepper. Heat a large stockpot over medium heat, and add the butter. When the butter foams, add the bones and cook for 3 to 4 minutes per side, turning occasionally, until the bones brown. Transfer the bones to a plate. Add the carrots, onion and garlic to the pan. Cook for 6 to 8 minutes, stirring often, until the vegetables brown. Return the bones to the pot, and fill the stockpot with water (about 3 litres), leaving at least a 1-cm-/½-in-space at the top of the pot.

RECIPE CONTINUES

TIP

Request beef shank bones *with marrow from the butcher, as they are usually not sold in the pre-packaged meat aisle.*

2 Add the vinegar, bay leaves and thyme, and bring to a boil. As soon as the mixture boils, reduce to a simmer, cover and cook for 8 hours, adding additional water as needed to keep the water level high.

3 Remove and discard the bones. Strain the broth into a large bowl, discarding the solids. Cool completely and store in an airtight container in the refrigerator for up to 1 week or in the freezer for up to 6 months.

To prepare bone broth in a slow cooker: Place all the ingredients in an 8-litre/7-quart slow cooker and cover with water. Set to low and cook for 10 hours until the marrow falls away from the bone. Discard the bones and strain. Discard the vegetables and marrow and let cool completely before storing in airtight containers in the refrigerator for up to 1 week or in the freezer for up to 6 months.

JALAPEÑO CHEDDAR
BROCCOLI SOUP

SERVES 4

If you are not a fan of spicy heat, this soup is surprisingly mild since the seeds (where the spicy compound capsaicin resides) of the jalapeños are removed. The melted cheese on top will make you feel as though you're getting a bistro treat; however, it tastes just as good without the cheese.

3 tablespoons olive oil

1 head broccoli, cut into florets

6 jalapeños, deseeded and diced

½ onion, chopped

1 teaspoon salt

½ teaspoon curry powder or ground turmeric

½ teaspoon freshly ground black pepper

2 tablespoons Atkins Flour Mix (page 126)

1 litre/35fl oz Basic Bone Broth (page 161), or unsalted chicken or beef stock

4 tablespoons double cream or tinned coconut milk

1 tablespoon hot sauce

4 slices (115g/4oz total) Cheddar cheese, optional

1 Warm the olive oil in a large stockpot over medium heat. Add the broccoli, jalapeños, onion, salt, curry powder or turmeric and pepper; cook for 5 to 6 minutes, stirring often, until the onion begins to brown. Sprinkle with the Atkins Flour Mix and cook for 1 minute more, stirring often, until the flour coats the vegetables. Add the broth and cover.

2 Cook for 10 to 15 minutes over medium heat, until the broccoli is fork tender. Using an immersion blender, blend until smooth. Stir in the cream or coconut milk and hot sauce. Set the oven to grill. Transfer the soup to four oven-safe bowls and top each with one slice of cheese, if using. Place under the grill for 2 to 3 minutes until the cheese is melted and bubbly. Serve immediately.

WITH CHEESE	
TIME	PER SERVING
Active: 10 minutes	Net Carbs: 9.1g
	Total Carbs: 13.5g
Total: 30 minutes	Fibre: 4.3g
	Protein: 18.9g
	Fat: 27.4g
	Calories: 365
	FV= 6.8

WITHOUT CHEESE	
TIME	PER SERVING
Active: 10 minutes	Net Carbs: 8.8g
	Total Carbs: 13.1g
Total: 30 minutes	Fibre: 4.3g
	Protein: 11.8g
	Fat: 18g
	Calories: 251
	FV=6.8

BONE BROTH
MINESTRONE

7.6g NET CARBS

SERVES 4

280 CALORIES

Minestrone, a chunky vegetable soup from Italy, usually has high-carb ingredients such as white rice, pasta and beans. This version features cauliflower instead and gets its rich savoury flavour from your homemade bone broth and tangy Parmesan cheese. *Buon appetito!*

45g/1½oz unsalted butter

½ head of cauliflower, chopped

1 courgette, diced

½ onion, diced

4 garlic cloves, sliced

1 teaspoon Italian seasoning or chopped fresh oregano

1 teaspoon salt

½ teaspoon freshly ground black pepper

1 tablespoon tomato purée

1 litre/35fl oz Basic Bone Broth (page 161) or beef stock

15g/½oz baby kale leaves

10g/⅓oz fresh basil leaves

15g/½oz Parmesan cheese, grated

1 Heat a large stockpot over medium heat and add the butter. When the butter foams, add the cauliflower, courgette, onion, garlic, Italian seasoning or oregano, salt and black pepper; cook for 3 to 4 minutes, stirring often. Decrease the heat to low and add the tomato purée. Cook for 2 to 3 minutes, stirring often, until the paste becomes fragrant. Add the broth, and simmer on medium heat for 10 minutes, until the cauliflower is tender.

2 Add the kale and basil, and cook for 3 minutes more until the kale wilts. Spoon into four bowls, sprinkle with the Parmesan and serve immediately.

TIME	PER SERVING
Active: 10 minutes	*Total Carbs:* **10.5g**
	Fibre: **3g**
Total: 40 minutes	*Protein:* **18.7g**
	Fat: **19.3g**
	FV=7

CAULIFLOWER
BISQUE

6.1g
NET CARBS

SERVES 4

339
CALORIES

Bisque is a smooth, creamy French soup that comes in many different flavours, from lobster to tomato and also cauliflower. Although this soup may appear to be a fine-dining treat, it's surprisingly easy to make and will satisfy any creamy craving.

TIME	PER SERVING
Active: 10 minutes	*Total Carbs:* **8.8g** *Fibre:* **2.7g**
Total: 30 minutes	*Protein:* **9.3g** *Fat:* **27g** *FV=5*

45g/1½oz unsalted butter

1 small head cauliflower, cut into florets

4 garlic cloves, chopped

½ teaspoon salt

½ teaspoon freshly grated nutmeg

¼ teaspoon freshly ground black pepper

1 litre/35fl oz Basic Bone Broth (page 161) or unsalted chicken or vegetable stock

1 tablespoon lemon juice

120ml/4fl oz double cream or tinned coconut milk

4 teaspoons olive oil

½ red pepper, deseeded and finely chopped

1 Place the butter in a large stockpot and warm over medium heat for about 1 minute, until the butter foams. Add the cauliflower, garlic, salt, nutmeg and pepper; cook for 5 to 6 minutes, stirring often, until the garlic begins to brown. Add the broth and lemon juice and cover.

2 Cook for 15 to 20 minutes, until the cauliflower is fork tender. Using an immersion blender, blend until smooth. Stir in the cream or coconut milk. Spoon into 4 bowls, garnish each serving with the olive oil and chopped pepper, and serve immediately.

TIP

You can also purée creamy soups in a standing blender. Before you do so, be sure that the soup has cooled to room temperature. When hot soup is blended, it creates steam that will force the lid off the blender, so leave the lid ajar as a safety precaution. Reheat the soup as needed.

SPICY
KOREAN
SOUP

with Spring Onions

4.7g NET CARBS

SERVES 4

322 CALORIES

Yukgaejang, a spicy shredded beef soup with vegetables, is the inspiration for this beef soup with spring onions. Depending on your carb intake, you can add 100g/3½oz of spiralized courgette noodles for an additional 3 grams of Net Carbs.

TIME	PER SERVING
Active: 15 minutes	*Total Carbs:* **6.4g**
	Fibre: **1.7g**
Total: 2 hours, 15 minutes	*Protein:* **29.7g**
	Fat: **21.1g**
	FV=3.9

- 450g/1lb flank steak
- ½ teaspoon freshly ground black pepper
- 3 tablespoons sesame oil
- 280g/10oz mushrooms, such as button, shiitake or chestnut
- 8 spring onions, thinly sliced
- 4 garlic cloves, finely chopped
- 1 to 2 teaspoons crushed chilli flakes
- ¼ teaspoon salt
- 2 tablespoons soy sauce or tamari
- 2 tablespoons apple cider vinegar
- 1 litre/35fl oz beef stock or Basic Bone Broth (page 161)

1 Place the flank steak in a large stockpot, and cover with water. Add the pepper and bring to a boil over high heat. Reduce the heat to low and simmer for 2 hours, covered, until the meat is very tender. Drain, discarding the liquid, and let the beef cool. Use a fork to shred the meat. Wash and dry the stockpot.

2 Warm the oil in the stockpot over medium-low heat. Add the mushrooms, spring onions, garlic, chilli flakes and salt, and cook for about 3 minutes, stirring often, until fragrant. Add the shredded beef, soy sauce or tamari, vinegar and stock. Bring to a simmer and cook for 4 to 5 minutes, until the mushrooms are tender. Serve immediately.

SALSA VERDE
CHICKEN SOUP

4.7g
NET CARBS

SERVES 4

322
CALORIES

Salsa verde, jarred or fresh, is a tangy green salsa made with tomatillos (husk tomatoes), onions and plenty of coriander. Hearty chicken, cauliflower and soured cream turn this flavourful soup into a satisfying meal. Even if you are not a coriander fan, you will enjoy cooked coriander, since its flavour mellows quite a bit.

TIME	PER SERVING
Active: 10 minutes	*Total Carbs:* **8.6g** *Fibre:* **2g**
Total: 45 minutes	*Protein:* **33.5g** *Fat:* **18.3g** *FV=5*

- **4 chicken breasts, on the bone, skin intact (about 680g/1½lb)**
- **½ teaspoon salt**
- **½ teaspoon mild chilli powder**
- **¼ teaspoon freshly ground black pepper**
- **2 tablespoons olive oil**
- **½ red or white onion, finely chopped**
- **140g/5oz cauliflower florets**
- **25g/1oz fresh coriander leaves and stems, chopped and divided**
- **4 garlic cloves**
- **1 litre/35fl oz unsalted chicken stock**
- **90g/3¼oz salsa verde from a jar**
- **4 tablespoons soured cream**

1 Sprinkle the chicken with the salt, chilli powder and pepper. Warm the oil in a large stockpot over medium heat. Add the chicken and cook for 7 to 8 minutes, turning a few times, until the chicken is well browned. Transfer the chicken to a plate. Add the onion, cauliflower, half the coriander and the garlic, and cook for 5 to 6 minutes more until the vegetables soften.

2 Return the chicken to the stockpot, and cover with the stock. Bring to a simmer over medium heat and cook for 20 to 25 minutes, until the chicken is cooked through. Transfer the chicken to a cutting board to cool. Discard the skin and bones, then shred the chicken. Return it to the soup, and top with the salsa verde and the remaining coriander. Serve with the soured cream.

TURMERIC CARROT
GINGER SOUP

9.6g NET CARBS · SERVES **4** · **310** CALORIES

Turmeric is one of the top healing spices; in fact, this powerful anti-inflammatory spice has more than seven hundred medical studies behind it! Turmeric, a relative of the ginger root, has a tart flavour that works well with sweeter foods such as carrot and is a great way to perk up mild-tasting proteins such as prawns.

TIME	PER SERVING
Active: 15 minutes	*Total Carbs:* **13.3g** *Fibre:* **3.7g**
Total: 25 minutes	*Protein:* **30g** *Fat:* **15.2g** *FV=***7.4**

60g/2oz unsalted butter

4 carrots, thinly sliced

140g/5oz cauliflower florets

4 garlic cloves, chopped

½ teaspoon salt

½ teaspoon freshly ground black pepper

1 small fresh turmeric root, chopped (about 2 teaspoons) or 1 teaspoon ground turmeric

1 tablespoon peeled, grated ginger

1 litre/35fl oz Basic Bone Broth (page 161) or chicken stock

450g/1lb king prawns (21 to 25 count), with heads

½ teaspoon hot or sweet paprika

¼ teaspoon freshly ground black pepper

TIP

For a restaurant-worthy garnish, *mix 2 tablespoons of chopped fresh coriander with a few teaspoons of water and drizzle it into the soup.*

1 Warm 45g/1½oz of the butter in a large stockpot over medium heat. Add the carrots, cauliflower, garlic, salt and pepper; cook for 5 to 6 minutes, stirring often, until the vegetables start to brown. Add the turmeric and ginger and cook for 1 minute more to blend the flavours.

2 Add the broth and cover, increasing the heat to medium-high. As soon as the soup comes to a boil, reduce the heat to low and cook for an additional 7 to 8 minutes, until the carrots and cauliflower are tender. Using an immersion blender, blend until smooth.

3 Warm the remaining butter in a large frying pan over medium heat. Add the prawns and sprinkle with the paprika and pepper. Cook for 6 to 8 minutes, turning the prawns often, until the shells are pink and the meat is no longer translucent inside. Divide the prawns among four soup bowls, ladle the soup over the prawns, and serve immediately.

THAI
TOM YUM SOUP

6.8g
NET CARBS

SERVES 4

274
CALORIES

Thai tom yum soup has a sweet and hot flavour that any chilli fan will enjoy, and it can easily be paired with your favourite protein. If you can't locate the tiny but pungent Thai chillies, look for serrano chillies or even a sliver of habanero to use instead. You can also take the hotness factor down a notch by cutting the amount of chillies and chilli paste in half.

TIME	PER SERVING
Active: 10 minutes	*Total Carbs:* **7.3g**
	Fibre: **0.5 gram**
Total: 20 minutes	**Protein: 29.9g**
	Fat: **12.4g**
	*FV=*2.9

1 litre/35fl oz chicken stock

1 stalk lemongrass, chopped

2.5-cm/1-in piece of ginger, peeled and finely chopped

2 small red or green chillies, such as Thai bird's eye chillies, halved

450g/1lb large prawns (31 to 35 count), peeled and deveined or 450g/1lb thinly sliced chicken

240ml/8fl oz tinned coconut milk

1 tablespoon red chilli paste

1 tablespoon fish sauce

2 spring onions, thinly sliced

10g/⅓oz fresh coriander leaves and stems

1 Place the stock in a large stockpot along with the lemongrass, ginger and chillies. Bring to a simmer over medium heat.

2 Add the prawns or chicken, coconut milk, chilli paste, fish sauce, spring onions and coriander. Turn the heat off, cover, and let rest for 5 to 6 minutes, until the prawns or chicken slices are cooked through. Remove and discard the lemongrass. Serve immediately.

CREAM OF
HEIRLOOM
TOMATO SOUP

5.8g NET CARBS

SERVES **4**

364 CALORIES

Like the cauliflower bisque, this silky soup, made from freshly roasted farmers' market tomatoes, will hit the spot when you're in the mood for something creamy and seasonal. If you can't find heirlooms, red tomatoes on the vine or beef tomatoes work well, too.

450g/1lb heirloom tomatoes, chopped

1 tablespoon olive oil

2 tablespoons tomato purée

1 teaspoon Italian seasoning or herb salt

1 litre/35fl oz Basic Bone Broth (page 161) or unsalted chicken stock

4 tablespoons double cream

10g/⅓oz Pecorino cheese, grated

2 tablespoons Atkins Flour Mix (page 126)

450g/1lb shredded or diced chicken (optional)

1 Preheat the oven to 200°C/400°F/Gas 6. Line a baking tray with kitchen foil. Place the tomatoes on the baking tray and drizzle them with the olive oil, dot with the tomato purée, and sprinkle them with the Italian seasoning or herb salt. Roast for 20 to 25 minutes, until the tomato purée starts to brown. Transfer to a large stockpot and add the broth. Bring to a simmer over medium heat and cook for 2 to 3 minutes, until the tomatoes begin to break apart.

2 Turn the heat off, and add the cream and Pecorino cheese. Sprinkle the flour mix over the surface of the soup. Use an immersion blender and blend until smooth. Top with the chicken, if desired.

TIME	PER SERVING
Active: 15 minutes	*Total Carbs:* **7.7g**
	Fibre: **1.9g**
Total: 30 minutes	*Protein:* **43.1g**
	Fat: **16.9g**
	FV=4

TUSCAN
KALE SOUP

8.1g
NET CARBS

SERVES
4

260
CALORIES

Cavolo nero (also known as Tuscan kale or lacinato kale), with its bumpy dark skin, is delicious cooked in soups, since it has a heartier texture with a hint of spice that pairs well with sausage. If you're a spice fan, go for spicy Italian sausage and a dash of chilli flakes.

Olive oil spray

5 sweet or hot Italian sausage links, chopped (85g/3oz each)

30g/1oz chopped cavolo nero (see Tip, page 187)

2 celery stalks, thinly sliced

4 garlic cloves, finely chopped

1 litre/35fl oz Basic Bone Broth (page 161), beef stock, or chicken stock

2 tablespoons tomato purée

½ teaspoon crushed chilli flakes (optional)

15g/½oz Parmesan cheese, grated

1 Coat a large stockpot with olive oil spray. Add the sausage, place over medium heat, and cook for 8 to 9 minutes, stirring often, until the sausage browns and is cooked through. Add the cavolo nero, celery, and garlic and cook for 1 to 2 minutes more, coating with the rendered fat from the sausage. Add the broth, tomato purée and chilli flakes, if using.

2 Bring to a simmer and cover. Cook for 2 to 3 minutes, until the cavolo nero is cooked through. Sprinkle with the Parmesan and serve immediately.

TIME	PER SERVING
Active: 15 minutes	Total Carbs: 9.7g Fibre: 1.6g
Total: 45 minutes	Protein: 26.4g Fat: 13.3g FV=5.2

CHILLED
AVOCADO
CRAB
GAZPACHO

3.9g
NET CARBS

SERVES
4

168
CALORIES

Gazpacho, a Spanish chilled soup made from tomatoes, is typically served as a starter to cool you down on a blistering hot day. This filling version, based on fibre-rich avocado, is also great for summer dining when you're ready to beat the heat and get out of the kitchen.

480ml/16fl oz unsalted chicken stock or Basic Bone Broth (page 161)

1 ripe Haas avocado, diced

1 cucumber, peeled and chopped

2 garlic cloves, peeled and cut in half

1 green pepper, deseeded and chopped

6g/¼oz fresh mint leaves

2 tablespoons red wine vinegar

½ teaspoon salt

¼ teaspoon freshly ground black pepper

225g/8oz crab meat, picked over for shells and cartilage

Place the stock, avocado, cucumber, garlic, green pepper, mint, vinegar, salt, and pepper in a blender, and process until smooth. Transfer to a large bowl, cover and refrigerate until chilled, at least 2 hours and up to 8 hours. Dish into four bowls, top with the crab meat, and serve immediately.

TIME	PER SERVING
Active: 10 minutes	Total Carbs: **8.1g**
	Fibre: **4.2g**
	Protein: **15.5g**
Total: 10 minutes	Fat: **8.6g**
	FV=**3.4**

ROPA VIEJA
SOUP

6.2g NET CARBS

SERVES 4

322 CALORIES

Ropa Vieja is a national dish from Cuba; in Spanish, it means 'old clothes,' since the tender, shredded beef resembles twisted old fabric. This soup skips the rice and beans of the traditional version but still has the great flavours of oregano, green pepper, coriander and tomato. You can serve this soup with cauliflower rice (page 232) instead of rice and beans.

- 450g/1lb flank steak
- 3 tablespoons olive oil
- 1 green pepper, deseeded and chopped
- ½ onion, chopped
- 6g/¼oz fresh coriander leaves and stems
- 4 garlic cloves, finely chopped
- 1 teaspoon dried oregano
- ½ teaspoon ground cumin
- ½ teaspoon salt
- ¼ teaspoon freshly ground black pepper
- 1 litre/35fl oz Basic Bone Broth (page 161) or beef stock
- 2 tomatoes, chopped
- 1 tablespoon tomato purée

1 Place the steak in a large stockpot and cover with water. Cook for 2 hours, covered, until the meat is very tender. Strain and set the beef aside. Using a fork, shred the meat.

2 Place the olive oil in a large stockpot over medium heat. Add the pepper, onion, coriander, garlic, oregano, cumin, salt and black pepper; cook for 5 to 7 minutes, stirring occasionally, until the onion is soft. Add the broth, tomatoes and tomato purée, along with the shredded beef. Bring to a simmer over medium heat and cover. Cook for 4 to 5 minutes more to allow the flavours to meld, then serve immediately.

TIME	PER SERVING
Active: 15 minutes	*Total Carbs:* **8.3g**
	Fibre: **2.1g**
Total: 2 hours 30 minutes	*Protein:* **27g**
	Fat: **21g**
	FV=6

HOT-AND-SOUR
SOUP

7.4g
NET CARBS

SERVES
4

318
CALORIES

Hot-and-sour soup, popular on Chinese take-away menus, combines Szechuan-based flavours such as spicy red chillies with savory vinegar and healing shiitake mushrooms. Hot-and-sour soup is typically made with pork – this one uses tender pork chop meat – but feel free to substitute the pork with equal portions of firm tofu or even peeled, deveined prawns.

TIME	PER SERVING
Active: 15 minutes	*Total Carbs:* **9.5g** *Fibre:* **2.1g** *Protein:* **22.9g**
Total: 30 minutes	*Fat:* **21g** *FV=***6.3**

3 tablespoons sesame oil

4 pork chops (450g/1lb total), thinly sliced against the grain, bone discarded

140g/5oz shiitake mushrooms, stems discarded, caps sliced

½ red onion, thinly sliced

3 garlic cloves, finely chopped

1 tablespoon peeled, grated ginger root

1 tablespoon crushed chilli flakes

120g/4¼oz thinly sliced cabbage

1 litre/35fl oz Basic Bone Broth (page 161), beef stock, or unsalted chicken stock

2 tablespoons tamari or soy sauce

2 tablespoons white distilled vinegar

1 teaspoon stevia

1 Put the sesame oil in a large stockpot over medium heat. Add the pork, shiitakes, onion, garlic, ginger and chilli flakes; cook for 4 to 5 minutes, stirring occasionally, until the pork starts to brown and the mushrooms are tender.

2 Add the cabbage, broth, tamari, vinegar and stevia. Bring to a simmer, and cook for 2 to 3 minutes more to allow the flavours to meld and the cabbage to soften. Serve immediately.

9

SALADS

FRESH VEGETABLES,

Leafy Greens and

FLAVOURFUL DRESSINGS

Salads are a staple of Atkins, because there are so many
delicious and naturally low-carb variations of vegetables, leafy greens,
fresh and creamy dressings, and meat, poultry, and fish that you
can put together in no time at all. If you're ready to break out of your
'same old' salad routine, these recipes are the key.

RECIPES

OLD BAY
SHRIMP
SALAD

3g NET CARBS

SERVES **4**

409 CALORIES

Old Bay seasoning – created in the 1930s in the Chesapeake Bay area of the US east coast – is the perfect flavouring for delicate seafood such as crab and prawns, with its blend of many savoury spices including celery salt, black pepper, bay leaf and red pepper. You can buy it online or in specialist food stores. This chilled salad is ideal picnic fare and a great low-carb swap for traditional potato salad.

TIME	PER SERVING
Active: 15 minutes	*Total Carbs:* **4.7g**
	Fibre: **1.8g**
Total: 30 minutes	*Protein:* **24.4g**
	Fat: **32.2g**
	*FV=***1.9**

450g/1lb frozen cooked baby prawns, defrosted

70g/2½oz cauliflower florets, chopped

2 celery stalks, thinly sliced

180g/6½oz mayonnaise

2 spring onions, thinly sliced

1 tablespoon Old Bay seasoning or seasoning salt (see Tip)

1 head Little Gem lettuce, broken into 12 leaves

Drain the prawns on kitchen paper to be sure they are dry. Transfer to a large bowl along with the cauliflower, celery, mayonnaise, spring onions and Old Bay seasoning. Stir well. Set the leaves out and divide the salad between the 12 leaves. Serve immediately.

TIP

If you want to sub out the Old Bay, *a blend of ¼ teaspoon each of sweet paprika, celery salt, garlic salt and black pepper is an option.*

WATERCRESS
BACON
SALAD
with Ranch Dressing

4.4g
NET CARBS

SERVES
4

353
CALORIES

Spicy watercress is part of the superhealing cruciferous family, which also includes kale, broccoli and cauliflower – some of the most nutrient-dense foods around. Watercress is most abundant in spring, and it adds the vitamins, fibre and anti-inflammatory nutrients your body thrives on. Topped with tomatoes, bacon and ranch dressing, this salad is jam-packed with flavour.

TIME	PER SERVING
Active: 15 minutes	*Total Carbs:* **9.6g** *Fibre:* **5.2g** *Protein:* **7.5g**
Total: 30 minutes	*Fat:* **33.2g** *FV=***3.8**

225g/8oz watercress

225g/8oz baby spinach

2 tomatoes, chopped

1 ripe Haas avocado, diced

4 rashers cooked bacon, crumbled

Combine the watercress and spinach, tossing well. Divide among four plates and top with the tomatoes, avocado and bacon. Serve immediately.

RANCH DRESSING

120g/4¼oz mayonnaise

2 tablespoons tinned coconut milk or double cream

1 teaspoon apple cider vinegar

½ teaspoon onion powder

½ teaspoon garlic salt

1 tablespoon chopped fresh dill or flatleaf parsley

¼ teaspoon freshly ground black pepper

Place the mayonnaise, coconut milk or cream, vinegar, onion powder, garlic salt, dill or parsley and black pepper in a large bowl. Whisk well to combine. Serve over the salad.

CRISPY DUCK

SPINACH SALAD

with Warm and Tangy
Turmeric Dressing

3.5g
NET CARBS

SERVES 4

333
CALORIES

Don't be daunted by the idea of cooking duck, which has delicious red meat that any steak lover will appreciate. Duck is traditionally paired with something sweet, so high-antioxidant raspberries provide a hint of sweetness without sugar overload.

TIME	PER SERVING
Active: 15 minutes	Total Carbs: 9.2g
	Fibre: 5.7g
Total: 30 minutes	Protein: 33.3g
	Fat: 18.5g
	FV=1

2 duck breasts, fat trimmed to 1cm/½in thick

¼ teaspoon salt

¼ teaspoon freshly ground black pepper

225g/8oz baby spinach

225g/8oz frisée or endive leaves, chopped

30g/1oz walnuts

120g/4¼oz fresh raspberries

1 Score the fat side of the duck breast with a sharp knife. Sprinkle the duck with half the salt and black pepper. Place the duck breast, fat side down, in a large, cold frying pan. Cook for 7 to 8 minutes, until the fat is crisp. Flip and cook for 4 to 5 minutes more until the duck is no longer translucent red inside but still pink. Remove the duck from the pan, reserving the fat. Let the duck rest for 5 minutes. Slice the duck across the grain. Make the dressing as directed.

2 Divide the spinach and frisée or endive among four plates and drizzle with the dressing. Top with the sliced duck, walnuts and raspberries. Serve immediately.

WARM & TANGY TURMERIC DRESSING

4 tablespoons red wine vinegar

¼ teaspoon salt

¼ teaspoon freshly ground black pepper

½ teaspoon ground turmeric

½ teaspoon sweet paprika

Add the vinegar to the warm reserved fat in the pan, along with the salt, pepper, turmeric and paprika, whisking well.

TIP

Look for duck breasts (magrets) at farmers' markets or in high-end supermarkets that handle specialty meats. Just trim away some of the 'fat cap,' or thick fat flap, that covers the breast meat of most commercial brands of duck, leaving the skin attached.

TIP

If you have time, refrigerate the duck breasts overnight, leaving the skin side uncovered, but the flesh protected with plastic wrap. This will air-dry and tighten the skin to release even more fat during cooking.

KALE
CAESAR
SALAD

with Creamy Meyer
Lemon Dressing

SERVES
4

Tired of the same old Caesar salad? This version uses the top superfood kale and Meyer lemon – a sweeter variety of lemon – to create a fresh take on an everyday classic. The Meyer lemon is a hybrid citrus fruit that isn't as sweet as an orange but is less tangy than a standard lemon. The secret to tender kale salad? Massage the leaves first.

400g/14oz extra-firm tofu, well drained

2 tablespoons Atkins Flour Mix (page 126)

½ teaspoon Old Bay seasoning (see page 182) or garlic salt

Olive oil spray

280g/10oz kale or cavolo nero (see Tip)

15g/½oz Parmesan cheese, shaved

1 Place the tofu onto kitchen paper and pat dry. Cut into 16 (2.5-cm/1-in) cubes. Place the Atkins Flour Mix and Old Bay seasoning on a plate. Mix well with your fingers or a fork. Dredge the tofu cubes in the flour mixture. Coat a large frying pan with olive oil spray and place over medium heat. Add the tofu cubes and cook for 3 to 4 minutes, adding more olive oil spray as necessary, until the tofu is crisp.

2 Place the kale in a large bowl, and toss with the dressing. Divide among four plates and top each with the tofu croutons and Parmesan shavings.

CREAMY MEYER LEMON DRESSING

4 tablespoons mayonnaise

4 tablespoons double cream or tinned coconut milk

½ teaspoon garlic salt

½ teaspoon onion powder

½ teaspoon freshly ground black pepper

2 tablespoons fresh Meyer lemon or regular lemon juice

Place the mayonnaise, cream, garlic salt, onion power, black pepper and lemon juice in a small bowl. Whisk well and set aside.

WITH TOFU	
TIME	PER SERVING
Active: 15 minutes	*Net Carbs:* **9g**
	Total Carbs: **12.2g**
Total: 30 minutes	*Fibre:* **3.2g**
	Protein: **19.5g**
	Fat: **24.2g**
	Calories: **340**
	*FV=***5.6**

WITH CHICKEN	
TIME	PER SERVING
Active: 15 minutes	*Net Carbs* **7.8g**
	Total Carbs: **9.7g**
Total: 30 minutes	*Fibre:* **1.9g**
	Protein: **20.1g**
	Fat: **22g**
	Calories: **310**
	*FV=***5.6**

To prep tougher, larger leaves *for kale salads, remove the tough bottom stem and thick rib that runs up the centre of the leaf. Tear the leaves into bite-sized pieces and squeeze them for about 1 minute to tenderize the kale.*

You can serve this salad as a **healthy side,** *without the tofu croutons, or, as a protein swap in place of the tofu, toss with cooked prawns, chicken or slices of grilled flank steak.*

BABY KALE

AND BLUE CHEESE SALAD

with Warm Hazelnut Dressing

4.5g
NET CARBS

SERVES 4

362
CALORIES

You can enjoy this salad any time of year, but if you want to go seasonal, start your autumn off with kale. Kale is best as the weather turns colder; it actually becomes sweeter when the first frost hits. Cooking hazelnuts in oil not only toasts them but also helps flavour this uniquely fragrant dressing.

TIME	PER SERVING
Active: 10 minutes	*Total Carbs:* **7.8g**
	Fibre: **3.3g**
Total: 10 minutes	*Protein:* **31.3g**
	Fat: **22.3g**
	FV=3.8

- 280g/10oz baby kale
- 30g/1oz blue cheese, crumbled
- 450g/1lb cooked prawns or shredded chicken

Place the kale in a large bowl, pour the dressing over the greens and toss well. Top with the blue cheese and prawns or chicken, and serve immediately.

WARM HAZELNUT DRESSING

- 4 tablespoons olive oil
- 30g/1oz skinned hazelnuts, chopped
- 4 large fresh sage leaves, chopped
- ½ teaspoon salt
- ¼ teaspoon freshly ground black pepper
- 4 tablespoons red wine vinegar

Warm the olive oil in a small frying pan over medium heat. Add the hazelnuts, sage, salt and pepper. Cook for 1 to 2 minutes, until the sage is crisp. Turn the heat off, add the vinegar, and stir well.

WILTED
BRUSSELS SPROUT
SALAD

with Warm Pancetta Dressing

4g
NET CARBS

SERVES 4

217
CALORIES

Think of Brussels sprouts as mini cabbages with all the same great nutrition and antioxidants, including vitamin C, vitamins B$_1$ and B$_6$, and folate. They are delicious raw, especially with a hot dressing made from pancetta dripping, which takes the place of the oil in standard dressings.

TIME	PER SERVING
Active: 15 minutes	*Total Carbs:* **8.1g**
	Fibre: **3.1g**
Total: 30 minutes	*Protein:* **13.5g**
	Fat: **14.7g**
	FV=3.8

225g/8oz Brussels sprouts

140g/5oz baby spinach or kale

4 hard-boiled eggs, quartered

115g/4oz pancetta, diced

1 Shred the Brussels sprouts in a food processor with the shredder attachment. Divide the spinach and Brussels sprouts among four plates. Divide the eggs among the plates.

2 Place the pancetta in a small frying pan over medium heat. Cook for 4 to 5 minutes, stirring occasionally, until well browned, reserving the fat in the pan. Make the dressing as directed. Divide the pancetta among the salad plates. Drizzle the dressing over the salad and serve immediately.

WARM PANCETTA DRESSING

4 garlic cloves, crushed

4 tablespoons apple cider vinegar

2 teaspoons Dijon mustard

Place the frying pan with the fat from the pancetta over a low heat and add the garlic; cook for 1 to 2 minutes, until fragrant. Turn the heat off, carefully add the vinegar and the mustard to the pan, and stir well, scraping up any brown bits sticking inside the pan.

CHILLED ROMAINE
WEDGE
SALAD

with Gorgonzola Dressing

5.2 NET CARBS

SERVES 4

367 CALORIES

Steak houses are famous for their iceberg wedge salads, which are delicious but offer few nutrients. This recipe uses vitamin A–rich romaine, a superfood, as its base, and teaches you a unique technique to make it just as crispy as a wedge of iceberg lettuce.

TIME	PER SERVING
Active: 15 minutes	*Total Carbs:* **8.7g**
	Fibre: **3.6g**
Total: 30 minutes	*Protein:* **21.3g**
	Fat: **27.8g**
	*FV=***1.9**

4 romaine lettuce hearts

4 rashers cooked bacon, crumbled

225g/8oz cooked prawns or chicken

Fill two large bowls with lukewarm water. Add the romaine hearts and soak for 3 to 4 minutes while you prepare the dressing. Drain the romaine, wrap in kitchen paper and chill in the fridge for at least 1 hour to crisp it up. Cut the romaine hearts in half and place two halves on each plate. Drizzle with the dressing and sprinkle with pepper. Top with the bacon and the prawns or chicken.

GORGONZOLA DRESSING

120g/4¼oz full-fat Greek yogurt

120g/4¼oz mayonnaise

30g/1oz Gorgonzola, cut into small pieces

2 tablespoons lemon juice

1 teaspoon onion powder

½ teaspoon garlic salt

¼ teaspoon freshly ground black pepper

¼ teaspoon sweet paprika

Place the yogurt, mayonnaise, Gorgonzola, lemon juice, onion powder, garlic salt, pepper and paprika in a bowl along with 2 tablespoons warm water and whisk well. Refrigerate until ready to serve.

MIXED
POWER GREENS

with Prosciutto-wrapped Chicken Tenders

4.8g
NET CARBS

SERVES 4

295
CALORIES

Some farms are calling their salad mixes 'power greens', since most of them are made up of superfood leafy greens such as beetroot tops, kale, red leaf and romaine. If you can't find 'power greens', you can still take advantage of the power of superfoods by using a mix of baby kale and spinach. 'Chicken tenders' are the mini fillets that come loosely attached to chicken breast fillets.

TIME	PER SERVING
Active: 15 minutes	*Total Carbs:* **9.3g**
	Fibre: **4.6g**
Total: 30 minutes	*Protein:* **33.5g**
	Fat: **13.1g**
	FV=4.5

Olive oil spray

4 slices prosciutto (about 30g/1oz total)

8 chicken mini fillets (about 450g/1lb total)

140g/5oz mixed 'power greens' or baby spinach

225g/8oz green beans or mangetout, trimmed and chopped

1   Preheat the oven to 200°C/400°F/Gas 6. Coat a baking sheet with olive oil spray. Cut the prosciutto slices in half diagonally, making a total of 8 pieces. Wrap each mini fillet in ½ slice of prosciutto and place on the baking sheet. Coat the tops of the fillets with olive oil spray and bake for 6 to 8 minutes, until the prosciutto is crisped and the chicken is cooked through and no longer pink in the centre when sliced.

2   Divide the greens among four plates along with the green beans. Transfer the chicken to the salad, and drizzle with the dressing. Serve immediately.

MUSTARD
VINAIGRETTE

3 tablespoons olive oil

2 tablespoons red wine or apple cider vinegar

1 teaspoon Dijon mustard

½ teaspoon garlic salt

¼ teaspoon freshly ground black pepper

Place the olive oil, vinegar, mustard, garlic salt and pepper in a small bowl and whisk well.

PEAR AND MANCHEGO

MESCLUN SALAD

with Caramelized Onions

7.8g
NET CARBS

SERVES
4

253
CALORIES

Juicy pear, salty Manchego and sweet caramelized onions make a delectable salad topping, especially when drizzled with a sweet and tangy apple cider dressing. Manchego is an aged sheeps' milk cheese from La Mancha, Spain, that you can find in most supermarkets, or you can use thinly sliced Parmesan in its place.

TIME	PER SERVING
Active: 15 minutes	*Total Carbs:* **11.5g**
	Fibre: **3.6g**
Total: 30 minutes	*Protein:* **8.9g**
	Fat: **20.2g**
	*FV=***1.5**

1 tablespoon olive oil

1 onion, thinly sliced

1 teaspoon stevia

225g/8oz 'power greens' (see page 193), mesclun, or spinach mixed with baby kale

3g/⅛oz fresh parsley leaves

½ pear, thinly sliced

115g/4oz Manchego cheese, thinly sliced

1 Warm the olive oil in a frying pan over medium heat. Add the onion and stevia; cook for 8 to 10 minutes, stirring often, until golden brown. Add a few tablespoons of water to keep the onions from sticking as they cook.

2 Divide the greens and parsley among four plates. Top with the pear slices, onions and Manchego cheese. Drizzle with the dressing and serve immediately.

APPLE CIDER DRESSING

2 tablespoons olive oil

1 tablespoon apple cider vinegar

1 teaspoon Dijon mustard

½ teaspoon salt

¼ teaspoon freshly ground black pepper

Place the olive oil in a bowl along with the vinegar, mustard, salt and pepper. Whisk well. Add one tablespoon of water and whisk again.

GREEN GODDESS

SALAD

with Lemon Tahini Dressing

7.7g
NET CARBS

SERVES
4

292
CALORIES

Tahini is a Middle Eastern sesame paste that you can find in most large supermarkets. Its texture makes an excellent smooth base for any salad dressing, and sesame seeds are high in iron (for healthy blood and heart) and zinc, an immune system booster.

TIME	PER SERVING
Active: 15 minutes	*Total Carbs:* **14.9g** *Fibre:* **7.2g**
Total: 15 minutes	*Protein:* **28.6g** *Fat:* **14.9g** *FV=***5.3**

140g/5oz mixed greens, 'power greens' (see page 193), or baby spinach

1 ripe Haas avocado, diced

2 tomatoes, diced

70g/2½oz pitted black olives

4 radishes, thinly sliced

225g/8oz alfalfa or other sprouts

450g/1lb cooked prawns or shredded chicken

Divide the greens among four plates, and top with the avocado, tomatoes, olives, radishes and sprouts. Drizzle with the dressing, then top with the prawns or chicken. Serve immediately.

LEMON TAHINI DRESSING

2 tablespoons well-stirred tahini

4 tablespoons water

1 spring onion, chopped

2 tablespoons fresh lemon juice

½ teaspoon garlic salt

¼ teaspoon stevia

Place the tahini, water, spring onion, lemon juice, garlic salt and stevia in a food processor, and process until smooth.

GARLIC BUTTER
LOBSTER
SALAD

5.3g
NET CARBS

SERVES 4

215
CALORIES

Even if you're not an expert chef, this upscale dish is incredibly easy to make and will make you look like a hero in the kitchen. It's perfect for date night or any celebration. For added creaminess, top with 1 avocado, thinly sliced.

TIME	PER SERVING
Active: **15 minutes**	*Total Carbs:* **9.4g**
	Fibre: **4g**
Total: **30 minutes**	*Protein:* **25.1g**
	Fat: **9.2g**
	*FV=***3.6**

Zest of 1 lemon, finely grated

1 tablespoon lemon juice

1 tablespoon mayonnaise

½ teaspoon seasoning salt or garlic salt

30g/1oz baby spinach or kale, chopped

2 celery stalks, finely chopped

1 head butter lettuce, divided into 8 leaves

4 raw lobster tails (see Tip)

450g/1lb asparagus, cut into 1-cm/½-in pieces

2 tablespoons unsalted butter, at room temperature

2 tablespoons finely chopped flatleaf parsley

1 garlic clove, crushed

4 radishes, thinly sliced

TIP

If you fear snipping the lobster tails, most fishmongers will do it for you at the fish counter.

1 Place the lemon zest and juice, mayonnaise, and seasoning salt or garlic salt in a large bowl and whisk until well combined. Add the spinach or kale and celery and toss well.

2 Prepare the lobster: Set the oven to grill. Using kitchen shears, snip through the hard top shell to expose the lobster meat. Transfer the tails to a baking tray and arrange the asparagus around the tails. Place the butter, parsley and garlic in a small bowl, mashing the ingredients together. Spread the butter mixture over the exposed meat of the lobster and place under the grill on the middle oven rack.

3 Cook for 8 to 9 minutes, until the meat is cooked through and the asparagus starts to brown. Transfer the asparagus to the bowl with the greens and toss well. Remove the lobster meat from the shells and chop. Divide the lettuce leaves among four plates and top with the salad mixture and the lobster. Garnish with the radishes and serve immediately.

MIXED
ASIAN GREENS

with Shredded Sesame Chicken

4.4g
NET CARBS

SERVES 4

301
CALORIES

You'll adore this creamy Asian dressing, which sneaks in one of the top healing spices, turmeric. Turmeric may seem exotic, but it is low in carbs and also makes food more visually appealing and fresh tasting, while adding health-promoting compounds, such as curcumin.

TIME	PER SERVING
Active: 15 minutes	*Total Carbs:* **7.6g**
	Fibre: **3.2g**
Total: 30 minutes	*Protein:* **31.1g**
	Fat: **17.1g**
	FV=2.9

450g/1lb boneless, skinless chicken breasts

2 jalapeños, deseeded and diced

2 tablespoons soy sauce or tamari

1 tablespoon sesame oil

Cooking spray

225g/8oz Asian greens or mesclun

1 Place the chicken breasts in a bag with the jalapeños, soy sauce or tamari and sesame oil. Marinate in the fridge for at least 6 hours or overnight. Coat a griddle pan with cooking spray and place over medium heat. Add the chicken and cook for 10 to 12 minutes, turning occasionally, until the chicken is brown and no longer pink inside when sliced with a knife.

2 Transfer the cooked chicken to a chopping board to rest for 5 minutes, then slice. Divide the greens among four plates, top with the chicken and drizzle with the dressing. Serve immediately.

CREAMY ASIAN DRESSING

4 tablespoons mayonnaise

2 tablespoons apple cider vinegar

2 tablespoons soy sauce or tamari

1 garlic clove, crushed

1 teaspoon sesame oil

¼ teaspoon ground turmeric

1 tablespoon toasted sesame seeds

Place the mayonnaise, vinegar, soy sauce or tamari, garlic, sesame oil, turmeric and sesame seeds in a small bowl and whisk until smooth and creamy.

10

APPETIZERS

SAVOURY BITES
AND SMALL PLATES

•

From fries to cheese-stuffed peppers, bruschetta, personal-sized pizza, and more, the dishes in this chapter replicate many favourite starters and small bites. The rich flavours and elegant presentations (as well as the fact that they are naturally low in carbs) are sure to impress your guests, but don't wait until you entertain to treat yourself to these appealing appetizers.

RECIPES

LOW-CARB
FLAX MEAL
BREAD

2.3g
NET CARBS

SERVES
8

220
CALORIES

This low-carb artisan bread is so easy to make, it will become your weekly baking habit! It's powered by the superseed flax and is rich in fibre, plant-based omega-3s, and manganese (which is great for blood sugar control and skin health). Don't be deceived by the small amount of batter; it puffs up dramatically when it bakes and fills the house with the comforting aroma of freshly baked bread.

Olive oil spray

75g/2¾oz 100% whole ground golden flaxseed meal

90g/3¼oz almond flour

25g/1oz Parmesan cheese, grated

1 tablespoon dried herbs, such as Italian seasoning or rosemary

2 teaspoons baking powder

2 teaspoons stevia

1 teaspoon crushed chilli flakes (optional)

5 eggs

1 tablespoon olive oil

1 tablespoon whole flaxseeds

1 tablespoon sunflower seeds

1 tablespoon pumpkin seeds

1 Preheat the oven to 180°F/350°F/Gas 4. Coat a 450-g/1-lb loaf pan with olive oil spray. Mix the flaxseed meal, almond flour, Parmesan, dried herbs, baking powder, stevia and chilli flakes, if using, in a large bowl, stirring well to combine.

2 Add the eggs and oil to the dry ingredients, using a wooden spoon to combine. Transfer to the prepared loaf pan and sprinkle with the three seeds. Bake for 35 to 40 minutes, until the loaf is firm to the touch and the crust starts to brown. Transfer to a wire rack to cool. Store, refrigerated, in an airtight container or kitchen foil for up to 5 days.

TIME	PER SERVING
Active: 15 minutes	*Total Carbs:* **6.6g**
	Fibre: **4.3g**
Total: 30 minutes	*Protein:* **12.5g**
	Fat: **16.5g**
	FV=0

CHIPOTLE LIME
COURGETTE CRISPS

2.3g
NET CARBS

SERVES 4

17
CALORIES

When baked at a low temperature, sliced courgette transforms into lovely crisps that will cure your salty crisp craving. Ground chipotle makes a tangy topping when paired with lime zest, but if you're not a spice lover, go for mild chilli powder or paprika.

TIME	PER SERVING
Active: 15 minutes	*Total Carbs:* **3.6g** *Fibre:* **1.3g**
Total: 30 minutes	*Protein:* **1.3g** *Fat:* **0.2g** *FV=*2.2

2 courgettes

Olive oil spray

1 teaspoon lime zest, finely grated

½ teaspoon ground chipotle

½ teaspoon garlic salt

¼ teaspoon freshly ground black pepper

1 Preheat the oven to 130°C/250°F/Gas 1. Using a Japanese mandoline, vegetable slicer or large knife, slice the courgettes into 5-mm-/⅛-in-thick slices and transfer to a baking sheet. Coat with a layer of olive oil spray on both sides. Combine the lime zest, chipotle, garlic salt and pepper in a small bowl, mix well, and sprinkle over the courgette slices.

2 Set the slices on a baking sheet in a single layer and bake for 1 hour, 10 minutes, turning once. Cool on the baking sheet, then serve immediately or transfer to an airtight container and store at room temperature for up to 3 days.

PORTOBELLO
PIZZA

5g NET CARBS | SERVES **4** | **179** CALORIES

A portobello mushroom makes a perfectly-sized personal pizza. Not only are mushrooms a tasty low-carb base for pizza, they are rich in important nutrients such as niacin, which helps your body regulate cholesterol levels, and selenium, which helps keep your thyroid healthy and aids hair growth.

Olive oil spray

4 large portobello mushrooms, stems removed

120g/4¼oz low-sugar tomato pasta sauce

60g/2oz grated mozzarella cheese

16 slices pepperoni or chorizo sausage

Preheat the oven to 190°C/375°F/Gas 5. Line a baking tray with baking parchment and coat with a layer of olive oil spray. Scrape out the dark gills from the mushrooms with a spoon, and discard the gills. Place the mushrooms, stem side up, on the baking tray and top each with 2 tablespoons of the sauce. Sprinkle each with 2 tablespoons of the mozzarella and 4 slices of pepperoni or chorizo. Bake for 20 to 25 minutes, until the cheese is bubbly and the mushrooms are soft. Serve immediately.

TIME	PER SERVING
Active: 10 minutes	*Total Carbs:* **7g**
	Fibre: **1.9g**
Total: 40 minutes	*Protein:* **10.7g**
	Fat: **12.6g**
	FV=4.2

CHIMICHURRI
STEAK BITES

1.6g
NET CARBS

SERVES 4

208
CALORIES

Chimichurri is a tasty parsley-based green sauce and marinade that hails from Argentina, where the locals are experts at flavouring their renowned beef. The parsley and coriander in this green sauce also happen to be high in antioxidants and antibacterial compounds; the two herbs also give the sauce flavour and colour.

TIME	PER SERVING
Active: 15 minutes	*Total Carbs:* **2.6g**
	Fibre: **1g**
Total: 30 minutes	*Protein:* **18.3g**
	Fat: **14.4g**
	*FV=***1.6**

20g/¾oz fresh flatleaf parsley leaves

20g/¾oz fresh coriander leaves and stems

4 garlic cloves

4 tablespoons red wine vinegar

4 tablespoons olive oil

½ teaspoon salt

¼ teaspoon freshly ground black pepper

680g/1½lb flank steak

Olive oil spray

½ head broccoli, cut into small florets

1 Place the parsley, coriander, garlic, vinegar, olive oil, salt and pepper in a blender and process until a smooth sauce forms.

2 Place the steak in a large zip-lock bag with half the sauce and shake well to coat the steak. Transfer to the fridge and marinate for at least 1 hour or overnight. Refrigerate the remaining sauce, as well. Bring the steak to room temperature before grilling (about 1 hour) to enhance juiciness.

3 Coat a large griddle pan with olive oil spray and place over high heat. Once hot, add the steak and cook for 15 to 20 minutes, turning occasionally, until the steak is no longer red in the centre but still pink. Transfer to a cutting board, and let rest for 5 minutes before slicing against the grain. Spear the slices on small skewers and top each with a broccoli floret. Serve immediately with the remaining sauce.

CLAM
LINGUINE

4.6g
NET CARBS

SERVES **4**

271
CALORIES

Tender freshly cooked clams smothered in a white Alfredo sauce are a feast fit for a king or queen, and are also perfect on a regular weeknight since this meal comes together in minutes. If you don't own a spiralizer or veggie noodle maker, many supermarkets sell courgette noodles already cut. To complete the meal, serve with a Caesar side salad, such as the Kale Caesar Salad with Creamy Meyer Lemon Dressing on page 186.

1 tablespoon unsalted butter

180ml/6fl oz double cream

4 tablespoons grated Parmesan cheese

5 tablespoons grated Romano cheese

½ teaspoon freshly ground black pepper

⅛ teaspoon freshly ground nutmeg

Olive oil spray

450g/1lb clams, such as Manila, well washed under cold running water

2 courgettes, spiralized into long noodle shapes

1 Make the cheese sauce: Melt the butter in a medium saucepan over medium heat. Add the cream and simmer until reduced to ½ cup, about 3 minutes. Remove from the heat. Stir in the Parmesan, Romano, pepper and nutmeg until the cheeses have melted and the sauce is smooth.

2 Coat a large sauté pan with the olive oil spray and place over high heat. Add the clams and cover; cook for 4 to 5 minutes, until the clams open. Add the courgette noodles and cook for an additional 4 to 5 minutes until the noodles are tender. Drain off any excess liquid and toss with the cheese sauce. Serve immediately.

TIME	PER SERVING
Active: **15 minutes**	*Total Carbs:* **5.8g**
	Fibre: **1.2g**
Total: **30 minutes**	*Protein:* **10g**
	Fat: **23.9g**
	*FV=***2.2**

MANCHEGO
MINI MUFFINS

2.1g
NET CARBS

SERVES 12

202
CALORIES

If you're missing your cornbread, this tasty muffin will hit the spot with a similar texture but far more protein. Manchego, a tangy Spanish cheese, is a perfect pairing with peppers, but feel free to mix it up with grated Asiago or even grated aged Gouda.

TIME	PER SERVING
Active: 10 minutes	*Total Carbs:* **3.4g** *Fibre:* **1.4g** *Protein:* **13.5g**
Total: 40 minutes	*Fat:* **15.4g** *FV=***0.1**

125g/4½oz unsalted butter, cut into pieces

100g/3½oz Atkins Flour Mix (page 126)

Olive oil spray

1 teaspoon baking powder

1 teaspoon ground mustard

½ teaspoon garlic salt

¼ teaspoon ground cayenne or mild chilli powder

4 eggs, whisked

90g/3¼ oz grated Manchego or Asiago cheese

2 jalapeños, deseeded and finely chopped

1 Preheat the oven to 190°C/375°F/Gas 5. Place the butter in a small frying pan and melt over low heat for 1 to 2 minutes. Set aside to cool. Coat a 24-hole mini muffin tin with olive oil spray.

2 Place the Atkins Flour Mix, baking powder, mustard, garlic salt and cayenne or chilli powder in a large bowl and whisk well to combine. Make a well in the centre of the flour mixture and add the eggs, melted butter, cheese and jalapeños. Stir to combine. Divide the batter evenly among the holes of the muffin tin.

3 Bake in the preheated oven until the muffins are golden around the edges and have puffed up, about 18 to 20 minutes. Cool in the muffin tin on wire racks for 10 to 15 minutes. Serve immediately, or store in an airtight container, refrigerated, for up to 3 days.

BOURBON PECAN PÂTÉ

1.4g NET CARBS

SERVES 4

264 CALORIES

Rich-tasting bourbon gives a hint of sweet aroma without adding carbs to this creamy, dreamy pâté. Chicken livers are incredibly high in energizing ingredients such as several B vitamins (to sooth your nerves) and iron (for energy and red blood cell production). Serve this uplifting dish with low-carb crackers and sliced cucumbers and celery.

TIME	PER SERVING
Active: 15 minutes	*Total Carbs:* **2.3g**
	Fibre: **0.8g**
Total: 30 minutes	*Protein:* **20.4g**
	Fat: **15.3g**
	FV=1

- 450g/1lb chicken livers
- 1 teaspoon salt
- ½ teaspoon freshly ground black pepper
- 2 tablespoons unsalted butter
- 4 garlic cloves, chopped
- 10g/⅓oz chopped fresh parsley
- 4 tablespoons bourbon, beef stock, Basic Bone Broth (page 161), or unsalted chicken stock
- 30g/1oz pecans, chopped
- 2 teaspoons fresh thyme leaves

1 Place the chicken livers in a large colander and rinse under cold running water. Drain them well, then transfer to a chopping board. Cut away and discard any of the white sinew that holds the livers together and discard. Dry the livers well with kitchen paper. Sprinkle them with the salt and pepper.

2 Warm the butter in a large frying pan over medium-high heat and add the livers, garlic and parsley. Cook for 10 to 12 minutes, turning once or twice, until the livers are cooked but still slightly pink (not red) in the centre when sliced. Turn the heat to low and carefully add the bourbon, stirring the mixture for about 1 minute to scrape up any brown bits sticking to the pan.

3 Turn the heat off, and let cool for 10 to 15 minutes. Transfer to a food processor and blend until smooth. Transfer to a 1-litre/35-fl oz airtight container and sprinkle with the pecans and thyme leaves. Chill for at least 1 hour before serving. Refrigerate any leftover pâté for up to 1 week.

FLATBREAD
DUET

SERVES 4

If you're living a low-carb lifestyle, it doesn't mean you have to give up all the recipes you love, like flatbread with two tasty toppings! The base of this flatbread is used for the Avocado Toast (page 142) and in a pinch can be a base for pizza, as well.

Flatbread dough

1 egg

1 tablespoon extra-virgin olive oil

4 tablespoons cold water

180g/6½oz almond flour

15g/½oz Parmesan cheese, grated

½ teaspoon baking powder

½ teaspoon stevia

¾ teaspoon dried oregano

¼ teaspoon crushed chilli flakes

1 To make the flatbread: Place the egg, olive oil and water in a large bowl and whisk well. Set aside. Place the almond flour, Parmesan, baking powder, stevia, oregano and chilli flakes in a large bowl and stir well with a wooden spoon. Add the wet ingredients, stirring to form a thick, sticky dough.

2 Coat 2 sheets of baking parchment with olive oil spray. Roll out the dough into a large rectangle about 5mm-/⅛in-thick between the sheets of sprayed baking parchment. Slide onto a baking sheet and put in the freezer. Freeze for 15 minutes to make the dough easier to handle.

3 Preheat the oven to 190°C/375°F/Gas 5. Discard the top parchment sheet. Score the dough into 8 equal rectangles. Leaving the dough on the parchment–lined baking sheet, bake for 20 to 25 minutes until crisp around the edges. Leave to cool completely on the baking sheet. Cut into pieces along the score marks. (Makes 4 servings of 2 flatbreads each.)

RECIPE CONTINUES

CRUST	
TIME	**PER SERVING**
Active: 15 minutes	*Net Carbs:* **7.3g** *Total Carbs:* **12.5g** *Fibre:* **5.2g** *Protein:* **22.1g** *Fat:* **39.1g** *Calories:* **466** *FV=* **1.3**
Total: 50 minutes	

TOMATO-MOZZARELLA TOPPING

2 small tomatoes, sliced lengthways

40g/1½oz mozzarella, sliced

2 tablespoons chopped fresh basil

1 tablespoon olive oil

Place the tomatoes, mozzarella, basil and olive oil in a bowl. Toss well and divide among 4 flatbreads.

CHEESE AND PROSCUITTO TOPPING

225g/8oz cottage cheese

1 tablespoon olive oil

**1 thin slice of proscuitto, or
    2 tablespoons crumbled cooked
    bacon or pancetta**

Place the cottage cheese and olive oil in a bowl and stir well. Divide among 8 flatbread pieces and top with a piece of the slice of proscuitto.

TOMATO-MOZZARELLA TOPPING	
TIME	PER SERVING
Active: 15 minutes	*Net Carbs:* **7.3g**
	Total Carbs: **12.5g**
Total: 50 minutes	*Fibre:* **5.2g**
	Protein: **22.1g**
	Fat: **39.1g**
	Calories: **466**
	FV = **1.2**

CHEESE & PANCETTA TOPPING	
TIME	PER SERVING
Active: 15 minutes	*Net Carbs:* **8.1g**
	Total Carbs: **13.2g**
Total: 50 minutes	*Fibre:* **5.1g**
	Protein: **23.3g**
	Fat: **36.1g**
	Calories: **449**
	FV = **0**

ARTICHOKE DIP—STUFFED
MUSHROOMS

4.3g
NET CARBS

SERVES
4

275
CALORIES

Two appetizers in one, artichoke dip and stuffed mushrooms, no crisps required! These richly stuffed, totally delicious mushrooms are ideal for parties and can even be served as a meal when paired with any of the salads from chapter 9.

280g/10oz button mushrooms

Olive oil spray

2 garlic cloves, crushed

10g/⅓oz chopped parsley

250g/9oz frozen artichokes, defrosted

120g/4¼oz mayonnaise

15g/½oz Parmesan cheese, grated

1 Preheat the oven to 200°C/400°F/Gas 6. Remove the stems from the mushrooms and chop them finely. Coat a large frying pan with olive oil spray and place over medium heat. Add the mushroom stems, garlic and parsley to the pan and cook for 3 to 4 minutes until soft.

2 Place the defrosted artichokes in the bowl of a food processor and pulse until finely chopped. Transfer the chopped artichokes to a clean tea towel and squeeze out the water. Add the artichokes to a bowl, along with the cooked mushroom mixture, mayonnaise and Parmesan. Mix well.

3 Fill the mushrooms with the artichoke mixture. Bake for 15 to 20 minutes until the tops are golden and the mushrooms are soft. Serve immediately.

TIME	PER SERVING
Active: 15 minutes	*Total Carbs:* **6.7g**
	Fibre: **2.4g**
Total: 40 minutes	*Protein:* **8.3g**
	Fat: **24.8g**
	FV= **3.8**

STEAMED
ARTICHOKES

with Homemade Lemon
Mayonnaise

7.2g
NET CARBS

SERVES
4

323
CALORIES

Artichokes, which are part of the thistle family, are also superhealing for your liver.[2] Artichokes are also a pre-biotic food, which means they are high in a certain kind of insoluble fibre that feeds the good bacteria in your gut and enhances digestion. If you want a healthier movie snack or finger food, this recipe is ideal, as you can pluck the artichoke leaves as you would popcorn and dip away!

TIME	PER SERVING
Active: **10 minutes**	*Total Carbs:* **14.4g**
	Fibre: **7.2g**
Total: **30 minutes**	*Protein:* **5.9g**
	Fat: **28.8g**
	FV=6.6

4 globe artichokes

1 egg

120ml/4fl oz grapeseed oil

Zest of 1 lemon, finely grated

1 tablespoon lemon juice

1 teaspoon Dijon mustard

½ teaspoon salt

¼ teaspoon freshly ground black pepper

¼ teaspoon mild paprika

1 Cut the tops of the artichokes off and discard. Using a pair of scissors, clip the tops of any artichoke leaves that have thorns. Peel the outside of the stalk using a potato peeler or paring knife, and trim the bottom of the stem, retaining as much length as possible.

 TIP

An immersion blender is a must-have in my kitchen because it allows me to make small portions of mayonnaise and hollandaise. Don't try to make these sauces in a food processor or standing blender, as they are too large and the recipes won't work.

2 Fit a large stockpot with a steamer basket and fill with water to the edge of the basket. Bring to a boil over high heat. Add the artichokes and steam for 15 to 20 minutes, or until the stems are tender when pierced with a knife.

3 While the artichokes are steaming, prepare the mayonnaise: Place the egg in the bottom of an immersion blender beaker. Add the oil, lemon zest, lemon juice, mustard, salt, pepper and paprika. Allow the egg to sink to the bottom. Add the nozzle of an immersion blender, pressing it to the bottom of the beaker, and blend until a thick white cloud forms. Continue to blend until all the oil is incorporated. Divide the artichokes among four plates and serve immediately with the mayonnaise.

BRIE-STUFFED
GRILLED JALAPEÑOS

3g NET CARBS

SERVES **4**

130 CALORIES

Jalapeño poppers are an American bar food which are loaded with carb-rich breadcrumbs that can spike your blood sugar and leave you craving more fried and breaded food. These grilled poppers are lighter and still filled with satisfying, gooey cheese.

TIME	PER SERVING
Active: 10 minutes	Total Carbs: **5.9g** Fibre: **2.9g** Protein: **6.8g** Fat: **10.1g** FV=**2.9**
Total: 20 minutes	

8 large jalapeños

85g/3oz Brie cheese, sliced into 8 pieces

Olive oil spray

¼ teaspoon salt

¼ teaspoon freshly grated black pepper

120g/4¼oz olive tapenade from a jar (see Tip)

1 Cut off the tops of the jalapeños. Use a small paring knife to remove the seeds. Place a piece of brie into each jalapeño.

2 Set the oven to grill. Coat a baking sheet with the olive oil spray. Coat the jalapeños with the olive oil spray and place on the baking sheet. Place them under the grill on the middle rack for 5 to 6 minutes, until the peppers start to blister and the cheese melts. Serve immediately with the tapenade.

TIP

If you can't find olive tapenade (an olive-based dip), try serving these with a few tablespoons of the Ranch Dipping Sauce from the Fried Green Tomatoes recipe (page 153).

TURMERIC ORANGE
SCALLOPS

9.4g
NET CARBS

SERVES
4

283
CALORIES

This gorgeous meal is ideal for your next dinner party or date night. Bright yellow turmeric gives a golden cast to the scallops and a flavourful health boost to your meal, since it is one of the most anti-inflammatory spices around. Pair it with black pepper, since the active compound in pepper, piperine, makes turmeric 100 percent more potent.[1] Cauliflower mash is a creamy, rich accompaniment to this special dish.

TIME	PER SERVING
Active: **15 minutes**	*Total Carbs:* **13.1g**
	Fibre: **3.7g**
Total: **30 minutes**	*Protein:* **20.7g**
	Fat: **16.1g**
	FV=3.8

Cauliflower Mash

1 small head cauliflower, cut into florets

240ml/8fl oz tinned coconut milk

½ teaspoon garlic powder

¼ teaspoon freshly ground black pepper

Scallops

450g/1lb sea scallops

½ teaspoon ground turmeric

½ teaspoon hot or sweet paprika

½ teaspoon salt

¼ teaspoon freshly ground black pepper

1 tablespoon unsalted butter

Zest of 1 orange, finely grated

1 Prepare the cauliflower mash: Place the cauliflower florets in a large stockpot and add 5cm/2 in of water. Bring to a boil over high heat. Steam for 4 to 5 minutes, until fork tender. Drain and transfer to a food processor along with the coconut milk, garlic powder and pepper. Process until smooth. Set aside.

2 Place the scallops on a plate and sprinkle both sides with the turmeric, paprika, salt and pepper. Warm the butter in a large frying pan over medium-high heat and stir in the orange zest. Add the scallops and cook for 2 to 3 minutes per side, until the scallops are well browned and no longer translucent when sliced with a knife. Serve immediately with the mash.

TURNIP
FRIES

9.8g
NET CARBS

SERVES 4

169
CALORIES

If you crave starchy fries, there's no reason to hit the drive-through when you can head to your oven for a tasty, fulfilling low-carb version: turnip fries! Turnips are the perfect vegetable to 'fry' in the oven; the result is a delicious treat that is crispy on the outside and tender on the inside.

680g/1½lb turnips

2 tablespoons olive oil

4 garlic cloves, crushed

15g/½oz Parmesan cheese, grated

½ teaspoon garlic salt

1 teaspoon sweet paprika (see Tip)

1 teaspoon onion powder

1 Preheat the oven to 220ºC/425°F/Gas 7. Line a baking sheet with a piece of baking parchment.

2 Peel the turnips and cut them into skinny French fry–sized sticks. Put them in a large bowl and toss with the olive oil and garlic to coat. Place the Parmesan, garlic salt, paprika and onion powder on a sheet of greaseproof paper and toss the fries in the mixture. Spread the fries out onto the prepared baking sheet. Bake until the outsides are crispy and the insides are tender, about 20 to 25 minutes. Serve immediately.

TIP

For flavour variations, you can replace the paprika with an equal amount of ground chipotle, herbes de Provence or lemon pepper.

TIME	PER SERVING
Active: 20 minutes	*Total Carbs:* **13.2g**
	Fibre: **3.4g**
Total: 40 minutes	*Protein:* **6.7g**
	Fat: **10.6g**
	FV=8.8

11

15-MINUTE MEALS

SIMPLE AND SATISFYING

MEALS FOR WEEKDAYS

Breakfast, Lunch and Dinner

These 15-minute miracles will take your weeknight meals
from everyday to extraordinary. Less active cooking time and more flavour?
Yes, please! From supercharged smoothie bowls to nutrient-filled, satisfying noodle
dishes to saucepan sensations inspired by traditional favourites around the world,
these recipes have you covered.

RECIPES

AVOCADO KALE BERRY
SMOOTHIE BOWL

12.5g
NET CARBS

SERVES
2

356
CALORIES

The vibrant colours of this spoonable smoothie bowl make it Instagram-worthy, but there's so much more to it – it is a blended plant-based meal that will supercharge your energy! Plus, blending breaks up plant fibres for easy digestion while you pack in nutrients for your thyroid, liver and gut health. Smoothie bowls can also double as a light meal – a real treat when you're looking to cool down during scorching days.

- 35g/1¼oz plain protein powder (see Tip, page 132)
- 240g/8½oz plain full-fat Greek yogurt
- 4 tablespoons water
- ½ ripe Haas avocado
- 15g/½oz kale leaves
- 2 tablespoons chopped fresh mint
- 1 teaspoon stevia
- 70g/2½oz fresh or frozen berries such as blackberries, strawberries, or raspberries
- 2 tablespoons almonds or walnut halves
- 2 tablespoons chia seeds

Place the protein powder, yogurt, water, avocado, kale, mint and stevia in a blender. Blend until smooth, then divide between two bowls. Sprinkle the berries, almonds or walnut halves and chia seeds over the smoothie. Serve immediately.

TIME	PER SERVING
Active: 10 minutes	*Total Carbs:* **24.2g**
	Fibre: **11.8g**
Total: 10 minutes	*Protein:* **32.2g**
	Fat: **15.6g**
	FV=3.5

ALMOND BUTTER

SMOOTHIE BOWL

12.5g
NET CARBS

SERVES 2

417
CALORIES

Nuts, seeds and greens are an energizing trio. High in hunger-busting, antioxidant-rich healthy fats, they also feature a wide spectrum of nutrients from which you can get most of your essential vitamins and some much-needed minerals (such as magnesium) in which many people are deficient.

TIME	PER SERVING
Active: 10 minutes	*Total Carbs:* **20g** *Fibre:* **7.5g**
Total: 10 minutes	*Protein:* **36.9g** *Fat:* **22.5g**

- 35g/1¼oz plain protein powder
- 240g/8½oz plain full-fat Greek yogurt
- 4 tablespoons water
- 225g/8oz spinach or kale
- 4 tablespoons almond or peanut butter
- 70g/2½oz fresh or frozen sliced strawberries
- 2 tablespoons chopped almonds
- 2 tablespoons ground flaxseed

Place the protein powder, yogurt, water, spinach or kale, and almond or peanut butter in a blender. Blend until smooth, then divide between two bowls. Sprinkle the strawberries, almonds and flaxseed over the smoothie bowl. Serve immediately.

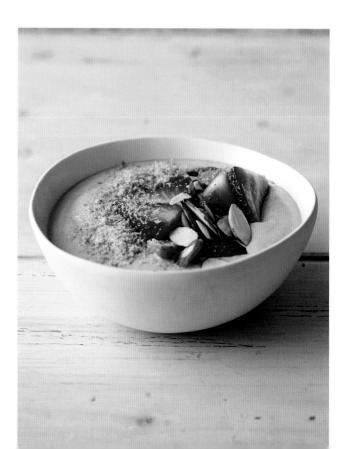

CARROT SPICE

SMOOTHIE BOWL

16.1g NET CARBS

SERVES 2

434 CALORIES

Carrot and spice and everything nice, this deliciously sweet smoothie bowl could double as dessert! If you can't nosh on this bowl right away, pack it in an airtight container and store in the fridge for up to 5 hours or even overnight. As the flax sits in the mixture, it takes on a lovely biscuity flavour.

TIME	PER SERVING
Active: 10 minutes	*Total Carbs:* **22g** *Fibre:* **5.9g**
Total: 10 minutes	*Protein:* **32.6g** *Fat:* **25.8g** *FV=2.5*

- 35g/1¼oz plain protein powder
- 240g/8½oz plain full-fat Greek yogurt
- 4 tablespoons water
- 1 carrot, peeled and chopped
- 4 tablespoons almond or peanut butter
- ½ teaspoon ground cinnamon
- ¼ teaspoon freshly grated nutmeg
- ¼ teaspoon ground turmeric
- 70g/2½oz fresh or frozen sliced strawberries
- 2 tablespoons ground flaxseed
- 2 tablespoons desiccated coconut or dried coconut flakes

Place the protein powder, yogurt, water, carrot, almond or peanut butter, cinnamon, nutmeg and turmeric in a blender. Blend until smooth, then divide between two bowls. Sprinkle the strawberries, flaxseed and coconut over the smoothie bowl. Serve immediately.

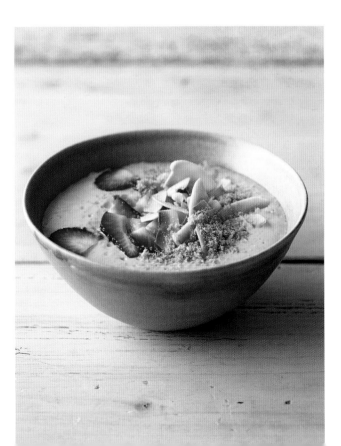

THAI PEANUT

BUDDHA BOWL

10.8g NET CARBS

SERVES 4

427 CALORIES

Buddha bowls are filling, colourful meals bursting from a large bowl packed with nutritious veggies. Drizzle this bowl with a delectable peanut sauce, which adds crave-worthy flavour to otherwise plain proteins and vegetables.

TIME	PER SERVING
Active: 15 minutes	*Total Carbs:* **18.1g**
	Fibre: **7.3g**
Total: 30 minutes	*Protein:* **21.8g**
	Fat: **30.7g**
	FV= 6.3

Olive oil spray

2 skinless, boneless chicken breasts (340g/12oz total)

120g/4¼oz peanut butter

3 tablespoons coconut milk

1 tablespoon fish sauce

2 teaspoons hot chilli sauce

2 garlic cloves, crushed

1 tablespoon grated fresh ginger

1 tablespoon sesame oil

3 tablespoons hot water

80g/2¾oz baby spinach

1 ripe Haas avocado, thinly sliced

1 courgette, spiralized into noodle shapes

2 carrots, spiralized into noodle shapes

2 radishes, thinly sliced

8 sprigs coriander

1 Preheat the oven to 200°C/400°F/Gas 6. Coat a small frying pan with olive oil spray. Add the chicken and cook for 3 to 4 minutes, turning once or twice to brown the chicken. Slide into the oven and bake for 6 to 8 minutes, until the chicken is cooked through and no longer pink in the centre when sliced with a knife. Set aside to rest for 5 minutes, then shred.

2 Place the peanut butter, coconut milk, fish sauce, chilli sauce, garlic, ginger, sesame oil and hot water in a large bowl. Whisk well until smooth. Divide the spinach and avocado among four bowls. Top with the chicken, courgette, carrots, radishes and coriander. Drizzle with the dressing, and serve immediately.

TIP

If you don't have a spiralizer, which is a convenient kitchen tool that allows you to slice vegetables such as courgettes, squash, carrots and cucumbers into thin noodle shapes, you can achieve a similar effect by using a vegetable peeler to shave thin ribbons. It's a little more time intensive and you won't get quite the same results as the 'noodles' you get from a spiralizer, but your dish will taste just as delicious. You can also use a mandoline vegetable slicer and then use a knife to cut the strips into even thinner noodlelike strips.

KUNG PAO
CHICKEN
with Cauliflower Rice

4.9g
NET CARBS

SERVES 4

366
CALORIES

Kung Pao Chicken gets its 'pow' from Szechuan chillies and hot peppercorns that come from a province of central China. Szechuan chillies can be difficult to find, so this version uses hot chilli paste, which you can find in the international aisle of your grocery store. The chopped peanuts and crisp radishes give this dish the classic 'crunch' that turns it into a truly authentic Kung Pao Chicken experience.

TIME	PER SERVING
Active: **15 minutes**	*Total Carbs:* **7.7g**
Total: **30 minutes**	*Fibre:* **2.7g**
	Protein: **35.5g**
	Fat: **22.2g**
	FV=2.9

½ head small cauliflower, cut into florets

4 tablespoons sesame oil

2 tablespoons Basic Bone Broth (page 161) or unsalted chicken stock

2 tablespoons tamari or soy sauce

1 to 2 tablespoons hot chilli paste

1 tablespoon chopped garlic

1 teaspoon distilled white vinegar

2 teaspoons stevia

3 skinless, boneless chicken breasts, thinly sliced (500g/18oz total)

2 tablespoons Atkins Flour Mix (page 126)

4 radishes, thinly sliced

35g/1¼oz chopped peanuts

2 spring onions, thinly sliced

1 Place the cauliflower florets in a food processor and chop roughly. You will need to do this in two batches. Warm half the oil in a large frying pan over medium heat and cook the cauliflower for 4 to 5 minutes, stirring occasionally, until it starts to brown and becomes tender. Transfer to a bowl and cover to keep warm.

2 In a medium bowl, whisk the broth, tamari or soy sauce, chilli paste, garlic, vinegar and stevia together. Toss the chicken in the Atkins Flour Mix. Heat the remaining oil in a large frying pan and add the coated chicken; cook for 5 to 6 minutes, turning often, until crisp and cooked through. Transfer to a plate. Add the sauce to the pan, and cook for 1 minute more, stirring often. Pour the sauce over the chicken and garnish with the radishes. Sprinkle with the peanuts and spring onions and serve immediately with the cauliflower rice.

LEMON PEPPER
PRAWNS
with Mangetout

4.8g
NET CARBS

SERVES
4

263
CALORIES

Bright lemon and pungent pepper flavour this fast meal that is just as delicious served hot or at room temperature (consider it for your next brunch buffet). For larger appetites or as part of a more elaborate meal, pair with a crepe (page 127) or a serving of Manchego Mini Muffins (page 211).

680g/1½lb prawns

Zest of 1 lemon, finely grated

1 teaspoon freshly ground black pepper

1 tablespoon olive oil

1 tablespoon unsalted butter

225g/8oz mangetout

115g/4oz watercress, baby spinach or baby kale

Combine the prawns, lemon zest and pepper in a large bowl, and toss well. Heat a large sauté pan over medium-high heat. Add the olive oil, butter, prawns and mangetout and cook for 5 to 6 minutes, tossing well, until the prawns are cooked through. Turn off the heat, add the greens and cover the pan and leave for about 1 minute to wilt them, Toss well, and serve immediately.

TIME	PER SERVING
Active: **15 minutes**	*Total Carbs:* **6.6g**
Total: **30 minutes**	*Fibre:* **1.9g** *Protein:* **36.6g** *Fat:* **9.4g** *FV=2.9*

GRILLED
MISO SALMON

9.1g
NET CARBS

SERVES 4

313
CALORIES

Miso is a fermented soybean paste that is bursting with savoury and salty flavour. You can keep leftover miso for up to 6 months in a refrigerated airtight container. The topping for this salmon also makes a tasty salad dressing (see Tip).

TIME	PER SERVING
Active: **5 minutes**	*Total Carbs:* **10.6g**
	Fibre: **1.5g**
Total: **15 minutes**	*Protein:* **27.9g**
	Fat: **17.7g**
	*FV=*1.8

Olive oil spray

225g/8oz baby spinach

4 tablespoons white miso paste

4 tablespoons lemon juice

2 teaspoons water

4 salmon fillets (115g/4oz each), skin on

115g/4oz shiitake mushrooms, thinly sliced

3 tablespoons sesame oil

½ teaspoon toasted sesame seeds

1 Cover a baking sheet with kitchen foil. Coat with a light layer of olive oil spray. Divide the spinach among four plates.

2 Set the oven to grill. Place the miso paste, lemon juice and water in a bowl and whisk well. Place the salmon in the bowl and spoon the mixture over the top. Adjust the oven rack to the middle. Place the salmon fillets on the prepared baking sheet, skin side down. Brush the remaining miso over the salmon. In a small bowl, toss the mushrooms in the sesame oil, then transfer them to the tray alongside the salmon.

3 Grill the salmon for 8 to 10 minutes, until it flakes when pressed with a fork. Check after 5 minutes so the miso does not burn. If the miso browns too quickly, cover the salmon loosely with a sheet of foil and return to the grill. After the salmon flakes, divide the vegetables among four plates. Top each with the salmon, sprinkle with the sesame seeds and serve immediately.

TIP

Mix the miso paste and lemon juice mixture with 1 tablespoon olive oil and 1 tablespoon water **for a salad dressing with a zing!** *It will make about four servings.*

If you wish, substitute 225g/8oz baby bok choy halves and 115g/4oz trimmed mangetout for the spinach. Just toss them in with the mushrooms, and surround the salmon with the vegetables.

MONGOLIAN
BEEF
WRAPS

4.6g NET CARBS **SERVES 4** **327** CALORIES

Mongolian beef is an American/ Asian restaurant creation that is usually packed with brown sugar and served over white rice, priming you for a sugar slump. This Atkins-approved makeover slashes the sugar (we swap the white rice for the pleasing crunch of a butter lettuce wrap) and lets the healing aromatic flavourings of ginger, garlic and chilli flakes shine through.

TIME	PER SERVING
Active: 15 minutes	*Total Carbs:* **7.9g**
	Fibre: **3.3g**
Total: 30 minutes	*Protein:* **30g**
	Fat: **20.9g**
	FV=3.5

- 450g/1lb flank steak, sliced against the grain
- 2 tablespoons Atkins Flour Mix (page 126)
- ½ teaspoon garlic salt
- 3 tablespoons sesame oil
- 1 bunch asparagus, trimmed and thinly sliced on the bias
- 2 garlic cloves, crushed
- 1 tablespoon grated fresh ginger
- ½ teaspoon crushed chilli flakes
- 2 tablespoons tamari or soy sauce
- 4 tablespoons water
- 1 head butter lettuce, broken into leaves, to serve
- 4 spring onions, thinly sliced

1 Place the steak on a plate and sprinkle it with the Atkins Flour Mix and garlic salt. Toss well to coat. Warm 2 tablespoons of the oil in a frying pan over medium heat and add the beef, cooking for 2 to 3 minutes, until the beef starts to brown. Transfer to a clean plate.

2 Warm the remaining sesame oil in the same pan. Add the asparagus, garlic, ginger and chilli flakes; cook for 4 to 5 minutes, stirring often, until the garlic becomes fragrant. Return the beef to the pan and reduce the heat to low. Add the tamari or soy sauce and water, tossing well until a thick sauce forms. Spoon the mixture into the lettuce leaves, sprinkle with the spring onions and serve immediately.

FRIED
SAGE CHICKEN
AND COURGETTE

4.5g
NET CARBS

SERVES 4

328
CALORIES

Sage has long been prized in folk medicine for its ability to cleanse and protect against illness, and now we know why! Medical studies have revealed that sage is rich in potent antibacterial and antioxidant compounds.[1] Its flavour can be a bit overwhelming when it is raw, but cooking it in rich fats mellows it and makes it a perfect pairing for bright flavours such as lemon.

TIME	PER SERVING
Active: 15 minutes	*Total Carbs:* **5.9g**
	Fibre: **1.4g**
Total: 30 minutes	*Protein:* **28.5g**
	Fat: **21.3g**
	FV=2.7

1 tablespoon unsalted butter

1 tablespoon olive oil

4 sage leaves, whole

10g/⅓oz chopped fresh parsley

2 garlic cloves, crushed

Zest of 1 lemon, finely grated

2 fresh sage leaves, thinly sliced

900g/2lb skinless, boneless chicken breast, sliced

2 courgettes, thinly sliced

15g/½oz Parmesan cheese, grated

120ml/4fl oz unsalted chicken stock

4 tablespoons double cream

2 tablespoons lemon juice

1 Place the butter and olive oil in a large frying pan over medium heat. When the mixture foams, add the whole sage leaves and fry until golden, 1 to 2 minutes. Remove the leaves from the pan and set aside on kitchen paper. Add the parsley, garlic and lemon zest; cook for about 1 minute, until fragrant. Add the sliced sage leaves and chicken; cook for 4 to 5 minutes more, until the chicken starts to brown. Add the courgettes and cook for 4 to 5 minutes, tossing well, until the courgettes are tender and the chicken is cooked through.

2 Reduce the heat to low, add the Parmesan, stock and double cream, and cook for 1 minute more, scraping any brown bits from the bottom of the pan. Add the lemon juice and mix. Garnish with the fried sage leaves and serve immediately.

CHOP SUEY

4.7g
NET CARBS

SERVES 4

353
CALORIES

Chop Suey is a classic American dish that has its roots in Asian flavours such as soy and sesame but has no historical background. We update this recipe by mixing mild-tasting (and heart-healthy) oils such as sesame or coconut oil with butter, yielding a rich, slightly sweet base for the veggie-centric dish, which provides more flavour.

- 3 large pork chops on the bone (680g/1½lb total)
- ¼ teaspoon garlic salt
- ¼ teaspoon freshly ground black pepper
- 2 tablespoons Atkins Flour Mix (page 126)
- 3 tablespoons sesame or coconut oil
- 1 tablespoon unsalted butter
- 140g/5oz thinly sliced pak choi
- 140g/5oz button or chestnut mushrooms, thinly sliced
- 2 celery stalks, thinly sliced
- 1 green pepper, thinly sliced
- 4 spring onions, thinly sliced
- 120ml/4fl oz Basic Bone Broth (page 161) or unsalted chicken stock
- 2 tablespoons soy sauce or tamari

1 Thinly slice the meat off the pork chops, and discard the bone. Sprinkle the pork with the garlic salt, pepper and Atkins Flour Mix.

2 In a large frying pan, warm the oil and butter over medium heat. Add the pork slices and brown them for 2 to 3 minutes, stirring occasionally. Add the pak choi, mushrooms, celery, pepper and spring onions; cook for 4 to 5 minutes, stirring often, until the vegetables are soft. Stir in the broth and soy sauce, scraping any brown bits from the bottom of the pan. Serve immediately.

TIP

For a heartier dish, *pair with 55g/2oz cauliflower rice (page 118) per person for 2 added grams of Net Carbs.*

TIME	PER SERVING
Active: 15 minutes	*Total Carbs:* **7.2g**
	Fibre: **2.6g**
Total: 30 minutes	*Protein:* **27.1g**
	Fat: **24.5g**
	FV=**3.5**

SUPERFAST
STROGANOFF

8.6g
NET CARBS

SERVES 4

425
CALORIES

Rich-tasting beef stroganoff has a gravy made by mixing soured cream with browned beef. It's a perfect cold-weather, creamy, iron-rich recipe that's fast to make and satisfying to eat. It's good enough to 'stick to your ribs' – but not to worry, it won't! Depending on your carb intake, you can serve this stroganoff on top of 100g/3½oz cooked spiralized courgette or with a veggie side that is lower in carbs, such as sautéed spinach.

TIME	PER SERVING
Active: 10 minutes	Total Carbs: **10.4g**
	Fibre: **1.8g**
Total: 20 minutes	Protein: **33.6g**
	Fat: **29g**
	FV=5

2 tablespoons unsalted butter

225g/8oz button or chestnut mushrooms, thinly sliced

1 onion, thinly sliced

2 garlic cloves, finely chopped

450g/1lb flank steak, sliced 1cm/½in thick

1 teaspoon garlic salt

240ml/8fl oz Basic Bone Broth (page 161)

1 teaspoon Worcestershire sauce

4 tablespoons Atkins Flour Mix (page 126)

240g/8½oz full-fat soured cream

1 Warm 1 tablespoon of butter in a large frying pan over medium heat, and add the mushrooms, onion and garlic; cook for 4 to 5 minutes, stirring often, until the mushrooms start to brown. Transfer to a plate. Sprinkle the steak with the garlic salt. Add the remaining butter to the pan over medium heat, then add the steak and cook for 2 to 3 minutes, stirring occasionally, to brown the beef. Transfer to the plate with the mushroom mixture.

2 Stir in the broth and Worcestershire sauce, scraping up any brown bits from the bottom of the pan. Whisk in the Atkins Flour Mix and simmer for 1 minute, until the sauce begins to thicken. Return the steak and mushroom mixture to the skillet and toss well. Turn the heat off. Stir in the soured cream, and serve immediately.

PARMESAN
SCALLOPS

14.3g
NET CARBS

SERVES
4

299
CALORIES

This speedy seafood dish is ideal when you're in the mood for Italian fare. Fresh broccoli florets add a pleasing crunch as well as a boost of fibre, while the medley of scallops, bubbling Parmesan cheese, bright flavours of fresh herbs and tangy tomato sauce completes the dish.

2 tablespoons olive oil

1 head broccoli, cut into small florets

¼ teaspoon garlic salt

¼ teaspoon freshly ground black pepper

480ml/16fl oz low-sugar tomato sauce from a jar

120ml/4fl oz water

450g/1lb fresh sea scallops (see Tip)

10g/⅓oz chopped fresh flatleaf parsley

15g/½oz Parmesan cheese, grated

1 Warm the olive oil in a large sauté pan or deep frying pan, with a heatproof handle, over medium heat. Add the broccoli, garlic salt and black pepper; cook for 7 to 8 minutes, until the broccoli starts to brown and soften. Set the oven to grill. Decrease the heat to low under the pan, carefully add the tomato sauce and water, and stir well. Smooth the top of the broccoli sauce mixture, and place the scallops on top.

2 Sprinkle with the parsley and Parmesan and place under the grill. Grill for 4 to 5 minutes, until the tops become golden and the scallops are cooked through and no longer translucent when sliced with a paring knife. Serve immediately.

TIP

Look for sea scallops that are 'dry', *not treated with phosphates, a preserving method that makes them stringy when they are cooked.*

TIME	PER SERVING
Active: 15 minutes	*Total Carbs:* **17.4g** *Fibre:* **4.1g** *Protein:* **29.2g**
Total: 30 minutes	*Fat:* **13.3g** *FV=* **9.8**

12
ONE-POT MEALS

EASY FAMILY FARE

for Tasty No-Fuss Meals

You'll love these budget-friendly, one-pot meals, which are
super easy to cook and simple to clean up after. They are flawless family
meals and excellent crowd-pleasers. Looking for something you can prepare
in advance? Try the Italian Stuffed Cabbage (page 251) or Year-Round Barbecued
Brisket (page 268), both of which are a breeze with the help of a slow cooker.
With their rich, hearty flavours and creamy sauces, you'll even discover
a few recipes perfect for a decadent date night!

RECIPES

CHICKEN PARMESAN

MEATBALLS

5.1g
NET CARBS

SERVES
4

359
CALORIES

Craving the flavour of chicken Parmesan but don't want to deal with the hassle and carbs of bread-crumbing the chicken? These meatballs are bound to become your go-to for Italian Sunday-night meals. Grinding the chicken meat in your food processor is vital to the texture of this dish, since pre-ground chicken meat is often loaded with water, making the meatball mixture too wet. Do it yourself for the flavour and the savings!

TIME	PER SERVING
Active: 15 minutes	*Total Carbs:* **6.7g**
	Fibre: **1.6g**
Total: 30 minutes	*Protein:* **37.7g**
	Fat: **21.3g**
	*FV=***1.8**

3 skinless, boneless chicken breasts (500g/1lb 2oz total), diced

50g/1¾oz Atkins Flour Mix (page 126)

120g/4¼oz full-fat cream cheese, room temperature

1 egg

2 garlic cloves, crushed

1 teaspoon dried oregano

½ teaspoon salt

Olive oil spray

240ml/8fl oz low-sugar tomato sauce from a jar

120ml/4fl oz Basic Bone Broth (page 161) or unsalted chicken stock

2 slices (25g/1oz total) mozzarella cheese

10g/⅓oz Parmesan cheese, grated

1 Place the chicken in the food processor, pulsing to chop for 6 to 7 minutes. Combine the chicken, Atkins Flour Mix, cream cheese, egg, garlic, oregano and salt in a large bowl. Mix well with your hands until well incorporated. Roll into 5-cm/2-in balls (about 12).

2. Coat a large deep frying pan or sauté pan with olive oil spray and place over medium heat. Add the meatballs and cook for 5 to 6 minutes, turning occasionally, until they are well browned. Reduce the heat to low and add the tomato sauce and broth. Cover and cook for 4 to 5 minutes more, until the meatballs are cooked through. Top with the sliced mozzarella and Parmesan. Cover and let rest for 1 minute to melt the cheese. Serve immediately.

TIP

If you have the time, put the diced chicken on a baking tray and freeze for about 1 hour, or until it is firmer but not solid, to help the chopping.

ROAST BEEF

with Greek Yogurt Horseradish Sauce

1.2g
NET CARBS

SERVES 14

223
CALORIES

Need to feed a crowd with minimal work? This traditional roast beef feast gets a spicy kick from the creamy horseradish sauce. Serve with a delectable side such as Cauliflower Mac & Cheese (page 267) without the sausage, Cheesy Spring Onion Cauliflower Mash (page 151), or sautéed spinach. Double the sauce and serve with prawns as a festive, low-carb surf 'n' turf starter to kick off an evening.

1 teaspoon garlic salt

1 teaspoon sweet paprika

1 teaspoon freshly ground black pepper

2.25-kg/5-lb top or bottom round beef roast

Preheat the oven to 190°F/375°F/Gas 5. Place the garlic salt, paprika and pepper in a small bowl, and mix well with a spoon. Sprinkle the roast with the spices and transfer to a 2-litre/2-quart baking dish. Transfer the roast to the oven and cook for 1 to 1½ hours, until the outside of the roast is golden brown but the meat is still pink when sliced. Set aside for 5 minutes to allow the juices to redistribute. Slice the roast beef and serve immediately with the Horseradish Sauce.

HORSERADISH SAUCE

2 tablespoons grated fresh horseradish

240g/8½oz full-fat Greek yogurt

1 tablespoon lemon juice

1 cucumber, peeled, deseeded and grated

Place the horseradish, yogurt, lemon juice and cucumber in a bowl. Stir well to combine and refrigerate until required.

TIME	PER SERVING
Active: 15 minutes	*Total Carbs:* **1.5g**
	Fibre: **0.3g**
Total: 1 hour 30 minutes	*Protein:* **37.7g**
	Fat: **6.3g**
	FV=0

ITALIAN
STUFFED CABBAGE

5.3g
NET CARBS

SERVES
6

291
CALORIES

Stuffed cabbage is a traditional Polish and Hungarian dish that's naturally healthy. Nutrient-dense cabbage is rich in vitamins C and K and fibre, and its softened leaves make the perfect casing for well-seasoned minced meat. This version uses Italian flavours, including basil and Parmesan, for a twist on an Eastern European classic.

TIME	PER SERVING
Active: 15 minutes	*Total Carbs:* **7g** *Fibre:* **1.7g** *Protein:* **29.7g**
Total: 3 hours. 30 minutes	*Fat:* **15.3g** *FV=***4.6**

- 15g/½oz Parmesan cheese, grated
- 1 tablespoon ground flaxseed
- 1 egg
- ½ teaspoon garlic salt
- ¼ teaspoon freshly ground black pepper
- 1 large Chinese cabbage
- 400g/14oz tin chopped tomatoes
- 240ml/8fl oz Basic Bone Broth (page 161) or beef stock
- 2 tablespoons tomato purée
- 680g/1½lb minced beef or pork
- 10g/⅓oz chopped basil leaves
- 1 teaspoon Italian seasoning or ½ teaspoon dried oregano
- ½ teaspoon ground turmeric
- **Fresh dill for garnish, if wished**

1 Stir together the Parmesan, flaxseed, egg, garlic salt and pepper in a large bowl. Let rest for 30 minutes to allow the flaxseed to soften.

2 Meanwhile, bring a large stockpot filled halfway with water to a boil over high heat. Trim the tough root end of the cabbage so that you can easily remove 24 of the outer leaves; reserve the remaining cabbage for another use, such as Hot-and-Sour Soup (page 179). When the water boils, turn off the heat and add half of the leaves, pressing to submerge them in the hot water. Cover the stockpot and let soak for 4 to 5 minutes until the leaves begin to soften. Remove the cabbage leaves with tongs, and drain them in a colander.

RECIPE CONTINUES

3 Bring the water to a boil again, and cook the remaining cabbage leaves until they slowly start to soften but aren't fully cooked. Drain them in a colander. Repeat with the remaining leaves. Alternatively, working in batches, wrap the leaves in damp kitchen paper and microwave for 1 minute, until softened. Set aside to cool.

4 Put the chopped tomatoes, broth and tomato purée into a slow cooker, and mix together.

5 Add the minced beef or pork, basil, Italian seasoning or oregano, and turmeric to the flaxseed mixture and mix together with your fingers. Place a cabbage leaf on a chopping board and trim off the tough bottom. Place 3 tablespoons of the meat mixture close to the bottom edge of the leaf and roll up. Tuck in the edges, and place the cabbage roll, seam side down, over the tomato mixture in the slow cooker. Repeat with the remaining leaves and filling.

6 Cover the slow cooker, and cook on the low setting for 3 to $3\frac{1}{2}$ hours, until the filling is cooked through and no longer pink in the middle. To check for doneness, slice a cabbage roll open with a knife. Transfer four stuffed cabbage leaves to each of 6 soup plates and serve immediately. Garnish with fresh dill, if you like.

MUSHROOM
SPINACH
EGG SKILLET

7.8g
NET CARBS

SERVES **4**

237
CALORIES

Of all the quick weeknight meals, this simple one-pot dish is the most beautiful. Serve it alongside one of our salad recipes for dinner, or for a relaxed weekend brunch along with some Cauliflower Hash Browns (page 118).

TIME	PER SERVING
Active: **15 minutes**	*Total Carbs:* **11.7g**
Total: **30 minutes**	*Fibre:* **3.9g**
	Protein: **16.2g**
	Fat: **15g**
	FV=6.5

Olive oil spray

450g/1lb baby spinach or spinach leaves, chopped

450g/1lb button or chestnut mushrooms, thinly sliced

½ small onion, finely chopped

3 small garlic cloves, crushed

½ teaspoon salt

¼ teaspoon freshly ground black pepper

¼ teaspoon freshly grated nutmeg

80ml/2½fl oz double cream

4 eggs

10g/⅓oz Parmesan cheese, grated

1 Coat a large deep frying pan with olive oil spray and place over high heat. Add the spinach in batches and stir to wilt, cooking each batch for 1 to 2 minutes and transferring the wilted spinach to a bowl as you work. Coat the pan with the olive oil spray again. Add the mushrooms, onion, garlic, salt, pepper and nutmeg. Cook for 4 to 5 minutes, stirring often, until the mushrooms and onions soften. Return the spinach to the pan and stir well. Turn the heat to low and stir in the cream. Using a wooden spoon, make four wells in the vegetable mixture to hold the eggs.

2 Crack the eggs into the wells and cover. Cook on low for 3 to 4 minutes. Sprinkle with the Parmesan and cover, cooking for 1 minute more until the Parmesan is melted and the egg whites are cooked through. Spoon out an egg and the vegetable mixture it is nestled in, and serve in a soup plate. Repeat with the remaining eggs.

GARLIC ROSEMARY
PORK LOIN
with Creamed Spinach

4.7g NET CARBS

 SERVES 4

429 CALORIES

Garlic and rosemary, two flavour staples of many cuisines, are also high in health-promoting antiviral and antibacterial compounds. Pork loin is a naturally low-fat cut of meat that benefits from the gentle roasting in this recipe. If your loin comes with a large fat cap (the fat on the top of the joint), you can trim it back before cooking.

TIME	PER SERVING
Active: **15 minutes**	*Total Carbs:* **7.9g**
	Fibre: **3.2g**
Total: **1 hour**	*Protein:* **37g**
	Fat: **28.1g**
	FV=2.5

450g/1lb boneless pork loin

Olive oil spray

1 tablespoon Dijon mustard

3 garlic cloves, crushed

2 tablespoons thinly sliced fresh rosemary

1 Preheat the oven to 180°C/350°F/Gas 4. Place the pork loin, fatty side down, in a frying pan over medium heat. Cook for 4 to 5 minutes to brown the top and render some of the fat.

2 Coat a 18-by-28-cm/ 7-by-11-in baking dish with olive oil spray. Place the pork loin into the dish. Put the mustard, garlic and rosemary in a small bowl and stir well. Spoon the mixture over the pork.

3 Bake for 45 minutes to 1 hour, until the loin is cooked through but still slightly pink in the centre. About 15 minutes before the loin is done, prepare the Creamed Spinach. When the pork is cooked, let rest 5 minutes before slicing. Slice and serve immediately with the creamed spinach.

CREAMED SPINACH

450g/1lb baby spinach or spinach leaves, chopped

2 tablespoons unsalted butter

2 tablespoons Atkins Flour Mix (page 126)

120ml/4fl oz double cream

120ml/4fl oz Basic Bone Broth (page 161)
or unsalted chicken stock

¼ teaspoon freshly grated nutmeg

Zest of 1 lemon

15g/½oz Parmesan cheese, grated

Heat a saucepan over high heat. Add the spinach in batches and stir to wilt, cooking each batch for 1 to 2 minutes and transferring the wilted spinach to a bowl as you work. Melt the butter in the same pan over medium heat. When the butter is melted, sprinkle in the Atkins Flour Mix and cook for 1 to 2 minutes, stirring often, until the flour coats the pan. Whisk in the cream, broth, nutmeg and lemon zest; cook for 1 minute more, until the mixture forms a thick sauce. Stir in the reserved spinach and the Parmesan, stirring well until smooth and creamy.

TIP

Creamed Spinach is a rich side dish that is a traditional steakhouse favourite. It pairs well with grilled steak, salmon, poultry or Year-Round Barbecued Brisket (page 268). Here are some other suggestions for starters and hearty sides to round out these meals.

- *Instead of bread, start with the Steamed Artichoke (page 219) or a crudité platter, which is a plate of sliced vegetables. Experiment with colourful vegetables that are in season, in addition to carrots, celery, peppers and cherry tomatoes. Try sliced beetroot, grilled radicchio or purple Brussels sprouts. You can also add marinated artichoke hearts, mushrooms and olives. Dip your veggies in hummus or any of the homemade salad dressings in Chapter 9.*

- *Skip the mashed potatoes in favour of Cheesy Spring Onion Cauliflower Mash (page 151) or steamed broccoli or asparagus drizzled with rich Hollandaise sauce.*

- *If you're still craving potatoes, cut up half a potato and toss it with olive oil and vegetables lower in carbs, such as pieces of sweet potato, cauliflower, broccoli and mushrooms. Season with salt and pepper and roast in the oven.*

CHICKEN
AND
DUMPLINGS

7.7g
NET CARBS

SERVES 4

346
CALORIES

Homey, creamy chicken topped with tender dumplings that steam directly inside the pot is the ultimate comfort food combination. If you've never had drop dumplings before, imagine cake-like clouds of goodness that you can use to sop up a delicious sauce.

TIME	PER SERVING
Active: 15 minutes	*Total Carbs:* **11.3g**
	Fibre: **3.6g**
Total: 30 minutes	*Protein:* **37.8g**
	Fat: **17.6g**
	FV=2.2

Chicken

- 2 tablespoons unsalted butter
- 2 skinless, boneless chicken breasts, diced (about 350g/12oz total)
- ½ teaspoon garlic salt
- ½ teaspoon paprika
- ¼ teaspoon freshly ground black pepper
- 140g/5oz chestnut or button mushrooms, thinly sliced
- 2 celery stalks, thinly sliced
- 4 garlic cloves, crushed
- 180ml/6fl oz Basic Bone Broth (page 161) or unsalted chicken stock
- 2 tablespoons full-fat cream cheese
- 10g/⅓oz chopped fresh flatleaf parsley

Dumplings

- 100g/3½oz Atkins Flour Mix (page 126)
- 2 teaspoons baking powder
- ½ teaspoon salt
- 4 tablespoons whole milk
- 2 teaspoons olive oil

1 Prepare the chicken: Warm the butter in a large saucepan over medium heat. Add the chicken and sprinkle with the garlic salt, paprika and pepper; cook for 4 to 5 minutes, stirring occasionally, until the chicken starts to brown. Add the mushrooms, celery and garlic; cook for 4 to 5 minutes more until the vegetables are tender. Add the broth, scraping up any brown bits from the bottom of the pan. Turn the heat to low and stir in the cream cheese and parsley.

2 Prepare the dumplings: Place the Atkins Flour Mix, baking powder and salt in a small bowl. Mix well. Stir in the milk and oil until a thick, wet dough forms. Spoon the dough on top of the chicken mixture in heaped spoonfuls, leaving 2.5cm/1in between as they will expand. Cover and simmer for 4 to 5 additional minutes to steam the dumplings. Serve immediately with the chicken.

GREEN BEAN
CHICKEN
ONE-POT

4.6g
NET CARBS

SERVES 4

384
CALORIES

This convenient one-pot dish is quick to make, protein-rich, and topped with a pleasingly crunchy, heart-healthy crumble of nuts and unsweetened coconut. To save time on prep, shop for pre-sliced green beans, meaning there is no need to chop them.

TIME	PER SERVING
Active: **15 minutes**	*Total Carbs:* **9g**
	Fibre: **4.4g**
Total: **30 minutes**	*Protein:* **28.1g**
	Fat: **27.5g**
	FV=2

- 4 skinless, boneless chicken breasts, diced (680g/1½1lb total)
- 2 tablespoons Atkins Flour Mix (page 126)
- ½ teaspoon garlic salt
- ½ teaspoon sweet paprika
- ¼ teaspoon freshly ground black pepper
- 2 tablespoons coconut or olive oil
- 225g/8oz green beans, trimmed, cut in half
- 180ml/6fl oz unsalted chicken stock or Basic Bone Broth (page 161)
- 2 tablespoons full-fat cream cheese
- 40g/1½oz unsweetened desiccated coconut
- 30g/1oz chopped pecans, macadamia nuts or walnuts

1 Place the chicken on a plate and sprinkle with the Atkins Flour Mix, garlic salt, paprika and pepper, tossing with tongs to coat evenly. In a large deep frying or sauté pan with a heatproof handle, heat 1 tablespoon of the oil over medium heat. Add the chicken and cook for 3 to 4 minutes until the it starts to brown. Transfer to a plate. Add the remaining oil and the green beans to the pan and cook for 6 to 8 minutes, until the green beans begin to soften.

2 Set the oven to grill. Return the chicken to the pan, add the stock and bring to a simmer; cook for 1 minute more, stirring well. Decrease the heat to low and stir in the cream cheese until it melts. Turn the heat off. Sprinkle the coconut and nuts over the chicken mixture and place under the grill on the middle rack for 30 to 40 seconds, or until the tops are golden brown. Serve immediately.

BOLOGNESE
FRYING-PAN
LASAGNE

8.7g NET CARBS

SERVES **4**

403 CALORIES

Lasagne, filled with a rich meat ragù, is delicious but a lot of work to assemble and cook. This 'cheat' version, which is made in one heavy frying pan, uses the crepe recipe (page 127) as the lasagne sheet and takes half the time. If you want to make this novel recipe for date night, just cut the ingredients in half, use a smaller pan, and serve it in the pan for just the two of you.

TIME	PER SERVING
Active: 25 minutes	*Total Carbs:* **10.7g**
	Fibre: **2.7g**
Total: 45 minutes	*Protein:* **45.8g**
	Fat: **26.1g**
	*FV=***4.9**

⅓ crepe recipe (page 127)

450g/1lb lean minced beef

½ teaspoon salt

¼ teaspoon freshly ground black pepper

Olive oil spray

4 garlic cloves, crushed

2 tablespoons tomato purée

400g/14oz tin chopped tomatoes

120ml/4fl oz dry white wine, Basic Bone Broth (page 161), beef stock, or chicken stock

6 fresh basil leaves

20g/¾oz chopped fresh flatleaf parsley

125g/4½oz thinly sliced fresh mozzarella

15g/½oz Parmesan cheese, grated

1 Prepare the 4 crepes, and set aside. Sprinkle the beef with the salt and pepper. Coat a large heavy frying pan with olive oil spray and place over medium heat. Add the beef and garlic; cook for 5 to 6 minutes, stirring occasionally, until the beef is well browned. Add the tomato purée and cook for 1 to 2 minutes more, until fragrant.

2 Add the tomatoes, wine, basil and parsley. Increase the heat to high and bring to a rapid simmer. Reduce the heat to low and cook, covered, for 25 to 30 minutes, stirring occasionally, until the sauce thickens. Top the sauce with the four crepes, layering them slightly over each other to completely cover the surface of the meat. Cover with the mozzarella slices and sprinkle with the Parmesan. Coat the inside of the pan lid with olive oil spray to prevent it from sticking, and cover the lasagne. Simmer for 10 to 15 minutes more, until the cheese is melted and bubbly. Serve immediately.

BEEF
BOURGUIGNON

7.2g
NET CARBS

SERVES 4

461
CALORIES

This delectable French stew gets its flavour from bacon, herbs and red wine. The combination of aromatic ingredients will make your home smell like a French bistro. Serve this stew over 70g/2½oz cup of steamed broccoli (for 4 grams of Net Carbs) or a simple mixed green side salad tossed in olive oil and a teaspoon of red wine vinegar (for 2 grams of Net Carbs). You don't have to be Julia Child to master this mouthwatering, home-cooked recipe.

TIME	PER SERVING
Active: 30 minutes	*Total Carbs:* **8.9g**
	Fibre: **1.7g**
Total: 3 hours	*Protein:* **28.2g**
	Fat: **30.3g**
	FV=3.7

- 450g/1lb stewing beef
- 1 tablespoon Atkins Flour Mix (page 126)
- ½ teaspoon salt
- ¼ teaspoon freshly ground black pepper
- 2 tablespoons unsalted butter
- 2 tablespoons olive oil
- 115g/4oz bacon, chopped
- 280g/10oz mushrooms, such as button or chestnut, trimmed and sliced
- ½ onion, chopped
- 4 garlic cloves, crushed
- 2 tablespoons tomato purée
- 1 teaspoon fresh thyme leaves
- 240ml/8fl oz red wine, Basic Bone Broth (page 161) or beef stock
- 480ml/16fl oz Basic Bone Broth (page 161) or beef stock
- Chopped fresh flatleaf parsley, to garnish (optional)

1 Place the beef on a plate, and sprinkle with the Atkins Flour Mix, salt and pepper. Toss to coat evenly. Set aside. Warm the butter and olive oil in a large staucepan over medium-high heat. Add the beef and cook for 4 to 5 minutes, turning occasionally, until the coating browns. Transfer the beef to a plate.

2 Add the bacon and cook for 4 to 5 minutes, stirring often and scraping up any brown bits that stick to the inside of the pan. Add the mushrooms, onion and garlic; cook for 4 to 5 minutes, stirring often, until the mushrooms soften and the onion is brown. Reduce the heat to low and add the tomato purée and thyme, cooking for 1 minute more, until the tomato purée is fragrant. Add the red wine and broth and increase the heat to high. Return the beef to the pan and bring the liquid to a boil, then immediately reduce to a simmer and cover. Cook for 2½ to 3 hours, until the beef is tender and the sauce thickens. Serve immediately. Garnish with chopped parsley, if desired.

CIOPPINO

13.2g NET CARBS | SERVES **4** | **372** CALORIES

Cioppino, a San Francisco tradition created by Italian immigrants who settled in California in the 1800s, is a delectable seafood stew bursting with the flavours of the sea in a savoury broth that is great for celebrations or date night. This dish is easy to make even if you're not used to cooking fish, and the minerals and B vitamins in the variety of seafood give your brain and energy levels a natural boost.

- 2 tablespoons olive oil
- 1 fennel bulb, thinly sliced, fronds reserved and chopped
- 2 shallots, chopped
- 2 large garlic cloves, finely chopped
- ½ teaspoon salt
- ¼ teaspoon freshly ground black pepper
- 1 teaspoon crushed chilli flakes
- 2 tablespoons tomato purée
- 400g/14oz tin chopped tomatoes
- 180ml/6fl oz dry white wine or unsalted chicken stock
- 480ml/16fl oz unsalted chicken stock
- 1 bay leaf
- 225g/8oz manila clams, scrubbed
- 225g/8oz mussels, scrubbed, debearded
- 225g/8oz uncooked large prawns (about 20), peeled and deveined
- 350g/12oz assorted firm-fleshed fish fillets such as halibut
- 1 lemon, quartered

1 Heat the oil in a large saucepan over medium heat. Add the fennel, shallots, garlic, salt, pepper and half the chilli flakes; cook for 8 to 10 minutes, stirring occasionally, until the vegetables start to brown. Stir in the tomato purée. Add the chopped tomatoes with their juice, wine, stock and bay leaf. Cover and bring to a simmer. Reduce the heat to medium-low. Cover and simmer on low for 10 minutes to allow the flavours to meld.

RECIPE CONTINUES

TIME	PER SERVING
Active: 15 minutes	*Total Carbs:* **15.8g**
	Fibre: **2.6g**
Total: 30 minutes	*Protein:* **41.8g**
	Fat: **12g**
	FV=7.7

TIPS

For date night, *cut the recipe in half and serve with Wilted Brussels Sprout Salad with Warm Pancetta Dressing (page 190) or Pear and Manchego Mesclun Salad with Caramelized Onions (page 195).*

Though crusty sourdough bread is traditionally used to sop up the savoury broth in this dish, depending on how many carbs you are consuming, a slice of **Low-Carb Flax Meal Bread** *(page 202) works equally well.*

2 Add the clams and mussels to the cooking liquid; cover and cook until the clams and mussels begin to open, about 4 to 5 minutes. Add the prawns and fish. Simmer for 4 to 5 minutes longer, stirring gently, until the fish and prawns are just cooked through and the clams are completely open (discard any clams and mussels that do not open). Remove the bay leaf, ladle the stew into bowls and garnish with the remaining chilli flakes, reserved fennel fronds and the lemon quarters.

ROASTED FENNEL AND
COD
with Moroccan Olives

6.4g
NET CARBS

SERVES
4

335
CALORIES

Refreshing, slightly sweet, aromatic fennel makes a light base for flaky, well-seasoned cod in this simple roasted fish recipe. Any olives will work for this dish, but to make it even more flavourful, look for firm, salty black Moroccan olives cured in oil. Or use large, tart Italian Cerignola olives, which are sold in Italian delis, removing the stones before you bake.

TIME	PER SERVING
Active: 15 minutes	*Total Carbs:* **11.2g**
	Fibre: **4.8g**
Total: 45 minutes	*Protein:* **32.4g**
	Fat: **18.4g**
	FV=5.3

- 2 fennel bulbs, trimmed and thinly sliced
- 1 lemon
- 1 tablespoon olive oil
- ½ teaspoon garlic salt
- 680g/1½lb cod fillets
- 70g/2½oz black Moroccan olives, pitted
- 10g/⅓oz chopped dill or coriander
- ½ teaspoon hot paprika or ¼ teaspoon crushed chilli flakes
- ¼ teaspoon salt
- ¼ teaspoon freshly ground black pepper
- 4 tablespoons unsalted butter

1 Preheat the oven to 200°C/400°F/Gas 6. Put the fennel in an 18-by-28-cm/7-by-11-in baking dish. Zest the lemon over the fennel and add the olive oil and garlic salt. Toss well. Transfer to the oven and bake for 10 to 15 minutes, until the edges of the fennel start to brown.

2 Cut the zested lemon into quarters. Place the fish on top of the fennel, as well as the lemon wedges, and sprinkle with the olives, dill or coriander, paprika or chilli flakes, salt and pepper. Place a tablespoon of butter onto each piece of fish. Bake for 20 to 25 minutes, until the fish flakes when pressed with a fork. Squeeze lemon juice from the lemon wedges over the fish and serve immediately.

CAULIFLOWER
MAC & CHEESE

SERVES 8

In this cheesy comfort food classic, tender cauliflower florets are a 'super' low-carb swap for pasta. Cauliflower, a member of the cruciferous family, is considered a superfood because it's rich in certain compounds that may ward off heart disease, plus it's a good source of fibre, vitamins and minerals. You'll be hooked when you pair it with a medley of bubbling cheeses and savoury chunks of chicken sausage, which turn it into a full, protein-rich meal.

- 1 small head cauliflower, cut into florets
- Olive oil spray
- 350g/12oz chicken sausage, chopped (optional)
- 2 tablespoons unsalted butter
- 4 garlic cloves, crushed
- 3 tablespoons Atkins Flour Mix (page 126)
- 120ml/4fl oz whole milk
- 120ml/4fl oz Basic Bone Broth (page 161) or unsalted chicken stock
- 80g/2¾oz Cheddar cheese, grated
- 30g/1oz Parmesan cheese, grated
- 115g/4oz full-fat cream cheese, room temperature
- ½ teaspoon freshly grated nutmeg
- 2 tablespoons chopped fresh chives

1 Place the cauliflower florets into a large saucepan and add water to a depth of 5cm/2in. Bring to a boil over high heat. Cook the cauliflower for 4 to 5 minutes, until fork tender. Drain and set aside.

2 Coat a large saucepan with olive oil spray and place over high heat. Add the sausage, if using, and cook for 8 to 10 minutes, stirring often, until browned and cooked through. Transfer to a plate. Reduce the heat to low, add the butter and garlic, and cook for 1 to 2 minutes, until the garlic is fragrant. Add the Atkins Flour Mix and cook for 1 to 2 minutes, whisking continuously until a thick paste forms. Add the milk, broth, Cheddar, Parmesan, cream cheese and half the nutmeg.

3 Reduce the heat to low, and cook 1 to 2 minutes, stirring well, until the cheese is melted and the mixture is smooth. Stir in the cauliflower and toss well to coat in the sauce. Sprinkle with the sausage, if using, garnish with the remaining nutmeg and the chives, and serve.

WITH SAUSAGE	
TIME	**PER SERVING**
Active: 15 minutes	*Net Carbs:* **5.7g**
	Total Carbs: **7.6g**
	Fibre: **1.9g**
Total: 30 minutes	*Protein:* **21.8g**
	Fat: **21.8g**
	Calories: **311**
	*FV=*2.2

WITHOUT SAUSAGE	
TIME	**PER SERVING**
Active: 15 minutes	*Net Carbs:* **5.1g**
	Total Carbs: **6.9g**
	Fibre: **1.9g**
Total: 30 minutes	*Protein:* **14.3g**
	Fat: **17.6g**
	Calories: **238**
	*FV=*2.2

YEAR-ROUND
BARBECUED
BRISKET

2.6g
NET CARBS

SERVES
14

270
CALORIES

Brisket is a barbecue treat that you can actually make easily at any time of year when you use a slow cooker. It's the perfect hands-off dish that takes minimal prep time – just throw the ingredients into your slow cooker, set the timer and forget about it until the pleasing aroma fills your house. So go ahead, have a picnic indoors anytime you get the hankering by pairing this with Cauliflower Mac and Cheese (page 267) without the sausage or Creamed Spinach (page 255).

TIME	PER SERVING
Active: 15 minutes	*Total Carbs:* **3.6g**
	Fibre: **1g**
Total: 10 hours	*Protein:* **35.1g**
	Fat: **12.3g**
	*FV=***1.7**

- 170-g/6-oz tin tomato purée
- 5 tablespoons apple cider vinegar
- 1 tablespoon chilli powder
- 2 teaspoons onion powder
- 2 teaspoons garlic salt
- 1 teaspoon freshly ground black pepper
- 1 teaspoon smoked paprika
- 1 teaspoon cayenne pepper
- 2 tablespoons stevia
- 2 tablespoons Atkins Flour Mix (page 126)
- 2.25-kg/5-lb piece of beef brisket

1 Place the tomato purée, vinegar, chilli powder, onion powder, garlic salt, black pepper, paprika, cayenne pepper, stevia and Atkins Flour Mix in the slow cooker. Whisk to combine. Spoon out 4 tablespoons of the sauce to top the brisket.

2 Add the brisket and top with the sauce. Set the slow cooker to low and cook for 9 to 10 hours, until the meat is very tender. Shred and serve immediately.

SMOKY
HABANERO
CHILLI

4.8g
NET CARBS

SERVES 8

296
CALORIES

Smoky sea salt and chillies lend fiery southwestern flavours to this delicious chilli that easily feeds a group. Pair this meat-centric dish with a leafy green salad, Sautéed Spinach with Caramelized Shallots (page 154), or steamed broccoli to make it more nutritionally balanced.

TIME	PER SERVING
Active: 15 minutes	*Total Carbs:* **6.1g**
	Fibre: **1.3g**
Total: 3 hours, 15 minutes	*Protein:* **23.1g**
	Fat: **19.5g**
	FV=2.7

- 900-g/2-lb piece of stewing beef
- 1 teaspoon smoked sea salt or steak seasoning
- 1 teaspoon freshly ground black pepper
- 2 tablespoons grapeseed oil
- 1 red onion, finely chopped
- 4 garlic cloves, crushed
- 1 habanero chilli, deseeded and finely chopped
- 2 tablespoons mild chilli powder
- 1 teaspoon crushed chilli flakes
- ¼ teaspoon dried oregano
- 2 tablespoons tomato purée
- 960ml/32fl oz Basic Bone Broth (page 161) or unsalted chicken stock
- 120g/4¼oz full-fat soured cream
- 20g/¾oz fresh coriander leaves and stems, chopped

1 Season the beef with the salt or steak seasoning and pepper. Warm the oil in a large saucepan over high heat. Add the beef, and cook for 3 to 4 minutes, turning occasionally, until it browns. Add the onion, garlic, habanero, chilli powder, chilli flakes, oregano and tomato purée, and cook for 2 to 3 minutes more, until fragrant.

2 Add the broth, and bring to a simmer. Cover and reduce the heat to low, and cook for 2½ to 3 hours, until the beef begins to fall apart. Shred the beef with a fork, and serve immediately with the soured cream and coriander.

13

JUST DESSERTS

THE GRAND FINALE IS JUST AS SWEET,
Minus the Carbs and Sugar

●

Desserts are definitely not a thing of the past if you're living a low-carb, low-sugar lifestyle. Guilty pleasures? Nothing could be further from the truth! Get ready to indulge in these sweet, sometimes no-bake, often chocolatey, deliciously sinful but guilt-free delicacies.

RECIPES

BUCKEYE
TRUFFLES

2.3g
NET CARBS

MAKES 24

141
CALORIES

Conkers, or 'buck eyes' as they are known in the States, are the inspiration for these sweets. They have a peanut butter 'truffle' filling, which is almost completely surrounded by anti-oxidant rich chocolate, leaving just a little of the filling showing to look like a conker.

TIME	PER SERVING
Active: 10 minutes	*Total Carbs:* **3.8g** *Fibre:* **1.5g**
Total: 45 minutes	*Protein:* **4.7g** *Fat:* **12.6g**

Truffles
240g/8½oz no-sugar-added peanut butter

120g/4¼oz unsalted butter, softened

50g/1¾oz stevia

35g/1¼oz plain protein powder

2 tablespoons ground flaxseed

1 teaspoon vanilla extract

Chocolate Coating
115g/4oz unsweetened chocolate, chopped

2 tablespoons unsalted butter

1 Make the truffles: place the peanut butter, butter, stevia, protein powder, flaxseed and vanilla extract in a stand mixer and blend until smooth.

2 Line a tray that will fit into your freezer with greaseproof paper. Using a soup spoon to scoop the peanut mixture, make 24 (2.5-cm/1-in) mounds. Transfer them to the prepared tray and freeze for 30 minutes. With wet fingers, roll into balls. Return to the freezer on a separate plate while you prepare the chocolate coating. Reserve the tray with the greaseproof paper for the dipped truffles.

3 Melt the chocolate and butter in a microwavable bowl for 30 seconds to 1 minute. Stir until smooth. Since the entire batch won't fit on one plate, dip half the batch while you keep the other half in the freezer (which also prevents the other half from melting while you dip the first half).

4 Insert a cocktail stick or small skewer in the centre of each peanut butter ball, and dunk in the melted chocolate.

5 Return the dipped truffles to the prepared baking sheet. Repeat with the remaining truffles. Keep refrigerated until ready to serve. You can also freeze these in an airtight container for up to 6 months.

CHOCOLATE
EGG CREAM

6.4g NET CARBS

 SERVES 2

208 CALORIES

Don't be fooled by the name 'egg cream'. This classic soda shop drink received that nickname from the frothy top, which is made with a combination of sparkling water and milk and is as light as whipped egg whites. It's the ideal low-carb swap when you crave chocolate milk or a chocolate milkshake.

TIME	PER SERVING
Active: 5 minutes	*Total Carbs:* **7.4g**
	Fibre: **1g**
Total: 5 minutes	*Protein:* **2.4g**
	Fat: **19.3g**

- 120ml/4fl oz tinned coconut milk
- 4 tablespoons double cream
- 4 tablespoons sugar-free chocolate syrup
- 360ml/12fl oz unflavoured sparkling water

Divide the coconut milk, double cream and chocolate syrup between two glasses. Stir each glass well. Top off each with half the sparkling water and serve immediately.

MEXICAN
WEDDING
COOKIES

2.4g
NET CARBS

MAKES 22

124
CALORIES

Almost every culture has its version of a crumbly nut-and-butter-based biscuit, such as Russian tea cake, butter balls and Italian wedding cookies. This version is made with fibre-rich almond flour spiked with healing spices – ground cardamom and cinnamon – that add another layer of wonderful flavour with each bite.

TIME	PER cookie
Active: **10 minutes**	*Total Carbs:* **4.2g**
	Fibre: **1.8g**
Total: **30 minutes**	*Protein:* **4.4g**
	Fat: **11.1g**

240g/8½oz almond flour

120g/4¼oz finely chopped walnuts

25g/1oz Atkins Flour Mix (page 126)

1 teaspoon baking powder

1 teaspoon ground cardamom

¼ teaspoon salt

4 tablespoons unsalted butter, softened

1 egg

1 teaspoon vanilla extract

100g/3½oz stevia

1 tablespoon ground cinnamon

1 Preheat the oven to 170°C/325°F/Gas 3 and line two baking sheets with baking parchment.

2 In a bowl, mix together the almond flour, walnuts, Atkins Flour Mix, baking powder, cardamom and salt.

3 In a large bowl, beat the butter until light and fluffy, about 2 minutes. Beat in the egg, vanilla extract and half the stevia, then beat in the almond flour mixture until the dough comes together. Form the dough into 2-cm/¾-in balls, and place on the baking sheets about 2.5cm/1in apart.

4 Bake for 16 to 18 minutes, until just lightly golden brown. In a bowl, add the remaining stevia and cinnamon and mix well. While the cookies are still warm, roll them around in the cinnamon mixture to coat. Transfer to a plate to cool completely. Serve or store in an airtight container at room temperature for up to 4 days.

LIME
COCONUT RUM
CUPCAKES

3.8g
NET CARBS

MAKES
12

260
CALORIES

Island flavours of lime, coconut and rum give an otherwise plain vanilla cupcake some serious gourmet flair. These are ideal for an adult birthday, paired with artisanal low-carb rum drinks, or for a kids' birthday bash, using vanilla extract and water in place of the rum. Zest the lime for the icing first, then juice the lime for the cupcakes.

TIME	PER SERVING
Active: 10 minutes	*Total Carbs:* **5g**
Total: 29 minutes	*Fibre:* **1.2g**
	Protein: **8g**
	Fat: **23.9g**

Cupcakes

120g/4¼oz unsalted butter, melted

100g/3½oz stevia

Juice of 1 lime

2 tablespoons rum or coconut rum or 1 teaspoon vanilla extract mixed with 1 tablespoon water

3 eggs

65g/2¼oz Atkins Flour Mix (page 126)

20g/¾oz unsweetened desiccated coconut

2 teaspoons baking powder

Icing

115g/4oz full-fat cream cheese, at room temperature

50g/1¾oz stevia

Zest of 1 lime, finely grated

1 teaspoon vanilla extract

120g/4¼oz unsalted butter, room temperature

40g/1½oz unsweetened desiccated coconut

1 Make the cupcakes: Heat the oven to 180°C/ 350°F/Gas 4. Line a 12-hole muffin tin with cupcake liners. Place the butter, stevia, lime juice and rum in a large bowl and beat with an electric mixer until smooth and creamy. Beat in the eggs. In a separate bowl place the Atkins Flour Mix, coconut and baking powder and stir well.

2 Using a stand or hand mixer, slowly add the flour and coconut mixture to the wet ingredients. Beat until smooth, about 1 minute. Pour into the prepared muffin tin. Bake for 12 to 14 minutes, until the cake springs back when lightly touched in the middle. Cool in the pan on a wire rack for 5 minutes.

3 Prepare the icing: Place the cream cheese in a mixing bowl along with the stevia, lime zest and vanilla extract. Whip well until smooth, 30 seconds to 1 minute. Add the butter, and whip until smooth. Ice the cooled cupcakes and sprinkle with the coconut. Serve immediately. Store in an airtight container at room temperature for up to 4 days.

SALTED CARAMEL
CHEESECAKE BITES

3.8g
NET CARBS

MAKES 18

260
CALORIES

Caramel fans will freak over these cheesecake bites that pack a creamy punch, with the perfect taste combo of sweet and salty. Xanthan gum will improve the texture, but if you don't have it to hand, you can leave it out.

TIME	PER SERVING
Active: 10 minutes	*Total Carbs:* **1.1g**
	Fibre: **0.3g**
Total: 1 hour, 10 minutes	*Protein:* **2.6g**
	Fat: **7.6g**

120ml/4fl oz double cream

35g/1¼oz plain protein powder

2 tablespoons stevia

170g/6oz full-fat cream cheese, at room temperature

40g/1½oz chopped almonds or macadamia nuts

1 tablespoon sugar-free caramel syrup

1 teaspoon vanilla extract

⅛ teaspoon xanthan gum (optional)

¼ teaspoon sea salt or Maldon sea salt flakes

1 Place the double cream in a large mixing bowl with the protein powder and stevia. Whisk until smooth. Add the cream cheese, almonds or macadamia nuts, caramel syrup and vanilla extract and blend until smooth. If the cream cheese clumps slightly, mix with a rubber spatula, breaking up the bits of cream cheese against the side of the bowl. Sprinkle the mixture with the xanthan gum, if using, and mix again for about 30 seconds. The mixture will thicken slightly.

2 Cover a tray that will fit into your freezer with a sheet of greaseproof paper. Using a soup spoon to scoop the mixture onto the tray, make 18 mounds. Alternatively, you can use silicone moulds or coat an empty ice cube tray with olive oil spray, and press the spoonfuls of the cheesecake mixture into 18 of the holes. Sprinkle with the sea salt. Freeze at least 1 hour before serving. Store in the freezer for up to 1 month.

TIP

Switch up flavours *by using sugar-free hazelnut syrup in place of the caramel and hazelnuts or walnuts instead of the almonds or macadamia nuts.*

DOUBLE CHOCOLATE
BROWNIES

2.1g
NET CARBS

MAKES 18

108
CALORIES

Chocolatey cakes, biscuits and brownies are sweets that may seem 'forbidden' when living a low-carb, low-sugar lifestyle. However, real chocolate, which you'll find in two forms here – bar and powdered – can actually double as a healing food when it's unsweetened. Recent studies show that chocolate is a powerful brain booster, with detoxifying compounds that may boost memory and help sweeten your cognition as you age.[1]

TIME	PER SERVING
Active: 15 minutes	*Total Carbs:* **3.3g** *Fibre:* **1.3g** *Protein:* **2.8g**
Total: 45 minutes	*Fat:* **10.7g** *FV=0*

Olive oil spray

115g/4oz unsweetened chocolate, chopped

120g/4¼oz unsalted butter

4 tablespoons tinned coconut milk

100g/3½oz stevia

30g/1oz almond flour

3 tablespoons unsweetened cocoa powder

1 teaspoon baking powder

4 eggs, whisked

1 Preheat the oven to 170ºC/325°F/Gas 3. Coat a 20-by-20-cm/8-by-8-in baking tin with olive oil spray. Place the chocolate, butter and coconut milk in a bowl and microwave on high power for about 2 minutes, or until the chocolate is melted. Whisk well and let cool for 5 minutes while you prepare the dry ingredients.

2 Place the stevia, almond flour, 2 tablespoons of the cocoa powder and the baking powder in a large bowl and mix well. Whisk in the eggs and the cooled chocolate mixture. Transfer to the prepared tin and smooth the top with a spatula. Bake for 20 to 25 minutes, until the edges are firm but the centre is still soft. Leave to cool completely in the pan, then cut into 18 pieces (three rows of six brownies). Sprinkle with the remaining cocoa powder. Store in an airtight container in the fridge for up to 5 days.

CHOCOLATE CHIP
COOKIES

1.4g NET CARBS

MAKES 24

111 CALORIES

Chocolate chip cookies can still be part of your low-carb lifestyle when made with nutritious almond flour and unsweetened chocolate.

Olive oil spray

120g/4¼oz coconut oil, at room temperature

2 eggs

1 teaspoon vanilla extract

½ teaspoon almond extract (optional)

180g/6½oz almond flour

50g/1¾oz stevia

½ teaspoon bicarbonate of soda

1 teaspoon ground cinnamon

¼ teaspoon salt

90g/3¼oz sugar-free chocolate chips

TIP

For a flavour twist and gooey, softer cookies, add 1 teaspoon sugar-free vanilla or caramel syrup to the batter, and bake for 1 to 2 additional minutes.

1 Preheat the oven to 170°C/375°F/Gas 3. Coat a large baking sheet with olive oil spray. Place the coconut oil, eggs, vanilla extract and almond extract (if using) in a large mixing bowl and beat with an electric mixer until smooth and creamy, 30 seconds to 1 minute.

2 In a bowl, whisk together the almond flour, stevia, bicarbonate of soda, cinnamon and salt. Beat the almond flour mixture into the wet ingredients until the dough comes together.

3 Drop the cookie dough onto the prepared baking sheet by teaspoonfuls. Gently flatten the cookies by pressing with a fork or spatula. Press a few chocolate chips onto the top of each cookie. Bake for 10 to 12 minutes until lightly browned. Remove the cookies from the baking sheet and place on a wire rack to cool completely, then serve. Store in an airtight container at room temperature for up to 4 days.

TIME	PER SERVING
Active: 10 minutes	*Total Carbs:* **2.5g**
	Fibre: **1.1g**
Total: 25 minutes	*Protein:* **2.4g**
	Fat: **10.1g**

APPLE
CRUMBLE

7.3g
NET CARBS

**SERVES
6**

227
CALORIES

This is the perfect summertime dessert that will bring back childhood memories, while satisfying your sweet tooth. This hybrid pie/crumble has bottom and top crusts to satisfy apple pie fans, and sandwiches a delectable filling that includes courgettes to help reduce the carbs of the typical apple dessert. Mild courgette mimics the apple flavour as they cook together and pick up the fragrance of spices.

TIME	PER SERVING
Active: 15 minutes	*Total Carbs:* **11g**
	Fibre: **3.7g**
Total: 40 minutes	*Protein:* **6.2g**
	Fat: **19.7g**

Topping
Olive oil spray

1 courgette, peeled and diced

1 apple, cored and diced

3 tablespoons stevia

1 tablespoon ground cinnamon

1 tablespoon Atkins Flour Mix (page 126)

1 tablespoon coconut oil

80ml/2½fl oz water

1 teaspoon vanilla extract

Crust
120g/4¼oz almond flour

2 tablespoons stevia

2 teaspoons Atkins Flour Mix (page 126)

¼ teaspoon salt

60g/2oz unsalted butter, chilled and cut into chunks

1 Preheat the oven to 180°C/350°F/Gas 8. Coat a 20-by-20-cm/8-by-8-in tin with olive oil spray. Place the courgette, apple, stevia, cinnamon and Atkins Flour Mix in a bowl. Mix well.

2 Heat the coconut oil in a saucepan over medium heat. Cook the courgette and apple mix, tossing well, for 1 to 2 minutes. Reduce the heat to low, add the water and cover. Simmer for 6 to 8 minutes until the courgette and apple are tender and a thick sauce forms. Set aside.

3 Combine the crust ingredients in a food processor and pulse until a crumbly dough forms. Press half the crust mixture into the prepared tin. Bake for 10 to 15 minutes, until the crust is golden. Spoon the courgette-apple mixture over the crust and sprinkle the remaining crust mixture on top. Return to the oven and bake for 8 to 10 minutes more, until the top starts to brown. Serve immediately or let cool to room temperature, then store in the fridge in an airtight container for up to 3 days.

YOU CAN CUSTOMIZE THE ATKINS PLAN OF YOUR CHOICE

with the following Acceptable Foods lists
for Atkins 20, 40 and 100,

plus learn about a variety of low-carb products found in
supermarkets to round out your meals and snacks. Last, but not least,
you can review the extensive list of scientific studies that
support your low-carb, low-sugar lifestyle.

This is an extensive list, but it may not include all
possible Acceptable Foods

FISH AND SHELLFISH

- Most fish and shellfish contain no carbs. All are acceptable with the following exceptions:
- Avoid pickled herring prepared with sugar, artificial crab (surimi) or seafood sticks, and other processed shellfish products.
- Oysters and mussels contain carbs, so limit to about 115 grams/4 ounces per day.
- Do not breadcrumb seafood.

POULTRY

- All pure poultry products are acceptable.
- Do not use any products with breadcrumbs or fillers.

MEAT

- All pure meat products are acceptable.
- Avoid any processed meats with fillers (some salami, pepperoni, hog dogs, sausages, meatballs) or breadcrumbs, or that are cured with sugar (bacon, ham).

EGGS

- Eggs in any style are acceptable.

SOY AND VEGETARIAN PRODUCTS

- Quorn products contain milk and eggs, making them unsuitable for vegans.

- Soy cheeses that contain casein, a milk product, are also unsuitable for vegans.

- Many veggie burgers have carb counts higher than 2 grams of Net Carbs and ingredients that may not be acceptable in Level 1.

PRODUCT	SERVING SIZE	NET CARBS (Grams)
Almond milk, unsweetened	240ml/8fl oz	1.0
Quorn burger	1	4.0
Quorn roast	115g/4oz	4.0
Quorn unbreaded cutlet	1	3.0
Seitan	1 piece	2.0
Shirataki noodles	85g/3oz	1.0
Soy 'cheese'	1 slice	1.0
Soy 'cheese'	28g/1oz	2.0
Soy milk, plain, unsweetened	225g/8oz	1.2
Tempeh	80g/2¾oz	3.3
Tofu, firm	115g/4oz	2.5
Tofu, silken, soft	115g/4oz	3.1
Tofu 'back bacon'	3 rashers	1.5
Tofu 'streaky bacon'	2 rashers	2.0
Tofu 'hot dogs' *(depending on brand)*	1	2.0–5.0
Tofu bulk 'sausage'	60g/2oz	2.0
Tofu link 'sausage'	2 links	4.0
Vegan 'cheese', no casein	1 slice	5.0
Vegan 'cheese', no casein	25g/1oz	6.0
Veggie burger	1 burger	2.0
Veggie 'meatballs'	4–5 balls	4.0

* Check individual products for exact carb counts.

CHEESE

- All cheese except ricotta and cottage cheese (they can be added in Level 2).

- Up to 115 grams/4 ounces a day. A tablespoon or two of any grated cheese contains a negligible amount of carbs.

- Avoid cheese spreads that contain other ingredients – for example, strawberry cream cheese, 'diet' cheese, 'cheese products' and whey cheeses – none of which is 100 percent cheese.

- Soy or rice 'cheese' is acceptable, but check the carb count.

FOUNDATION VEGETABLES

These include both salad vegetables and others that are usually cooked.

Salad Vegetables

- Measure the following salad vegetables raw (except for artichoke hearts).

- Tomatoes, onions and peppers are higher in carbs than other salad vegetables, so use them in smaller portions.

- Included are fruits generally thought of as vegetables, such as avocados and olives.

VEGETABLE	SERVING SIZE	NET CARBS (Grams)
Alfalfa sprouts	15g/½oz	0.2
Artichoke hearts, tinned	1	1.0
Artichoke hearts, marinated	4 pieces	2.0
Avocado, Haas	½ fruit	1.8
Beans, green, snap, string, wax	85g/3oz, raw	2.1
Broccoli florets	35g/1¼oz, raw	0.8
Butterhead lettuce	55g/2oz, raw	0.8
Cabbage, green, red, Savoy	30g/1oz	1.1
Cauliflower florets	35g/1¼oz, raw	1.4
Celeriac	80g/2¾oz, grated	3.5
Celery	1 stalk	0.8
Chicory greens	15g/½oz	0.1
Chinese cabbage	30g/1oz	0.0
Chives	1 tbsp	0.1
Cucumber	50g/1¾oz	1.0
Daikon radish	50g/1¾oz	1.0
Endive	25g/1oz	0.4
Escarole	75g/2¾oz	0.1
Fennel	50g/1¾oz	1.8
Greens, mixed	50g/1¾oz	0.4
Iceberg lettuce	70g/2½oz	0.2
Jicama	60g/2oz	2.5
Loose-leaf lettuce	35g/1¼oz	1.0
Mesclun	35g/1¼oz	0.5
Mung bean sprouts	55g/2oz	2.1
Mushrooms, button, fresh	50g/1¾oz	1.2
Olives, black	5	0.7
Olives, green	5	0.0
Onion	2 tablespoons, chopped	0.5
Pak choi	70g/2½oz	0.4
Parsley (and all fresh herbs)	1 tablespoon	0.1
Pepper, green	60g/2oz	2.1
Pepper, red	60g/2oz	2.9
Radicchio	20g/¾oz	0.7
Radishes	6	0.5
Rhubarb, unsweetened	60g/2oz	1.7
Rocket	20g/¾oz	0.4
Romaine lettuce	50g/1¾oz	0.4
Spinach	20g/¾oz	0.2
Spring onion/green onion	25g/1oz	1.2
Tomato	1 small (85–115g/3–4oz)	2.5
Tomato	1 medium	3.3
Tomato, cherry	5	2.2
Watercress	10g/⅓oz	0.0

Cooked Vegetables

- Some also appear on the salad vegetable list, but cooking compacts them, which explains the differences in carb counts.

- Some, such as celeriac, kohlrabi, leeks, mushrooms, onions and pumpkin, are higher in carbs than most, which accounts for the smaller portions.

- Vegetables *not* on this list should not be consumed in Level 1.

VEGETABLE	SERVING SIZE	NET CARBS (Grams)
Artichoke	½ medium	3.5
Asparagus	6 spears	2.4
Aubergine	50g/1¾oz	2.0
Bamboo shoots, tinned, sliced	65g/2¼oz	1.2
Beans, green, wax, string, snap	65g/2¼oz	2.9
Beetroot greens	70g/2½oz	3.7
Broccoli	80g/2¾oz	1.7
Broccoli raab	65g/2¼oz	2.0
Brussels sprouts	75g/2¾oz	1.8
Cabbage, green	30g/1oz	1.6
Cabbage, red	30g/1oz	2.0
Cabbage, Savoy	30g/1oz	1.9
Cauliflower	80g/2¾oz	0.9
Celery	60g/2oz	1.2
Chard, Swiss	85g/3oz	1.8
Courgette	90g/3¼oz	1.5
Dandelion greens	50g/1¾oz	1.8
Escarole	75g/2¾oz	0.1
Fennel	50g/1¾oz	1.5
Hearts of palm	1	0.7
Kale	65g/2¼oz	2.4
Kohlrabi	40g/1½oz	2.3
Leeks	50g/1¾oz	3.4
Mangetout/sugar snap peas in the pod	50g/1¾oz	3.4
Mushrooms, button	25g/1oz	2.3
Mushrooms, shiitake	25g/1oz	4.4
Mustard greens	70g/2½oz	0.1
Okra	80g/2¾oz	2.4
Onion	50g/1¾oz	4.3
Pak choi	85g/3oz	0.2
Peppers, chopped	55g/2oz	1.9
Pumpkin	50g/1¾oz	2.4
Rhubarb, unsweetened	120g/4¼oz	1.7
Sauerkraut	70g/2½oz	1.2
Shallots	2 tablespoons	3.1
Spring onions	40g/1½oz	2.4
Sorrel	85g/3oz	0.2
Spaghetti squash	40g/1½oz	2.0
Spinach	90g/3¼oz	2.2
Summer squash	120g/4¼oz	2.6
Tomatillo	60g/2oz	2.6
Tomato	60g/2oz	4.3
Turnips, white, mashed	115g/4oz	3.3
Water chestnuts, tinned	55g/2oz	3.5

SALAD DRESSINGS

- Any salad dressing with no more than 2 grams of Net Carbs per 2-tablespoon serving is acceptable.
- Do *not* use sugar, honey, maple syrup or other caloric sweeteners in salad dressings.

FATS AND OILS

- Butter, rapeseed oil, coconut oil, flaxseed oil, grapeseed oil, olive oil, high-oleic safflower oil, sesame oil and walnut oil are acceptable.
- Oils labelled 'cold pressed' or 'expeller pressed' are preferable.
- Mayonnaise should be made with olive, rapeseed or high-oleic safflower oil.
- Use extra-virgin olive oil for dressing salads and vegetables and sautéing.
- Use olive, rapeseed or high-oleic safflower oil for other cooking.
- Use walnut, sesame or other speciality oils to season a dish after removing it from the heat.
- Avoid products labelled 'lite' or 'low fat' and all margarines and shortening products, which contain small amounts of trans fats.
- Avoid corn, soy, sunflower and other vegetable oils.

NON-CALORIC SWEETENERS

- The following are acceptable in moderation: Splenda (sucralose), Truvia or SweetLeaf (stevia), Sweet'N Low (saccharin), xylitol.

BEVERAGES

The following are acceptable:

- Broth/bouillon
- Club soda
- Cream, double or single, or half-and-half (25 to 40 millilitres/1 to 1.5 fluid ounces a day)
- Caffeinated or decaffeinated coffee and tea
- Diet soda sweetened with non-caloric sweeteners
- Lemon juice or lime juice; limit to 2 to 3 tablespoons a day.
- Plain or flavoured sparkling water (must say 'no calories')
- Herb tea (without added barley or fruit sugars)
- Unsweetened, unflavoured soy or almond milk

CONDIMENTS, HERBS AND SPICES

- All herbs, spices and seasonings are acceptable.
- Avoid herb or spice mixtures that contain added sugar.
- Avoid condiments made with added sugar or flour, cornflour, and other carb-filled thickeners.

CONDIMENT, HERB OR SPICE	SERVING SIZE	NET CARBS (Grams)
Ancho chilli pepper	1	5.1
Anchovy paste	1 tablespoon	0.0
Black bean sauce	1 teaspoon	3.0
Capers	1 tablespoon	0.1
Chipotle en adobe	2	2.0
Clam juice	240ml/8fl oz	0.0
Enchilada sauce	60ml/2fl oz	2.0
Fish sauce	1 teaspoon	0.2
Garlic	1 large clove	0.9
Ginger	1 tablespoon grated root	0.8
Horseradish sauce	1 teaspoon	0.4
Jalapeño pepper	45g/1½oz, sliced	1.4
Miso paste	1 tablespoon	2.6
Mustard, Dijon	1 teaspoon	0.5
Mustard, yellow	1 teaspoon	0.0
Olives, black	5	0.7
Olives, green	5	2.5
Pasilla pepper	1	1.7
Pesto sauce	1 tablespoon	0.6
Pickapeppa sauce	1 teaspoon	1.0
Pickle, dill or kosher	½	1.0
Pimento/roasted red pepper	25g/1oz	2.0
Salsa, green (no added sugar)	1 tablespoon	0.6
Salsa, red (no added sugar)	1 tablespoon	1.0
Serrano chilli pepper	50g/1¾oz	1.6
Soy sauce	1 tablespoon	0.9
Tabasco or other hot sauce	1 teaspoon	0.0
Taco sauce	1 tablespoon	1.0
Tahini (sesame paste)	2 tablespoons	1.0
Vinegar, balsamic	1 tablespoon	2.3
Vinegar, cider	1 tablespoon	0.9
Vinegar, red wine	1 tablespoon	1.5
Vinegar, rice (unsweetened)	1 tablespoon	0.0
Vinegar, sherry	1 tablespoon	0.9
Vinegar, white wine	1 tablespoon	1.5
Wasabi paste	1 teaspoon	0.0

ATKINS 20 LEVEL 2 ACCEPTABLE FOODS

In addition to the Acceptable Foods for Level 1, the following foods are acceptable in Level 2.

NUTS AND SEEDS

- Most nuts and seeds and butters made from them are acceptable.
- Consume no more than 60 grams/ 2 ounces per day.
- Nut meals and flours broaden your cooking options.
- Avoid honey-roasted and smoked products.
- Chestnuts are very starchy and high in carbs, making them unsuitable for this phase.
- Avoid products such as Nutella that include sugar or other sweeteners.

The following listing provides portions equivalent to 28 grams/1 ounce.

NUT OR SEED	SERVING SIZE	NET CARBS (Grams)
Almonds	24	2.3
Almond butter	1 tablespoon	2.5
Almond meal/flour	30g/1oz	3.0
Brazil nuts	5	2.0
Cashew butter	1 tablespoon	4.1
Cashew nuts	9	4.4
Coconut, desiccated, unsweetened	20g/¾oz	1.3
Cashew butter	1 tablespoon	4.1
Hazelnuts	12	0.5
Macadamias	6	2.0
Macadamia butter	1 tablespoon	2.5
Peanuts	22	1.5
Peanut butter, crunchy	1 tablespoon	2.4
Peanut butter, smooth	1 tablespoon	2.2
Pecans	10 halves	1.5
Pine nuts	2 tablespoons	1.7
Pistachios	25	2.5
Pumpkin seeds, hulled	2 tablespoons	2.0
Sesame seeds	2 tablespoons	1.6
Soy 'nuts'	2 tablespoons	2.7
Soy 'nut' butter	1 tablespoon	3.0
Sunflower seeds, hulled	2 tablespoons	1.1
Sunflower seed butter	1 tablespoon	0.5
Tahini (sesame paste)	1 tablespoon	0.8
Walnuts	7 halves	1.5

BERRIES AND OTHER FRUITS

- All berries are acceptable, as are melon (but not watermelon) and cherries.
- All fruits should be regarded as garnishes, not major components of a dish.
- Also acceptable are small (1-tablespoon) portions of preserves made without added sugar. Each tablespoon should provide no more than 2 grams of Net Carbs.

FRUIT	SERVING SIZE	NET CARBS (Grams)
Blackberries	30g/1oz	2.7
Blueberries	35g/1¼oz	4.1
Boysenberries	35g/1¼oz	2.7
Cherries, sour	30g/1oz	2.8
Cherries, sweet	30g/1oz	4.2
Cranberries, raw	25g/1oz	2.0
Gooseberries, raw	75g/2¾oz	4.4
Loganberries, raw	40g/1½oz	2.7
Melon, cantaloupe balls	45g/1½oz	3.7
Melon, honeydew balls	45g/1½oz	3.6
Raspberries	30g/1oz	1.5
Strawberries, sliced	35g/1¼oz	1.8
Strawberry, whole	1 large	1.0

FRESH CHEESE AND OTHER DAIRY PRODUCTS

- You can now reintroduce the remaining fresh cheeses.
- Use only plain, unsweetened, whole milk yogurt or Greek yogurt.
- Avoid processed yogurt made with fruit or other flavourings or with any added sugar.
- Avoid low-fat and no-fat cottage cheese and yogurt products.

CHEESE OR DAIRY PRODUCT	SERVING SIZE	NET CARBS (Grams)
Cottage cheese	115g/4oz	4.1
Cottage cheese, creamed	115g/4oz	2.8
Milk, whole, evaporated	2 tablespoons	3.0
Ricotta, whole milk	120g/4¼oz	3.8
Yogurt, low carb	115g/4oz	3.0
Yogurt, plain, unsweetened, whole	115g/4oz	5.5
Yogurt, Greek, plain, unsweetened whole	115g/4oz	3.5

LEGUMES

- Use small portions and regard legumes as a garnish.

- Avoid baked beans, which are full of sugar, and other products such as beans in tomato sauce with sugar or starches and bean dips.

- Black soybeans are far lower in carbs than black (or turtle) beans with no trade-off in taste.

LEGUME	SERVING SIZE	NET CARBS (Grams)
Black-eyed peas	40g/1½oz	6.2
Black/turtle beans	40g/1½oz	6.5
Broad beans	35g/1¼oz	6.0
Butter beans	50g/1¾oz	6.5
Cannellini beans	40g/1½oz	8.5
Chickpeas/garbanzo beans	40g/1½oz	6.5
Haricot beans	50g/1¾oz	9.1
Hummus	2 tablespoons	4.6
Kidney beans	40g/1½oz	5.8
Lentils	50g/1¾oz	6.0
Peas, split	50g/1¾oz	6.3
Pigeon peas	50g/1¾oz	7.0
Pinto beans	40g/1½oz	7.3
Refried beans, tinned	55g/2oz	6.5
Soybeans, green edamame	35g/1¼oz	3.1

Note: *Serving sizes for dried legumes are after cooking. Serving sizes for fresh legumes are for shelled beans.*

VEGETABLE AND FRUIT JUICES

- Most fruit juices are completely off limits.

- In Level 2, you can double the amount of lemon and lime juice.

- You can now also introduce small portions of tomato juice or tomato juice cocktail.

JUICES	SERVING SIZE	NET CARBS (Grams)
Lemon juice	60ml/2fl oz	5.2
Lime juice	60ml/2fl oz	5.6
Tomato juice	120ml/4fl oz	4.2
Tomato juice cocktail	120ml/4fl oz	4.5

LOW-CARB PRODUCTS SUITABLE FOR LEVEL 2

- In each case, we've provided the *maximum* acceptable carb count for a single serving. If the carb count of a specific product exceeds the amount listed below, pass it up.

LOW-CARB PRODUCT	SERVING SIZE	NET CARBS (Grams)
Low-carb bagels	1	5.0
Atkins All Purpose Bake Mix	75g/2¾oz	5.0
Low-carb bread	1 slice	6.0
Low-carb chocolate/candy	65g/2¼oz	3.0
Low-carb dairy drink	240ml/8fl oz	4.0
Low-carb pancake mix	2 pancakes	6.0
Low-carb pita	One 15-cm/6-in	4.0
Low-carb roll	1	4.0
Low-carb soy chips	25g/1oz	5.0
Low-carb tortillas	One 18-cm/7-inch	4.0
No-added-sugar ice cream	70g/2½oz	4.0

APPENDIX C

ATKINS 20 LEVELS 3 & 4 ACCEPTABLE FOODS

In addition to the foods you can eat in Levels 1 and 2, the
following foods are acceptable in Levels 3 and 4.

FRUITS OTHER THAN BERRIES

- All fruit is high in sugar and should be treated as a garnish.
- Avoid tinned fruit, even packed in juice concentrate or 'light' syrup.
- Continue to avoid fruit juice, other than lemon and lime juice.
- Avoid dried fruit.

The following carb counts are for fresh fruit:

FRUIT	SERVING SIZE	NET CARBS (Grams)
Apple	½ medium	8.7
Apricot	3 medium	9.2
Banana	1 small	21.2
Carambola (star fruit)	55g/2oz sliced	2.8
Cherimoya	80g/2¾oz	24.3
Figs, fresh	1 small	6.4
Grapes, green	80g/2¾oz	13.7
Grapes, purple Concord	80g/2¾oz	7.4
Grapes, red	80g/2¾oz	13.4
Grapefruit, red	½	7.9
Grapefruit, white	½	8.6
Guava	80g/2¾oz	5.3
Kiwi	1	8.7
Kumquat	4	7.5
Loquat	10	14.2
Lychee	95g/3½oz	14.5
Mango	85g/3oz	12.5
Orange	1 medium	12.9
Orange sections	90g/3¼oz	8.4
Nectarine	1 medium	13.8
Papaya	½ small	6.1
Passion fruit	60g/2oz	7.7
Peach	1 small	7.2
Pear, Bartlett	1 medium	21.1
Pear, Bosc	1 small	17.7
Persimmon	½	12.6
Pineapple	85g/3oz	8.7
Plantain	75g/2¾oz	21
Plum	1 small	3.3
Pomegranate	¼	6.4
Quince	1	12.3
Tangerine	1	6.2
Watermelon	75g/2¾oz balls	5.1

STARCHY VEGETABLES

All vegetables are measured after cooking, except for Jerusalem artichoke.

VEGETABLES	SERVING SIZE	NET CARBS (Grams)
Beetroot	85g/3oz	6.8
Burdock	60g/2oz	12.1
Carrot	1 medium	5.6
Cassava (yuca), mashed	100g/3½oz	25.1
Corn on the cob	1 ear	17.2
Jerusalem artichoke	75g/2¾oz	11.9
Parsnips, cooked	80g/2¾oz	10.5
Potato, baked	½	10.5
Squash, acorn, baked	100g/3½oz	7.8
Squash, butternut, baked	100g/3½oz	7.9
Swede	85g/3oz	5.9
Sweetcorn	80g/2¾oz	12.6
Sweet potato, baked	½	12.1
Taro	65g/2¼oz	19.5
Yam, sliced	65g/2¼oz	16.1

WHOLE GRAINS

- Note that these are *whole* grains, not simply grains.
- Avoid refined grains, such as white flour, 'enriched flour', and white rice.
- Baked goods should be made with 100 percent whole grains.
- All measurements are for cooked grains, except for cornmeal, oat bran, rolled oatmeal, and steel cut oatmeal.

WHOLE GRAIN	SERVING SIZE	NET CARBS (Grams)
Barley, hulled	90g/3¼oz	13.0
Barley, pearled	80g/2¾oz	19.0
Bulgur wheat	70g/2½oz	12.8
Cornmeal	2 tablespoons	10.6
Couscous, whole wheat	70g/2½oz	17.1
Cracked wheat	80g/2¾oz	15.0
Hominy	80g/2¾oz	9.7
Kasha (buckwheat groats)	90g/3¼oz	14.0
Millet	90g/3¼oz	19.5
Oat bran	2 tablespoons	6.0
Oatmeal, rolled	30g/1oz	19.0
Oatmeal, steel cut	40g/1½oz	19.0
Quinoa	30g/1oz	27.0
Rice, brown	60g/2oz	20.5
Rice, wild	90g/3¼oz	16.0
Wheat berries	85g/3oz	14.0

DAIRY PRODUCTS

- You can also add small portions of whole milk (120ml/4fl oz contain almost 6 grams of Net Carbs) or buttermilk.
- Avoid skim, nonfat, and low-fat milk.

APPENDIX D
ATKINS 40 & ATKINS 100 ACCEPTABLE FOODS

On Atkins 40 and Atkins 100, you can eat all the foods
shown previously for Atkins 20, Levels 1 through 4, in addition to the
following foods, which are listed with serving sizes that
correspond to either 5 or 10 grams of Net Carbs, so that you can easily
keep track. An asterisk indicates a rounded Net Carbs value.

NUTS AND SEEDS AND THEIR BUTTERS

NUTS OR SEEDS	SERVING SIZE	NET CARBS (Grams)
Almonds	70g/2½oz	5*
Almond butter	60g/2oz	5*
Brazil nuts	100g/3½oz	5*
Cashews	2 tablespoons	5*
Cashew butter	1 tablespoon	5*
Coconut, unsweetened	400g/14oz	5*
Hazelnuts	60g/2oz	5*
Macadamia nuts	65g/2¼oz	5*
Peanuts	3 tablespoons	5*
Peanut butter	3 tablespoons	5*
Pecans	120g/4¼oz	5*
Pine nuts	60g/2oz	5*
Pistachios	3 tablespoons	5*
Pumpkin seeds	70g/2½oz	5*
Sesame seeds	35g/1¼oz	5*
Soy nuts	3 tablespoons	5*
Sunflower seeds	70g/2½oz	5*
Walnuts	90g/3¼oz	5*

CHEESE AND OTHER DAIRY PRODUCTS

CHEESE & OTHER DAIRY	SERVING SIZE	NET CARBS (Grams)
Almond milk (unsweetened, plain)	240ml/8fl oz	1
Blue cheese	2 tablespoons	.4
Brie	25g/1oz	.1
Buttermilk	240ml/8fl oz	5*
Cheddar	25g/1oz	.4
Coconut milk (unsweetened, plain)	240ml/8fl oz	1
Colby cheese	25g/1oz	.7
Cottage cheese	120g/4¼oz	5*
Cream, double (liquid)	180ml/6fl oz	5*
Cream, soured	180ml/6fl oz	5*
Cream cheese (full fat, plain)	5 tablespoons	5*
Feta	25g/1oz	1.2
Goats' cheese (chèvre)	25g/1oz	.3
Gouda	25g/1oz	.6
Half-and-half	240ml/8fl oz	5*
Havarti	25g/1oz	0
Jarlsberg	25g/1oz	1.2
Laughing Cow	1 wedge	1
Milk, whole	120ml/4fl oz	5*
Mozzarella (whole milk)	25g/1oz	.6
Parmesan, chunk	25g/1oz	.9
Parmesan, grated	1 tablespoon	.2
Ricotta (whole milk)	60g/2oz	2
Romano (chunk)	25g/1oz	1
Soy milk (unsweetened, plain)	240ml/8fl oz	2
String cheese (whole milk)	25g/1oz	1
Swiss cheese	25g/1oz	1.5
Yogurt, Greek, plain, unsweetened whole milk	120ml/4fl oz	5*

LEGUMES

LEGUME	SERVING SIZE	NET CARBS (Grams)
Black beans	3 tablespoons/80g (2¾oz)	5/10*
Black-eyed peas	3 tablespoons/80g (2¾oz)	5/10*
Butter beans	3 tablespoons/125g (4½oz)	5/10*
Cannellini	3 tablespoons/80g (2¾oz)	5/10*
Chickpeas	2 tablespoons/40g (1½oz)	5/10*
Edamame	2 tablespoons/35g (1¼oz)	5/10*
Haricot beans	2 tablespoons/40g (1½oz)	5/10*
Hummus, plain	5 tablespoons/160g (5¾oz)	5/10*
Kidney beans	3 tablespoons/80g (2¾oz)	5/10*
Peas, split	3 tablespoons/100g (3½oz)	5/10*
Pinto beans	3 tablespoons/120g (4¼oz)	5/10*
Soybeans, white	55g (2oz)/110g (4oz)	5/10*

FRUIT

FRUIT	SERVING SIZE	NET CARBS (Grams)
Apple	⅓/⅔	5/10*
Apricot	½/⅓	5/10*
Blackberries	90g (3¼oz)/165g (5¾oz)	5/10*
Banana (small)	¼/½	5/10*
Blueberries	35g (1¼oz)/70g (2½oz)	5/10*
Boysenberries	105g (3¾oz)/210g (7¼oz)	5/10*
Cantaloupe	85g (3oz)/175g (6¼oz)	5/10*
Clementine	130g (4½oz)/260g (9¼oz)	5/10*
Cranberries	65g (2¼oz)/130g (4½oz)	5/10*
Cherries	3 tablespoons/6 tablespoons	5/10*
Coconut	80g (2¾oz)/160g (5¾oz)	5/10*
Dates	½/1	5/10*
Figs	¾/1½	5/10*
Gooseberries	50g (1¾oz)/100g (3½oz)	5/10*
Grapefruit	¼/½	5/10*
Grapes	3 tablespoons/6 tablespoons	5/10*
Guava	55g (2oz)/110g (4oz)	5/10*
Honeydew melon	55g (2oz)/110g (4oz)	5/10*
Kiwi	⅔/1⅓	5/10*
Lemon juice	5 tablespoons/10 tablespoons	5/10*
Lime juice	4½ tablespoons/9 tablespoons	5/10*
Mango	40g (1½oz)/80g (2¾oz)	5/10*
Orange	½/1	5/10*
Peach	½/1	5/10*
Pear	¼/½	5/10*
Pineapple	35g (1¼oz)/70g (2½oz)	5/10*
Plum	¾/1½	5/10*
Raisins	¾ tablespoon/1½ tablespoons	5/10*
Raspberries	90g (3¼oz)/165g (5¾oz)	5/10*
Rhubarb	180g (6½oz)/365g (13oz)	5/10*
Strawberries	60g (2oz)/120g (4¼oz)	5/10*
Watermelon	75g (2¾oz)/150g (5¼oz)	5/10*

STARCHY VEGETABLES

STARCHY VEGETABLE	SERVING SIZE	NET CARBS (Grams)
Acorn squash	50g (1¾oz)/100g (3½oz)	5/10*
Beetroot	45g (1½oz)/85g (3oz)	5/10*
Butternut squash	65g (2¼oz)/135g (4¾oz)	5/10*
Carrots, sliced	70g (2½oz)/140g (5oz)	5/10*
Parsnips	40g (1½oz)/75g (2¾oz)	5/10*
Peas	40g (1½oz)/80g (2¾oz)	5/10*
Potato, baked, small	¼/½	5/10*
Swede	120g (4¼oz)/240g (8½oz)	5/10*
Sweetcorn	40g (1½oz)/80g (2¾oz)	5/10*
Sweet potato, baked, medium	¼/½	5/10*

WHOLE GRAINS

GRAIN	SERVING SIZE	NET CARBS (Grams)
Barley, cooked	2 tablespoons/50g (1¾oz)	5/10*
Brown rice, cooked	2 tablespoons/30g (1oz)	5/10*
Coconut flour	2½ tablespoons/35g (1¼oz)	5/10*
Couscous, cooked	2½ tablespoons/60g (2oz)	5/10*
Grits, cooked	2½ tablespoons/45g (1½oz)	5/10*
Millet, cooked	2 tablespoons/45g (1½oz)	5/10*
Oat bran, raw	2 tablespoons/4 tablespoons	5/10*
Oatmeal, steel cut, dry	2 tablespoons/40g (1½oz)	5/10*
Polenta, dry	1 tablespoon/2 tablespoons	5/10*
Quinoa, cooked	2½ tablespoons/40g (1½oz)	5/10*
Wheat bran, raw	6 tablespoons/45g (1½oz)	5/10*
Wheat germ	2 tablespoons/20g (¾oz)	5/10*
Whole wheat bread	½ slice/1 slice	5/10*
Whole wheat pasta, cooked	2½ tablespoons/35g (1¼oz)	5/10*

ALCOHOLIC BEVERAGES

BEVERAGE	SERVING SIZE	NET CARBS (Grams)
Beer, light	360ml/12fl oz	5.6
Beer, low carb	360ml/12fl oz	2.5
Bourbon	25ml/1fl oz	0
Champagne	25ml/1fl oz	2–3
Rum	25ml/1fl oz	0
Scotch	25ml/1fl oz	0
Vodka	25ml/1fl oz	0
Wine, red	100ml/3½fl oz	2.6
Wine, white	100ml/3½fl oz	2

APPENDIX E
PRODUCTS FOR YOUR LOW-CARB LIFESTYLE

You can find a variety of delicious low-carb products,
and the selections and quality continue to expand, which
makes snacking or meal times that much easier.

GENERAL

CARBLIFE
Stocks a huge range of low-carb
products, including Atkins products,
bakery goods, syrups, sweet treats
and even cocktail mixes
www.carblife.co.uk

HOLLAND AND BARRETT
A large range of health products,
including natural sugar substitutes such
as xylitol, stevia and coconut sugar
www.hollandandbarrett.com

BREADS, TORTILLAS, NOODLES, AND PASTA

HOVIS
Now do a low-carb range of breads
made with plenty of seeds
www.hovis.co.uk

HI-LO BREAD
Low-carb bread, stocked at a range of
supermarkets
www.hi-lo-bread.co.uk

CARBZONE
Low-carb tortillas and wraps, breads,
pasta and snack bars
www.carbzone.co.uk

ZERO NOODLES
Almost zero-calorie and no-carb
noodles and rice made from the natural
soluable fibre of the konjac plant
www.zeronoodles.com

SNACKS

JULIAN BAKERY
Low-carb crackers in salt-and-pepper
and organic Parmesan flavours.
Available online in the UK
www.julianbakery.com

THE FOOD DOCTOR
A range of low-carb snacks, such as
roasted soy beans and seed and protein
mixes. Check individual products for
net carbs
www.thefooddoctor.com/

GRAZE
Portioned punnets of snacks, delivered
to your door or desk. Protein, kale and
nut mixes are all good choices, but
check individual products for details
as some of the sweeter choices may
not be suitable
www.graze.com

UNEARTHED
Produce biltong, a meat snack which
is cured without sugar, as well as a
range of delicious antipasti that are
naturally low in carbs, such as olives
and chargrilled artichokes
www.foodsunearthed.co.uk

ITSU
For their bags of crispy seaweed
snacks, which are low in carbs. Available
in supermarkets as well as in their
restaurants
www.itsu.com

MEALS AND SNACKS

ATKINS NUTRITIONALS, INC.
Low-carb nutrition bars and shakes,
treats, snacks, and frozen meals
https://uk.atkins.com

THE NATURAL LOW-CARB STORE
Stock a range of low-carb snacks and
treats, such as fruit and nut bars and
pork crackling, as well as pre-prepared
low-carb meals for home delivery
www.natural-low-carb-store.co.uk

ICE CREAM

OPPO
A new range of healthy ice cream in
indulgent flavours, sweetened with
natural sweeteners and superfoods
such as lucuma
www.oppoicecream.co.uk

PERFECT WORLD
Low-calorie, low-sugar, dairy-free ice
cream in a variety of delicious flavours
www.perfectworldicecream.co.uk

BEVERAGES

TORANI
Sugar-free flavoured syrups
Available online in the UK
www.torani.com

STUR
Natural water flavourings sweetened
with stevia leaf and suitable for
diabetics and low-carb diets
www.sturdrinks.eu

APPENDIX F
SCIENTIFIC STUDIES SUPPORTING
ATKINS 20, 40 & 100

ATKINS 20

Austin, G. L., Dalton, C. B., Hu, Y., Morris, C. B., Hankins, J., Weinland, S. R., et al. (2009). A very-low-carbohydrate diet improves symptoms and quality of life in diarrhea-predominant irritable bowel syndrome. *Clinical Gastroenterology and Hepatology* 7(6). doi:10.1016/j.cgh.2009.02.023.

Bailes, J. R., Strow, M. T., Werthammer, J., McGinnis, R. A., & Elitsur, Y. (2003). Effect of low-carbohydrate, unlimited calorie diet on the treatment of childhood obesity: a prospective controlled study. *Metabolic Syndrome and Related Disorders* 1(3): 221–225. doi:10.1089/154041903322716697.

Ben-Avraham, S., Harman-Boehm, I., Schwarzfuchs, D., & Shai, I. (2009). Dietary strategies for patients with type 2 diabetes in the era of multi-approaches; review and results from the Dietary Intervention Randomized Controlled Trial (DIRECT). *Diabetes Research and Clinical Practice* 86. doi:10.1016/s0168-8227(09)70008-7.

Boden, G., Sargrad, K., Homko, C., Mozzoli, M., & Stein, T. P. (2005). Effect of a low-carbohydrate diet on appetite, blood glucose levels, and insulin resistance in obese patients with type 2 diabetes. *Annals of Internal Medicine* 142(6): 403. doi:10.7326/0003-4819-142-6-200503150-00006.

Brinkworth, G. D., Noakes, M., Buckley, J. D., Keogh, J. B., & Clifton, P. M. (2009). Long-term effects of a very-low-carbohydrate weight loss diet compared with an isocaloric low-fat diet after 12 mo. *American Journal of Clinical Nutrition* 90(1): 23–32. doi:10.3945/ajcn.2008.27326.

Coleman, M. D., & Nickols-Richardson, S. M. (2005). Urinary ketones reflect serum ketone concentration but do not relate to weight loss in overweight premenopausal women following a low-carbohydrate/high-protein diet. *Journal of the American Dietetic Association* 105(4), 608–611. doi:10.1016/j.jada.2005.01.004.

Davis, N. J., Tomuta, N., Schechter, C., Isasi, C. R., Segal-Isaacson, C. J., Stein, D., et al. (2009). Comparative study of the effects of a 1-year dietary intervention of a low-carbohydrate diet versus a low-fat diet on weight and glycemic control in type 2 diabetes. *Diabetes Care* 32(7): 1147–1152. doi:10.2337/dc08-2108.

DiLorenzo, C., Curra, A., Sirianni, G., Coppola, G., Bracaglia, M., Cardillo, A., et al. (2013). Diet transiently improves migraine in two twin sisters: possible role of ketogenesis? *Functional Neurology* 28(4): 305–308. doi:10.11138/FNeur/2013.28.4.305.

Fine, E. J., Segal-Isaacson, C., Feinman, R. D., Herszkopf, S., Romano, M. C., Tomuta, N., et al. (2012). Targeting insulin inhibition as a metabolic therapy in advanced cancer: a pilot safety and feasibility dietary trial in 10 patients. *Nutrition* 28(10): 1028–1035. doi:10.1016/j.nut.2012.05.001.

Foster, G. D. (2010). Weight and metabolic outsomes after 2 years on a low-carbohydrate versus low-fat diet. *Annals of Internal Medicine* 153(3): 147. doi:10.7326/0003-4819-153-3-201008030-00005.

Foster, G., Wyatt, H., Hill, J., McGuckin, B., Brill, C., Mohammed, B., et al. (2003). A randomized trial of a low-carbohydrate diet for obesity. *New England Journal of Medicine* 348(21): 2082–2090. https://www.ncbi.nlm.nih.gov/pubmed/12761365.

Friedman, A., Ogden, L., Foster, G., Klein, S., Stein, R., Miller, B., et al. (2012). Comparative effects of low-carbohydrate high-protein versus low-fat diets on the kidney. *Clinical Journal of the American Society of Nephrology* 7(7): 1103–1111. doi:10.2215/CJN.11741111.

Gann, D. (2004). A low-carbohydrate diet in overweight patients undergoing stable statin therapy raises high-density lipoprotein and lowers triglycerides substantially. *Clinical Cardiology* 27(10): 563–564. doi:10.1002/clc.4960271008.

Gardner, C. D., Kiazand, A., Alhassan, S., Kim, S., Stafford, R. S., Balise, R. R., .et al. (2007). Comparison of the Atkins, Zone, Ornish, and LEARN diets for change in weight and related risk factors among overweight premenopausal women. *Journal of the Americasn Medical Association* 297(9): 969. doi:10.1001/jama.297.9.969.

Hickey, J. T., Hickey, L., Yancy, W. S., Hepburn, J., & Westman, E. C. (2003). Clinical use of a carbohydrate-restricted diet to treat the dyslipidemia of the metabolic syndrome. *Metabolic Syndrome and Related Disorders* 1(3): 227–232. doi:10.1089/154041903322716705.

Hussain, T. A., Mathew, T. C., Dashti, A. A., Asfar, S., Al-Zaid, N., & Dashti, H. M. (2012). Effect of low-calorie versus low-carbohydrate ketogenic diet in type 2 diabetes. *Nutrition* 28(10): 1016–1021. doi:10.1016/j.nut.2012.01.016.

Krebs, N. F., Gao, D., Gralla, J., Collins, J. S., & Johnson, S. L. (2010). Efficacy and safety of a high protein, low carbohydrate diet for weight loss in severely obese adolescents. *Journal of Pediatrics* 157(2): 252–258. doi:10.1016/j.jpeds.2010.02.010.

Martin, C. K., Rosenbaum, D., Han, H., Geiselman, P. J., Wyatt, H. R., Hill, J. O., et al. (2011). Change in food cravings, food preferences, and appetite during a low-carbohydrate and low-fat diet. *Obesity* 19(10): 1963–1970. doi:10.1038/oby.2011.62.

Mavropoulos, J., Yancy, W., Hepburn, J., & Westman, E. (2005). The effects of a low-carbohydrate, ketogenic diet on the polycystic ovary syndrome: a pilot study. *Nutrition and Metabolism* 2(35). https://www.ncbi.nlm.nih.gov/pubmed/16359551.

McAuley, K. A., Hopkins, C. M., Smith, K. J., Mclay, R. T., Williams, S. M., Taylor, R. W., & Mann, J. I. (2004). Comparison of high-fat and high-protein diets with a high-carbohydrate diet in insulin-resistant obese women. *Diabetologia* 48(1): 8–16. doi:10.1007/s00125-004-1603-4.

Morgan, L., Griffin, B., Millward, D., Delooy, A., Fox, K., Baic, S., et al. (2008). Comparison of the effects of four commercially available weight-loss programmes on lipid-based cardiovascular risk factors. *Public Health Nutrition* 12(6): 799. doi:10.1017/s1368980008003236.

Paoli, A., Grimaldi, K., D'Agostino, D., Cenci, L., Moro, T., Bianco, A., & Palma, A. (2012). Ketogenic diet does not affect strength performance in elite artistic gymnasts. *Journal of the International Society of Sports Nutrition* 9(1): 34. doi:10.1186/1550-2783-9-34.

Phinney, S., Bistrian, B., Wolfe, R., & Blackburn, G. (1983). The human metabolic response to chronic ketosis without caloric restriction: physical and biochemical adaptation. *Metabolism* 32(8): 757–768. doi:10.1016/0026-0495(83)90105-1.

Seshadri, P., Iqbal, N., & Stern, L. (2005). A randomized study comparing the effects of a low-carbohydrate diet and a conventional diet on lipoprotein subfractions and C-reactive protein levels in patients with severe obesity. *ACC Current Journal Review* 14(1): 19. doi:10.1016/j.accreview.2004.12.027.

Sharman, M., & Volek, J. (2004). Weight loss leads to reductions in inflammatory biomarkers after a very-low-carbohydrate diet and a low-fat diet in overweight men. *Clinical Science* 107(4): 365–369. doi:10.1042/cs20040111.

Tay, J., Brinkworth, G. D., Noakes, M., Keogh, J., & Clifton, P. M. (2008). Metabolic effects of weight loss on a very-low-carbohydrate diet compared with an isocaloric high-carbohydrate diet in abdominally obese subjects. *Journal of the American College of Cardiology* 51(1): 59–67. doi:10.1016/j.jacc.2007.08.050.

Thomson, C. A., Stopeck, A. T., Bea, J. W., Cussler, E., Nardi, E., Frey, G., & Thompson, P. A. (2010). Changes in body weight and metabolic indexes in overweight breast cancer survivors enrolled in a randomized trial of low-fat vs. reduced carbohydrate diets. *Nutrition and Cancer* 62(8): 1142–1152. doi:10.1080/01635581.2010.513803.

Vernon, M. C., Kueser, B., Transue, M., Yates, H. E., Yancy, W. S., & Westman, E. C. (2004). Clinical experience of a carbohydrate-restricted diet for the metabolic syndrome. *Metabolic Syndrome and Related Disorders* 2(3): 180–186. doi:10.1089/met.2004.2.180.

Vernon, M. C., Mavropoulos, J., Transue, M., Yancy, W. S., & Westman, E. C. (2003). Clinical experience of a carbohydrate-restricted diet: effect on diabetes mellitus. *Metabolic Syndrome and Related Disorders* 1(3): 233–237. doi:10.1089/154041903322716714.

Westman, E. C., Yancy, W. S., Mavropoulos, J. C., Marquart, M., & McDuffie, J. R. (2008). The effect of a low-carbohydrate, ketogenic diet versus a low-glycemic index diet on glycemic control in type 2 diabetes mellitus. *Nutrition & Metabolism* 5(1): 36. doi:10.1186/1743-7075-5-36.

Westman, E. C., Yancy, W. S., Edman, J. S., Tomlin, K. F., & Perkins, C. E. (2002). Effect of 6-month adherence to a very low carbohydrate diet program. *American Journal of Medicine* 113(1): 30–36. doi:10.1016/s0002-9343(02)01129-4.

Yancy, W. S., Westman, E. C., McDuffie, J. R., Grambow, S. C., Jeffreys, A. S., Bolton, J., et al. (2010). A randomized trial of a low-carbohydrate diet vs Orlistat plus a low-fat diet for weight loss. *Archives of Internal Medicine* 170(2), 136. doi:10.1001/archinternmed.2009.492.

Yancy, W. S., Almirall, D., Maciejewski, M. L., Kolotkin, R. L., McDuffie, J. R., & Westman, E. C. (2009). Effects of two weight-loss diets on health-related quality of life. *Quality of Life Research* 18(3): 281–289. doi:10.1007/s11136-009-9444-8.

Yancy, W., Foy, M., Chalecki, A., Vernon, M., & Westman, E. (2005). A low-carbohydrate, ketogenic diet to treat type 2 diabetes. *Nutrition & Metabolism* 2(34). https://www.ncbi.nlm.nih.gov/pubmed/16318637.

Yancy, W. S. (2004). A low-carbohydrate, ketogenic diet versus a low-fat diet to treat obesity and hyperlipidemia. *Annals of Internal Medicine* 140(10): 769. doi:10.7326/0003-4819-140-10-200405180-00006.

Yancy, W. S., Vernon, M. C., & Westman, E. C. (2003). A pilot trial of a low-carbohydrate, ketogenic diet in patients with type 2 diabetes. *Metabolic Syndrome and Related Disorders* 1(3):, 239–243. doi:10.1089/154041903322716723.

Yancy, W., Provenzale, D., & Westman, E. (2001). Improvement of gastroesophageal reflux disease after initiation of a low-carbohydrate diet: five brief case reports. *Alternative Therapies in Health and Medicine* 7(6): 116–119. https://www.ncbi.nlm.nih.gov/pubmed/11712463.

ATKINS 40

Ballard, K., et al. (2013). Dietary carbohydrate restriction improves insulin sensitivity, blood pressure, microvascular function, and cellular adhesion markers in individuals taking statins. *Nutrition Research* 33(11): 905–912. doi: 10.1016/j.nutres.2013.07.022.

Bazzano, L. A., et al. (2014). Effects of low-carbohydrate and low-fat diets: a randomized trial. *Annals of Internal Medicine* 161(5): 309–318. doi:10.7326/M14-0180.

Brehm, B. J., et al. (2003). A randomized trial comparing a very low carbohydrate diet and a calorie-restricted low fat diet on body weight and cardiovascular risk factors in healthy women. *Journal of Clinical Endocrinology and Metabolism* 88(4): 1617–1623. doi:10.1210/jc.2002-021480.

Brehm, B. J., et al. (2005). The role of energy expenditure in the differential weight loss in obese women on low-fat and low-carbohydrate diets. *Journal of Clinical Endocrinology and Metabolism* 90(3): 1475–1482. doi:10.1210/jc.2004-1540.

Dashti, H. M., et al. (2004). Long-term effects of a ketogenic diet in obese patients. *Experimental & Clinical Cardiology* 9(3): 200–205. https://www.ncbi.nlm.nih.gov/pubmed/19641727.

Dashti, H. M., et al. (2003). Ketogenic diet modifies the risk factors of heart disease in obese patients. *Nutrition* 19(10): 901–902. https://www.ncbi.nlm.nih.gov/pubmed/14559328.

Ebbeling, C. B., et al. (2012). Effects of dietary composition on energy expenditure during weight-loss maintenance. *Journal of the American Medical Association* 307(24): 2627–2634. doi:10.1001/jama.2012.6607.

Forsythe, C. E., et al. (2008). Comparison of low fat and low carbohydrate diets on circulating fatty acid composition and markers of inflammation. *Lipids* 43(1): 65–77. doi:10.1007/s11745-007-3132-7.

Forsythe, C. E., et al. (2010). Limited effect of dietary saturated fat on plasma saturated fat in the context of a low carbohydrate diet. *Lipids* 45(10): 947–962. doi:10.1007/s11745-010-3467-3.

Iqbal, N., et al. (2010). Effects of a low-intensity intervention that prescribed a low-carbohydrate vs. a low-fat diet in obese, diabetic participants. *Obesity* (Silver Spring) 18(9): 1733–1738. doi:10.1038/oby.2009.460.

Nickols-Richardson, S. M., et al. (2005). Perceived hunger is lower and weight loss is greater in overweight premenopausal women consuming a low-carbohydrate/high-protein vs high-carbohydrate/low-fat diet. *Journal of the American Dietary Association* 105(9): 1433–1437. http://dx.doi.org/10.1016/j.jada.2005.06.025.

O'Brien, K. D., et al. (2005). Diet-induced weight loss is associated with decreases in plasma serum amyloid and C-reactive protein independent of dietary macronutrient composition in obese subjects. *Journal of Clinical Endocrinology & Metabolism* 90(4): 2244–2249. doi:10.1210/jc.2004-1011.

Paoli, A., et al. (2013). Long term successful weight loss with a combination biphasic ketogenic Mediterranean diet and Mediterranean diet maintenance protocol. *Nutrients* 5(12): 5205–5217. doi:10.3390/nu5125205.

Ruth, M. R., et al. (2013). Consuming a hypocaloric high fat low carbohydrate diet for 12 weeks lowers C-reactive protein, and raises serum adiponectin and high density lipoprotein-cholesterol in obese subjects. *Metabolism* 62(12): 1779–1787. doi:10.1016/j.metabol.2013.07.006.

Saslow, L. R., et al. (2014). A randomized pilot trial of a moderate carbohydrate diet compared to a very low carbohydrate diet in overweight or obese individuals with type 2 diabetes mellitus or prediabetes. *PLOS ONE*. http://dx.doi .org/10.1371/journal.pone.0091027.

Sharman, M. J., et al. (2002). A ketogenic diet favorably affects serum biomarkets for cardiovascular disease in normal-weight men. *Journal of Nutrition* 132(7): 1879–1885. http://jn.nutrition .org/content/132/7/1879.abstract.

Sharman, M. J., et al. (2004). Weight loss leads to reductions in inflammatory biomarkers after a very-low-carbohydrate diet and a low-fat diet in overweight men. *Clinical Science* 107(4): 365–369. doi:10.1042/CS20040111.

Siegel, R. M., et al. (2009). A 6-month, office-based, low-carbohydrate diet intervention in obese teens. *Clinical Pediatrics* 48(7): 745–749. doi:10.1177/0009922809332585.

Sondike, S. B., et al. (2003). Effects of a low-carbohydrate diet on weight loss and cardiovascular risk factor in overweight adolescents. *Jounal of Pediatrics* 142(3): 253–258. doi:10.1067/ mpd.2003.4.

Stern, L., et al. (2004). The effects of low-carbohydrate versus conventional weight loss diets in severely obese adults: one-year follow-up of a randomized trial. *Annals of Internal Medicine* 140(10): 778–785. https://www.ncbi.nlm.nih.gov/ pubmed/15148064.

Tay, J., et al. (2014). A very low carbohydrate, low saturated fat diet for type 2 diabetes management: a randomized trial. *Diabetes Care*. doi:https://doi.org/10.2337/dc14-0845.

Velhorst, M. A., et al. (2010). Presence or absence of carbohydrates and the proportion of fat in a high-protein diet affect appetite suppression but not energy expenditure in normal-weight human subjects fed in energy balance. *British Journal of Nutrition* 104(9), 1395–1405. doi:10.1017/ S0007114510002060.

Volek, J. S., et al. (2000). Fasting lipoprotein and postprandial triacylglycerol responses to a low-carbohydrate diet supplemented with n-3 fatty acids. *Journal of the American College of Nutrition* 19(3): 383–391. https://www.ncbi.nlm.nih. gov/pubmed/10872901.

Volek, J. S., et al. (2002). Body composition and hormonal responses to a carbohydrate-restricted diet. *Metabolism* 51(7): 864–870. https://www.ncbi.nlm.nih.gov/pubmed/12077732.

Volek, J. S., et al. (2004). Comparison of a very low-carbohydrate and low-fat diet on fasting lipids, LDL subclasses, insulin resistance, and postprandial lipemic responses in overweight women. *Journal of the American College of Nutrition* 23(2): 177–184. https://www.ncbi.nlm.nih .gov/pubmed/15047685.

Volek, J. S., et al. (2004). Comparison of energy-restricted very low-carbohydrate and low-fat diets on weight loss and body composition in overweight men and women. *Nutrition & Metabolism* 1(13). doi:10.1186/1743-7075-1-13.

Volek, J. S., et al. (2009). Effects of dietary carbohydrate restriction versus low-fat diet on flow-mediated dilation. *Metabolism* 58(12): 1769–1777. doi:10.1016/j. metabol.2009.06.005.

Walsh, C. O., et al. (2013). Effects of diet composition on postprandial energy availability during weight loss maintenance. *PLOS ONE* 8(3). doi:10.1371/journal.pone.0058172.

ATKINS 100

Accurso, A., Bernstein, R., Dahlqvist, A., Draznin, B., Feinman, R., Fine, E., et al. (2008). Dietary carbohydrate restriction in type 2 diabetes millitus and metabolic syndrome: time for a critical appraisal. *Nutrition & Metabolism* 5(9). doi:10.1186/1743-7075-5-9.

Ajala, O., English, P., & Pinkney, J. (2013). Systematic review and meta-analysis of different dietary approaches to the management of type 2 diabetes. *American Journal of Clinical Nutrition* 97(3): 505–516. doi:10.3945/ajcn.112.042457.

Aude, Y. W., Agatston, A. S., Lopez-Jimenez, F., Lieberman, E. H., Almon, M., Hansen, M., et al. (2004). The National Cholesterol Education Program diet vs a diet lower in carbohydrates and higher in protein and monunsaturated fat. *Archives of Internal Medicine* 164(19): 2141. doi:10.1001/archinte.164.19.2141.

Bueno, N. B., Melo, I. S., Oliveira, S. L., & Ataide, T. D. (2013). Very-low-carbohydrate ketogenic diet v. low-fat diet for long-term weight loss: a meta-analysis of randomised controlled trials. *British Journal of Nutrition* 110(7): 1178–1187. doi:10.1017/ s0007114513000548.

Chiu, S., Bergeron, N., Williams, P., Bray, G., Sutherland, B., & Krauss, R. (2015). Comparison of the DASH (Dietary Approaches to Stop Hypertension) diet and a higher-fat DASH diet on blood pressure and lipids and lipoproteins: a randomized controlled trial. *American Journal of Clinical Nutrition* 103(2): 341–347. doi:10.3945/ajcn.115.123281.

Daly, M. E., Paisey, R., Paisey, R., Millward, B. A., Eccles, C., Williams, K., et al. (2006). Short-term effects of severe dietary carbohydrate-restriction advice in Type 2 diabetes—a randomized controlled trial. *Diabetic Medicine* 23(1): 15–20. doi:10.1111/j.1464-5491.2005.01760.x.

DeSouza, R. J., Mente, A., Maroleanu, A., Cozma, A., Ha, V., Kishibe, T., et al. (2015). Intake of saturated and trans unsaturated fatty acids and risk of all cause mortality, cardiovascular disease, and type 2 diabetes: systematic review and meta-analysis of observational studies. *British Medical Journal.* doi:10.1136/bmj.h3978.

DiNicolantonio, J. (2014). The cardiometabolic consequences of replacing saturated fats with carbohydrates or ŒΩ-6 polyunsaturated fats: do the dietary guidelines have it wrong? *Open Heart (British Medical Journal* 1(1). http://dx.doi.org/10.1136/openhrt-2013-000032.

Feinman, R. D., Pogozelski, W. K., Astrup, A., Bernstein, R. K., Fine, E. J., Westman, E. C., et al. (2015). Dietary carbohydrate restriction as the first approach in diabetes management: critical review and evidence base. *Nutrition* 31(1), 1–13. doi:10.1016/j.nut.2014.06.011.

Gannon, M. C., & Nuttall, F. Q. (2004). Effect of a high-protein, low-carbohydrate diet on blood glucose control in people with type 2 diabetes. *Diabetes* 53(9), 2375–2382. doi:10.2337/diabetes.53.9.2375.

Gutierrez, M., Akhavan, M., Jovanovic, L., & Peterson, C. M. (1998). Utility of a short-term 25% carbohydrate diet on improving glycemic control in type 2 diabetes mellitus. *Journal of the American College of Nutrition* 17(6): 595–600. doi:10.1080/07315724.1998.10718808.

Hays, J. H., Gorman, R. T., & Shakir, K. M. (2002). Results of use of metformin and replacement of starch with saturated fat in diets of patients with type 2 diabetes. *Endocrine Practice* 8(3), 177–183. doi:10.4158/ep.8.3.177.

Johnston, B. C., Kanters, S., Bandayrel, K., Wu, P., Naji, F., Siemieniuk, R. A., et al. (2014). Comparison of weight loss among named diet programs in overweight and obese adults. *Journal of the American Medical Association* 312(9): 923. doi:10.1001/jama.2014.10397.

Lin, P.-J., & Borer, K. T. (2016). Third exposure to a reduced carbohydrate meal lowers evening postprandial insulin and GIP responses and HOMA-IR estimate of insulin resistance. *PLOS ONE* 11(10): e0165378. https://doi.org/10.1371/journal.pone.0165378.

Maekawa, S., Kawahara, T., Nomura, R., Murase, T., Ann, Y., Oeholm, M., & Harada, M. (2014). Retrospective study on the efficacy of a low-carbohydrate diet for impaired glucose tolerance. *Diabetes, Metabolic Syndrome and Obesity: Targets and Therapy* 195. doi:10.2147/dmso.s62681.

Meckling, K. A., O'Sullivan, C., & Saari, D. (2004). Comparison of a low-fat diet to a low-carbohydrate diet on weight loss, body composition, and risk factors for diabetes and cardiovascular disease in free-living, overweight men and women. *Journal of Clinical Endocrinology & Metabolism* 89(6): 2717–2723. doi:10.1210/jc.2003-031606.

Moreno, B., Bellido, D., Sajoux, I., Goday, A., Saavedra, D., Crujeiras, A. B., & Casanueva, F. F. (2014). Comparison of a very low-calorie-ketogenic diet with a standard low-calorie diet in the treatment of obesity. *Endocrine* 47(3): 793–805. doi:10.1007/s12020-014-0192-3.

Nielsen, J. V., & Joensson, E. A. (2008). Low-carbohydrate diet in type 2 diabetes: stable improvement of bodyweight and glycemic control during 44 months follow-up. *Nutrition & Metabolism* 5(1): 14. doi:10.1186/1743-7075-5-14.

Rosedale, R., Westman, E., & Konhilas, J. (2009). Clinical experience of a diet designed to reduce aging. *Journal of Applied Research* 9(4): 159–165. https://www.ncbi.nlm.nih.gov/pmc/articles/PMC2831640/.

Sackner-Bernstein, J., Kanter, D., & Kaul, S. (2015). Dietary intervention for overweight and obese adults: comparison of low-carbohydrate and low-fat diets. A meta-analysis. *PLOS ONE* 10(10). doi:10.1371/journal.pone.0139817.

Samaha, F. F., Iqbal, N., Seshadri, P., Chicano, K. L., Daily, D. A., Mcgrory, J., et al. (2003). A low-carbohydrate as compared with a low-fat diet in severe obesity. *New England Journal of Medicine* 348(21): 2074–2081. doi:10.1056/nejmoa022637.

Santos, F. L., Esteves, S. S., Pereira, A. D., Yancy Jr., W. S., & Nunes, J. P. (2012). Systematic review and meta-analysis of clinical trials of the effects of low carbohydrate diets on cardiovascular risk factors. *Obesity Reviews* 13(11): 1048–1066. doi:10.1111/j.1467-789x.2012.01021.x.

Sasakabe, T., Haimoto, H., U., & W. (2011). Effects of a moderate low-carbohydrate diet on preferential abdominal fat loss and cardiovascular risk factors in patients with type 2 diabetes. *Diabetes, Metabolic Syndrome and Obesity: Targets and Therapy* 167. doi:10.2147/dmso.s19635.

Shai, I., Spence, J. D., Schwarzfuchs, D., Henkin, Y., Parraga, G., Rudich, A., . . . et al. (2010). Dietary intervention to reverse carotid atherosclerosis. *Circulation* 121(10): 1200–1208. doi:10.1161/circulationaha.109.879254.

Shai, I., Schwarzfuchs, D., Henkin, Y., Shahar, D., Witcow, S., Greenberg, I., et al. (2008). Weight loss with a low-carbohydrate, Mediterranean, or low-fat diet. *New England Journal of Medicine* 359(20): 2169–2172. doi:10.1056/nejmc081747.

Siri-Tarino, P. W., Sun, Q., Hu, F. B., & Krauss, R. M. (2010). Meta-analysis of prospective cohort studies evaluating the association of saturated fat with cardiovascular disease. *American Journal of Clinical Nutrition* 91(3): 535–546. doi:10.3945/ajcn.2009.27725.

Stewart, K. J., Dobrosielski, D. A., Sibler, H. A., Zakaria, S., Shapiro, E. P., & Ouyang, P. (2011). Losing 10 lbs with a low-CHO diet plus exercise does not impair vascular function. *Medicine & Science in Sports & Exercise* 43(suppl. 1): 154. doi:10.1249/01.mss.0000400404.56488.57.

Tirosh, A., Golan, R., Harman-Boehm, I., Henkin, Y., Schwarzfuchs, D., Rudich, A., et al. (2013). Renal function following three distinct weight loss dietary strategies during 2 years of a randomized controlled trial. *Diabetes Care* 36(8): 2225–2232. doi:10.2337/dc12-1846.

Volek, J. S., Volk, B. M., & Phinney, S. D. (2012). The twisted tale of saturated fat. *Lipid Technology* 24(5): 106–107. doi:10.1002/lite.201200189.

Volek, J. S., & Westman, E. C. (2002). Very-low-carbohydrate weight-loss diets revisited. *Cleveland Clinic Journal of Medicine* 69(11): 849, 853, 856–8 passim. doi:10.3949/ccjm.69.11.849.

Volk, B. M., Kunces, L. J., Freidenreich, D. J., Kupchak, B. R., Saenz, C., Artistizabal, J. C., et al. (2014). Effects of step-wise increases in dietary carbohydrate on circulating saturated fatty acids and palmitoleic acid in adults with metabolic syndrome. *PLOS ONE* 9(11). doi:10.1371/journal.pone.0113605.

Westman, E. C., Mavropoulos, J., Yancy, W. S., & Volek, J. S. (2003). A review of low-carbohydrate ketogenic diets. *Current Atherosclerosis Reports* 5(6), 476–483. doi:10.1007/s11883-003-0038-6.

Yamada, Y., Uchida, J., Izumi, H., Tsukamoto, Y., Inoue, G., Watanabe, Y., et al. (2014). A non-calorie-restricted low-carbohydrate diet is effective as an alternative therapy for patients with type 2 diabetes. *Internal Medicine* 53(1), 13–19. doi:10.2169/internalmedicine.53.0861.

ACKNOWLEDGEMENTS

I'm proud to say that writing this book was a team effort. It began with the realization that we had this amazing opportunity to speak to a very important part of our population that is interested in making small changes and embracing a better way of eating by learning how to live a low-carb, low-sugar lifestyle. You are done with diets, but you are passionate about the quality and quantity of the food you eat and how it impacts your overall health and wellness.

I am thankful to the leadership and vision of Scott Parker, Chief Marketing Officer (CMO) at Atkins, and Jennifer Livingston, Director of Public Relations, who were enormously helpful with insightful comments and additions from the very beginning, when this book was simply just a glimmer in our eyes, and during the continual process of bringing it to life. Gretchen Ferraro, freelance writer, was the Editorial Director who collaborated with me, and without her contributions, this book would not have been possible. Nutritionist Vicki Cox, Director of Nutrition Communications at Atkins, pored over every word for accuracy and supplied scientific references and insight where needed. Jennifer Knollenberg created our delicious and useful meal plans, which incorporated the recipes in this book; it was no easy task to meet all our nutritional targets, but she did it. And I would like to extend a special thanks to Joe Scalzo, Atkins' Chief Executive Officer, and Hanno Holm, Atkins' Chief Operations Officer, for their insights in supporting this book and assembling this talented team.

The key to this book is the mouthwatering low-carbohydrate and low-sugar recipes created by Jennifer Iserloh, which demonstrate once and for all that eating the Atkins way – eating right, not less – is wonderfully flexible and can be personalized to suit your individual needs. With Atkins, food should be an experience worth sharing and savouring with others, and these recipes are a testament to that.

Finally, this book would not have been possible without Joy Tutela, from the David Black Literary Agency, who went above and beyond in coordinating the moving pieces, and many thanks to the superb editorial efforts of Cara Bedick, Senior Editor at Touchstone/Simon & Schuster.

Last, but far from least, I am so thankful to Ellen Silverman for contributing her beautiful photography to this project. I knew the first time I saw her work that I wanted her and her team to work on this book. The end result is a dream come true: a coffee table–worthy book that showcases how delicious living a low-carb lifestyle can truly be.

NOTES

CHAPTER 1: THE HIDDEN SUGAR EFFECT

1. Institute for Health Metrics and Evaluation (2015). https://vizhub.healthdata.org/obesity/

2. Hulsegge, Gerben, H. S. J. Picavet, A. Blokstra, et al. (2013) Today's adult generations are less healthy than their predecessors: generation shifts in metabolic risk factors: the Doetinchem Cohort Study. *European Journal of Preventive Cardiology* April 2013: 1134–1144.

3. *USDA Dietary Guidelines 2015–2020.* Appendix 7, Nutritional goals for age-sex groups based on dietary reference intakes and dietary guidelines recommendations. (2016, January).

4. Menke, A., S. Casagrande, & L. Geiss, (2015). Prevalence of and trends in diabetes among adults in the United States, 1988–2012. *Journal of the American Medical Association* 314(10): 1021–1029.

5. Martin, C. K., D. Rosenbaum, H. Han, P. J. Geiselman, H. R. Wyatt, J. O. Hill, et al. (2011). Change in food cravings, food preferences, and appetite during a low-carbohydrate and low-fat diet. *Obesity* 19(10): 1963–1970.

CHAPTER 2: HOW ATKINS WORKS

1. Schwingshackl, L., G. Hoffmann, T. Kalle-Uhlmann, M. Arregui, B. Buijsse and H. Boeing (2015). Fruit and vegetable consumption and changes in anthropometric variables in adult populations: a systematic review and meta-analysis of prospective cohort studies. *PLOS ONE* 10(10): e0140846. doi:10.1371/journal.pone.0140846. L. Dauchat, P. Amouyel, S. Hercberg, and J. Dallongeville (2006). Fruit and vegetable consumption and risk of coronary heart disease: a meta-analysis of cohort studies. *Journal of Nutrition* 136(10): 2588–2593. jn.nutrition.org/content/136/10/2588.abstract. H. Boeing, A. Bechthold, A. Bub, S. Ellinger, D. Haller, A. Kroke, et al. (2012). Critical review: vegetables and fruits in the prevention of chronic diseases. *European Journal of Nutrition* 51(6): 637–663.

CHAPTER 3: LET'S GET STARTED

1. U.S. Food and Drug Administration. (2017, February 10).
How to understand and use the nutrition facts label. www.fda.gov/Food/IngredientsPackagingLabeling/LabelingNutrition/ucm274593.htm#overview.

2. American Heart Association. (2016). The American Heart Association recommendations for physical activity in adults. http://www.heart.org/HEARTORG/HealthyLiving/Physical Activity/FitnessBasics/American-Heart-Association-Recommendations-for-Physical-Activity-Infographic_UCM_450754_SubHomePage.jsp.

3. Harvard Health Publications, Harvard Medical School. (2011, February). Mindful eating. www.health.harvard.edu/staying-healthy/mindful-eating.

4. Turner-Mcgrievy, G. M., and D. F. Tate, (2013). Weight loss social support in 140 characters or less: use of an online social network in a remotely delivered weight loss intervention. *Translational Behavioral Medicine* 3(3), 287–294. R. R. Wing, and R. W. Jeffery (1999). Benefits of recruiting participants with friends and increasing social support for weight loss and maintenance. *Journal of Consulting and Clinical Psychology* 67(1): 132–138.

CHAPTER 4: ATKINS YOUR WAY

1. Martin, C. K., D. Rosenbaum, H. Han, P. J. Geiselman, H. R. Wyatt, J. O. Hill, et al. (2011). Change in food cravings, food preferences, and appetite during a low-carbohydrate and low-fat diet. *Obesity (Silver Spring)* 19(10): 1963–70. C. Heimowitz, M. Abdul, Q. Hu, N. Le, K. Bingham, V. Cox, et al. (2017). Changes in food cravings during dietary carbohydrate-restriction. *FASEB Journal* 31(5). www.fasebj.org/content/31/1_Supplement/643.23.

CHAPTER 5: LIVING A LOW-CARB AND LOW-SUGAR LIFESTYLE: SMALL CHANGES = BIG RESULTS

1. Jones, P. J., V. K. Senanayake, S. Pu, D. J Jenkins, P. W. Connelly, B. Lamarche, et al. (2014). DHA-enriched high-oleic acid canola oil improves lipid profile and lowers predicted cardiovascular disease risk in the canola oil multicenter randomized controlled trial. *American Journal of Clinical Nutrition* 100(1): 88–97.

2. Cardoso, D. A., A. S. Moriera, G. M. De Oliveria, L. R. Raggio, and G. Rosa (2015). A coconut extra virgin oil–rich diet increases HDL cholesterol and decreases waist circumference and body mass in coronary artery disease patients. *Nutrición Hospitalaria* 32(5): 2144–2152.

3. Marco, M. L., D. Heeney, S. Binda, C. J. Cifelli, P. D. Cotter, B. Foligné, et al. (2016). Health benefits of fermented foods: microbiota and beyond. *Current Opinion in Biotechnology* 44, 94–102.

4. Kong, A., et al. (2012). Self-monitoring and eating-related behaviors are associated with 12-month weight loss in postmenopausal overweight-to-obese women. *Journal of the Academy of Nutrition and Dietetics* 112(9): 1428–1435.

CHAPTER 6: BREAKFAST

1. Giusti, M. M. (2015). Anthocyanins. *Advances in Nutrition* 6: 620–622.

CHAPTER 7: SNACKS AND SIDES

1. Round, J. L., and S. K. Mazmanian, (2009). The gut microbiota shapes intestinal immune responses during health and disease. *Nature Reviews Immunology* 9(5): 313–323.

CHAPTER 10: APPETIZERS

1. Weil, A. (2016, November 1). Curcumin or turmeric? https://www.drweil.com/vitamins-supplements-herbs/herbs/curcumin-or-turmeric/.

2. Salem, M. B., H. Affes, K. Ksouda, R. Dhouibi, Z. Sahnoun, = S. Hammami, and K. M. Zeghal (2015). Pharmacological studies of artichoke leaf extract and their health benefits. *Plant Foods for Human Nutrition* 70(4): 441–453.

CHAPTER 11: 15-MINUTE MEALS

1. Hamidpour, M., R. Hamidpour, S. Hamidpour, and M. Shahlari (2014). Chemistry, pharmacology, and medicinal property of sage (salvia) to prevent and cure illnesses such as obesity, diabetes, depression, dementia, lupus, autism, heart disease, and cancer. *Journal of Traditional and Complementary Medicine* 4(2): 82–88.

CHAPTER 13: JUST DESSERTS

1. Brookshire, B. (2014). Cocoa antioxidant sweetens cognition in elderly. *Science News*. https://www.sciencenews.org/article/cocoa-antioxidant-sweetens-cognition-elderly.

INDEX

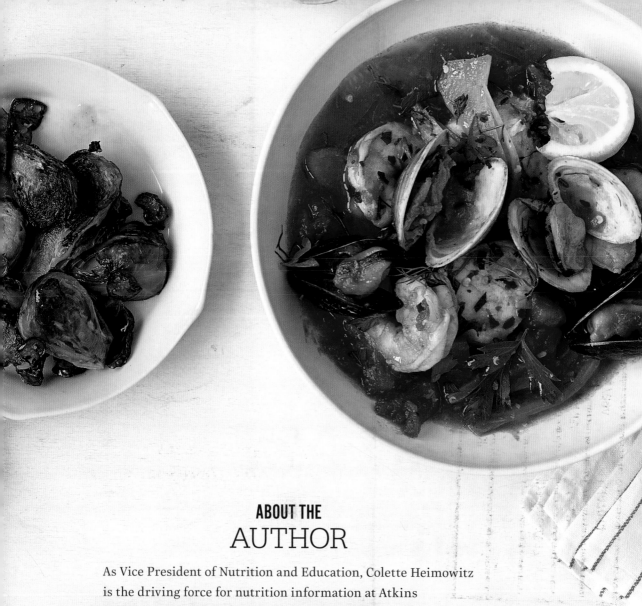

ABOUT THE
AUTHOR

As Vice President of Nutrition and Education, Colette Heimowitz
is the driving force for nutrition information at Atkins
Nutritionals, Inc. She is the nutritionist face of the Atkins
Community, which is dedicated to helping people reach their
weight-loss goals. As part of this initiative, she publishes a
weekly Nutritionist Blog, creates content devoted to educating
new members about the programme, and stays up to date on
emerging research on human nutrition.

Colette has been a guest on American national radio
programmes, as well as on television networks including CNN,
Fox News and MSNBC. She has more than twenty-five years of
experience as a nutritionist and received her M.Sc. in clinical
nutrition from Hunter College of the City University of New York.